FINISH LINE
New York
ELA
THIRD EDITION

Continental

CREDITS

Illustrations: Page 17: Jane Yamada; Pages 33, 232: Margaret Lindmark; Pages 40, 128, 158, 180, 184, 185, 212, 214, 216, 218, 220, 239, 243, 244, 247, 248, 252 *house,* 256 *earth:* Laurie Conley; Page 54: Harry Norcross; Page 124: Marty Husted; Page 240: Marilee Harrald-Pilz; Page 252 *toys:* Deborah C. Johnson; Page 257: Cindy Shaw

Photos: Page 63: Alan D. Carey; Page 68: Library of Congress, Prints and Photographs Division, LC-D418-9832; Page 73: Image used under Creative Commons from Rico Shen; Page 75: Library of Congress, Prints and Photographs Division, LC-USZC4-1291; Page 77: www.photos.com; Page 92: www.istockphoto.com/Xavier Pironet; Page 96: AP Photo/Tom Strattman; Page 100: Image used under Creative Commons from Michael Gäbler; Page 104: Image used under Creative Commons from Solid State Survivor; Page 108: www.istockphoto.com/Gijs Bekenkamp; Page 113: Francis M. Fritz; Page 169: Image used under Creative Commons from Mark Gstohl; Page 170: www.istockphoto.com/John Pitcher; Page 173: US Fish and Wildlife Service; Page 182: www.shutterstock.com, Maksym Gorpenyuk; Page 191: www.shutterstock.com, David Alexander Liu; Page 207: Henry Shipler; Page 254: Courtesy of Team Romero; Page 259: © Bettmann/CORBIS

Pages 64 and 65: LEGO® is a registered trademark of the LEGO Group.

ISBN 978-0-8454-7918-6

Copyright © 2015 The Continental Press, Inc.

TABLE OF CONTENTS

About Finish Line New York ELA

Finish Line New York ELA, Third Edition will give you practice in the reading and writing skills necessary to be an effective communicator in the 21st century. It will also help you to prepare for tests that assess your skills and knowledge.

The material in this book is written to the Common Core Learning Standards (CCLS) developed by your state. The book is divided into units of related lessons. The reading passages in a unit center around a common theme related to content taught at the grade level. Each reading lesson concentrates on one main standard and is broken into four parts:

 Introduction

The Introduction of each lesson reviews the standard you are going to study and explains what it is and how you use it. You may work with example text, pictures, or graphic organizers to help you better understand the skill.

 Focused Instruction

The Focused Instruction guides you through reading a passage. In this section, you will work with a partner, in small groups, or as a class to practice the skill. You will read a story, poem, play, or nonfiction piece and work through a series of questions to help you organize your thoughts. There are hints and reminders along the sides of the pages to help you remember what you have learned.

 Guided Practice

The third part is Guided Practice, where you will work alone to answer questions. The format of these items is similar to many test questions— multiple choice and short answer. Again, there will be hints and reminders to help you answer the questions.

(4) Independent Practice

Finally, you will complete the Independent Practice by yourself. These questions will be a variety of types—one- and two-part multiple choice, short response, and extended response or essay. The Independent Practice does not have hints or reminders. You must use everything you learned in the first three parts to complete this section.

At the end of each unit is a unit review. You will review all the skills you worked on in that unit to answer questions. You will see different item types, just like the Independent Practice section. There will not be any hints or reminders.

A glossary of key terms from the book appears at the end of the book for reference.

Now you are ready to begin. Good Luck!

Sometimes, reading is like being a detective! Detectives look closely for clues, and when you read, so do you! As you are reading a story, poem, or play, be on the lookout for the theme. Also, be sure to pay attention to details that are important to the plot and the characters. When you pay attention to these details, you will be able to summarize the text, and this will help you understand it better.

LESSON 1 Determining the Theme of a Story or Play will help you when you read stories and plays to look for the theme, or what the author wants you to know or learn. You will look for clues in the story or play that could help you find the message or lesson in the story.

LESSON 2 Determining the Theme of a Poem is about looking for themes in poetry. You will think about what the poet is describing, how the poem makes you feel, and what details from the poem help support the theme.

LESSON 3 Describing Characters in a Play focuses on telling about the characters in a play. You will read plays and think about each character's personality and actions, while finding details that support your opinion.

LESSON 4 Describing Settings and Events in a Story will help you read stories and pay attention to the setting and plot. You will think about how one action or event leads to the next, as well as how the setting can affect a story.

LESSON 5 Drawing Inferences from Literary Texts is about reading the story and looking for clues to help you make inferences, or guesses about what the author does not state directly. Paying attention to the details of a story will help you to make better inferences.

LESSON 6 Summarizing Literary Texts focuses on summarizing stories, plays, and poems in your head, aloud, or on paper. By summarizing what you read, you can think about the details and ideas, and find the theme.

LESSON 1

Determining the Theme of a Story or Play

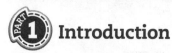 **Introduction**

THEME: ⟫ **The Story Inside**

The **theme** is the story's message, or what the author wants the reader to know. Sometimes the theme is not stated directly, but it holds the story together and gives it meaning. You must make an **inference,** or logical guess, about the theme based on what you know and what the text says.

> **Read the story. Note how story details give clues to a theme.**
>
> Maria was so tired when she got home that all she wanted to do was go to bed. Then she saw her neighbor, Mr. Sanchez, raking leaves in his yard. "Hello, Maria," he said. "Can you help me finish this job? It looks like it's going to rain, and I want to have these leaves raked up before the storm."
>
> Maria did not want to rake leaves. But Mr. Sanchez looked tired, and it really did look like it was going to rain. "Sure, I will help you," she said. "That's what neighbors do."

One way to determine a theme is to look for clues about how characters change over the course of the story and why.

Complete the chart with details about Maria's actions and the theme.

Story Details	Theme
What Maria does: 1. Maria is tired and does not want to help Mr. Sanchez. 2. Maria notices that Mr. Sanchez looks tired, too, and that it looks like rain. 3. *She did not want to rake levs but she did* 4. *because thats what neighbors do.*	*To help other people even if your tird too.*

Read the first part of the story. Then answer the questions.

adapted from Laetitia and the Redcoats
by Lillian L. Price

1   Laetitia burst through her grandparents' door, pulling her hood off her curls. With great pains she said, "Neighbor Paxton has just told me something awful. Oh, Grandmother, the British are crossing the valley. Master Paxton says they will camp here at nightfall! He says you and Grandfather must depart at once."

2   "Calm thyself, Laetitia. For these times of trouble are not for the children and the old. We have strong men that are fighting for us. You must be brave." Grandfather looked Laetitia squarely in the face. "We will move the family to the mountain until they leave."

Think About It

How does Laetitia's grandfather react when she is upset? The question asks you to tell what Laetitia's grandfather does when Laetitia learns that the British are coming. Finding key ideas and details in the story will help you understand story events and characters' feelings. Look for what the characters do and say.

Underline the dialogue that provides clues about how Laetitia feels.

Write the sentence that tells why Laetitia is upset. _____

_____

What is the first thing that Grandfather tells her? _____

_____

Why does Grandfather tell her his plan? _____

_____

Based on Grandfather saying, "You must be brave," it seems that he is teaching

Laetitia to be brave when _____.

Continue reading the story. Then answer the question.

A CLOSER LOOK

Think about how Laetitia's idea helps to save her home. Circle phrases in this part of the story that show how Laetitia's letter affected the soldiers.

3 "I will then, Grandfather. Not a tear will I shed." She could not imagine British soldiers clanking about the house. Her eyes filled with soft tears. Out of the corner of her watery eye, she saw pen and ink. Just then she had an idea. First, across one sheet she wrote and then across the other:

TO THE REDCOATS:

I am Laetitia Wright, aged 14, who lives in this house with my grandparents. I pray you, dear Redcoats, spare their home to them, and do not burn nor ruin their house. Perhaps, thou hast a little maid like me in England and old parents. Thou couldst not turn the roof from over their heads, and in such pity and mercy, spare ours! We leave thee much to eat and would leave thee more, were our store larger.

Signed, LAETITIA WRIGHT

4 Before they left for the safety of the mountain, Laetitia put the letter in the doorknocker. After they reached safety, the British soldiers occupied their home. An officer found Laetitia's letter, and it brought tears to his eyes. *How bold this little girl is to write such a letter,* he thought. *We shall not destroy anything in this town.*

5 A few days later, the bugle blew. Folks knew it was safe to return. When Laetitia arrived, she found a note from a soldier.

"Sweet Mistress Wright,
Though redcoats we be, you plainly will see,
We know how to grant a petition.
With rough soldier care, we've endeavored to spare
Your homes in a decent condition."

6 The letter was signed by the colonel. When Laetitia told her grandparents what she had done, they kissed and thanked her.

What do Laetitia's actions tell you about the story's lesson or message?

What is the theme of the story?

A It is easy to be brave.

B Fighting is best left to other people.

C Anyone can take action to make things better.

D Sometimes running away is the best thing to do.

 DISCUSS IT

How did Laetitia's actions save her home and the homes of her neighbors? Talk to another student about why Laetitia's actions were a success.

Read the passage. Then answer the questions.

excerpted from The Secret Garden

by Frances Hodgson Burnett

1   One place she went to oftener than to any other. It was the long walk outside the gardens with the walls round them. There were bare flowerbeds on either side of it, and against the walls, ivy grew thickly. There was one part of the wall where the creeping dark green leaves were more bushy than elsewhere. It seemed as if for a long time that part had been neglected. The rest of it had been clipped and made to look neat, but at this lower end of the walk, it had not been trimmed at all.

2   A few days after she had talked to Ben Weatherstaff, Mary stopped to notice this and wondered why it was so. She had just paused and was looking up at a long spray of ivy swinging in the wind when she saw a gleam of scarlet and heard a brilliant chirp, and there, on the top of the wall, forward perched Ben Weatherstaff's robin redbreast, tilting forward to look at her with his small head on one side.

3   "Oh!" she cried out, "is it you—is it you?" And it did not seem at all queer to her that she spoke to him as if she were sure that he would understand and answer her.

4   He did answer. He twittered and chirped and hopped along the wall as if he were telling her all sorts of things. It seemed to Mistress Mary as if she understood him, too, though he was not speaking in words. It was as if he said:

5   "Good morning! Isn't the wind nice? Isn't the sun nice? Isn't everything nice? Let us both chirp and hop and twitter. Come on! Come on!"

6   Mary began to laugh, and as he hopped and took little flights along the wall, she ran after him.

7   "I like you! I like you!" she cried out, pattering down the walk; and she chirped and tried to whistle, which last she did not know how to do in the least. But the robin seemed to be quite satisfied and chirped and whistled back at her. At last, he spread his wings and made a darting flight to the top of a tree, where he perched and sang loudly. That reminded Mary of the first time she had

A CLOSER LOOK

The robin is important to Mary. Circle a detail in the story that shows Mary's feelings.

The robin is in a secret place. Circle the part of the story that shows what Mary thinks about where the bird is.

seen him. He had been swinging on a treetop then and she had been standing in the orchard. Now she was on the other side of the orchard and standing in the path outside a wall—much lower down—and there was the same tree inside.

8 "It's in the garden no one can go into," she said to herself. "It's the garden without a door. He lives in there. How I wish I could see what it is like!"

> How does Mary behave when she is with the robin?

1 How does the robin make Mary feel?

A excited

B sad

C upset

D worried

> What does Mary say when she sees the robin fly into the tree at the end of the passage?

2 How does Mary know the robin is in the secret garden?

A The robin is in a tall tree.

B The robin is in the same orchard.

C There is no way to get into the garden.

D The wall is too high for Mary to see over.

> Mary imagines having a conversation with the robin. Look at this part of the story to find details that give clues to the theme.

3 One theme of the story might be: *It is fun to make unusual friends.* Which story details support this theme? Cite at least two details from the story to support your answer.

_____

_____

_____

_____

_____

_____

Read the play. Then answer the questions.

Oliver Joins the Circus

CAST:

OLIVER RYAN

THOMAS, *Oliver's neighbor*

MOTHER, *Oliver's mother*

MR. KLEIN, *Oliver's teacher*

act 1

Oliver's backyard. OLIVER is standing on a swing.

OLIVER: Presenting Oliver Ryan, the best acrobat on Earth!" (OLIVER *jumps off the swing and lands with his arms spread out. OLIVER bows.)*

Oliver's neighbor, THOMAS, *leans over the fence. He is laughing.*

THOMAS: You mean, presenting Oliver, the silliest boy on Earth. No one joins the circus—not even clowns like you!

OLIVER's *shoulders slump, and he walks over to sit on his back steps.*

OLIVER: Thomas is right. How can I join the circus? It's not like I can go to circus school or answer a want ad on the computer.

Oliver's MOTHER *comes outside. She is holding her purse and car keys.*

MOTHER: Oliver, there you are! I've been looking all over for you. Hurry up and get in the car. I have a surprise for you, and we don't want to be late.

End of act 1

act 2

Downtown at the community center. OLIVER *and his* MOTHER *get out of their car. In front of the center is a large poster that reads, "Join the circus! Take part in our summer Circus Camp!"*

OLIVER: *(yelling)* Circus Camp! What a great idea!

MOTHER: I saw an ad in the newspaper and signed you up over the phone. *(She kisses* OLIVER *good-bye.)* I'll be back at lunchtime. Have fun!

OLIVER: There sure are a lot of kids here. I guess I'm not the only person who loves the circus. Well, I might as well go in and find out what this is all about.

End of act 2

act 3

Several weeks later inside the community center. The stage is set up with a low trapeze and a tightrope, along with small platforms. Bright colors and streamers are everywhere. The seats in the audience are full. OLIVER *and his teacher,* MR. KLEIN, *are standing at the side of the stage.* OLIVER *is wearing a brightly colored costume.*

OLIVER: There are so many people here! I see a lot of my classmates. *(He groans.)* Oh, no! My neighbor Thomas is here. He's always making fun of me because I want to be in the circus.

MR. KLEIN: He's here to see a great show, just like everyone else, and that's what you are going to do. You're great at walking on a tightrope and swinging from a trapeze, remember?

OLIVER: Yes, but what if he laughs at me? I feel really nervous.

MR. KLEIN: The show must go on, no matter what.

End of act 3

act 4

The show is over, and OLIVER *is surrounded by his classmates and* THOMAS.

THOMAS: Oliver, that was great! I couldn't believe my eyes when you flipped off that trapeze into your partner's arms. You are really talented! How did you learn all those tricks?

OLIVER: *(grinning)* I joined the circus for the summer!

1 Part A

How does Thomas make Oliver feel about wanting to join the circus?

_____

_____

Part B

What detail from the story shows Oliver's feelings about Thomas's words?

A Oliver wants to go to circus camp.

B Oliver is having fun jumping off the swing.

C Oliver pretends he is an acrobat in the circus.

D Oliver stops playing and his shoulders slump.

2 What is Oliver worried about before he goes onstage?

   A   He is eager to show off his tricks.

   B   He is happy his friends will see him.

   C   He thinks Thomas will laugh at him.

   D   He is afraid he will not be able to perform.

3 Why does Mr. Klein say, "The show must go on"?

_____

_____

4 The theme of this story is that you should find a way to make your dreams come true, no matter what other people think. List at least three details from the story that support this theme.

   1. _____

   _____

   2. _____

   _____

   3. _____

   _____

LESSON 2

Determining the Theme of a Poem

 **Introduction**

THEME: »» **The Story Inside**

A poem has a **theme,** or an important idea that the poet wants readers to understand. The poet reveals the theme through the details, images, and events in the poem.

A poem does not always state the theme plainly. Some poems do not have characters or a plot to help explain the theme. In these poems, you need to understand the implied meaning of events or details in the poem.

Read the poem "Goodbye to a Friend."

> I had a friend I loved so much,
> He was with me every day.
> We played and laughed and worked together—
> I thought he'd always stay.
>
> 5   Then one sad day, my friend had news:
> He had to go away.
> I cried and cried but it was no use—
> He left that very day.
>
> As time went by, I missed my friend,
> 10 But one thing I now say:
> My memories can never be taken;
> In my heart my friend will stay.

Complete the sentences about the theme.

The poet feels _____ when the friend leaves, but the poet

later realizes that she will never _____ the friend. The theme

of the poem is that even if friends leave, they live on _____.

It is important to figure out a poem's theme as you read. The theme is the central message. While a poem might tell a story or describe a scene, the details work together to create a deeper meaning that is the theme of the poem.

Read the first part of the poem. Then answer the questions.

Only the Moon and Stars

On the western horizon, the sunset signals
the sleeping of the sun, yellow and pink.
The last rays of light go home,
Twilight brings the dawning of the dark.

5   Day animals sleep in dreams,
Houses sit quiet, dark, and still.
In the blackness, the night comes alive,
And creatures of the dark awake.

Think About It

What is this part of the poem about? You can find the answer by looking at the details in the poem and thinking about what these details mean. Look for descriptive phrases and see how they are linked by a common topic or theme.

Read the beginning of the poem again. As you read, underline the lines that describe what is happening.

What does the poet describe in lines 1–4? _____

_____

What details or images help you know the time of day? _____

_____

The details show that the world is _____

_____ .

A CLOSER LOOK

Circle phrases in this part of the poem that show key details about the sounds of the night.

Continue reading the poem. Then answer the question.

Powdery moths are drawn to lamps,
10 They lightly tap on window screens.
Around the pond, bullfrogs call jug-o-rum, jug-o-rum,
While green frogs sing their high-pitched songs.
In grassy fields, crickets chirp,

Field mice sniff and snuffle,
15 Raccoons, busy bodies clunking,
Searching trash cans for their food.

Coyotes howl, calling out in the blackness,
Stray cats yowl, looking for their friends,
From a tree, the haunting owl watches
20 And asks hoo-hoo-hoo, hoo-hoo-who?

An acrobatic cloud of bats,
Storms silently across the sky.
Only the moon and stars linger,
As witnesses to the creatures of the night.

How do the final two lines of the poem provide clues to the theme?

Which tells the poem's theme?

A   Wild animals come out at night.

B   There are a lot of animals in the world.

C   It is noisier at night than during the day.

D   The world is an active place, even at night.

 DISCUSS IT

Think about how the details of the poem describe what it is like during sundown and at night. How do the first eight lines fit in with the rest of the poem? Talk with another student about how this poem makes you feel.

Read the poem. Then answer the questions.

The Night Wind

by Eugene Field

Have you ever heard the wind go "Yooooo"?
'T is a pitiful sound to hear!
It seems to chill you through and through
With a strange and speechless fear.
5   'T is the voice of the night that broods outside
When folk should be asleep,
And many and many's the time I've cried
To the darkness brooding far and wide
Over the land and the deep:
10 "Whom do you want, O lonely night,
That you wail the long hours through?"
And the night would say in its ghostly way:
"Yoooooooo!"

My mother told me long ago
15 (When I was a little tad)
That when the night went wailing so,
Somebody had been bad;
And then, when I was snug in bed,
Whither I had been sent,
20 With the blankets pulled up round my head,
I'd think of what my mother'd said,
And wonder what boy she meant!
And "Who's been bad today?" I'd ask
Of the wind that hoarsely blew,
25 And the voice would say in its meaningful way:
"Yoooooooo!"

That this was true I must allow—
You'll not believe it, though!
Yes, though I'm quite a model now,
30 I was not always so.
And if you doubt what things I say,
Suppose you make the test;
Suppose, when you've been bad some day
And up to bed are sent away
35 From mother and the rest—
Suppose you ask, "Who has been bad?"
And then you'll hear what's true;
For the wind will moan in its ruefulest tone:
"Yoooooooo!"

A CLOSER LOOK

How does the poet's mother contribute to his feelings about the wind? Circle the part of the poem that shows what his mother says about the wind.

What does the poet do when he hears the wind in stanzas 1 and 2?

1 How does the wind make the poet feel?

A angry

B excited

C sad

D guilty

How do the poet's feelings show the theme of the poem?

2 Why does the poet's mother tell him the wind is saying someone has been bad?

A to help him go to sleep when he is scared

B to make him feel guilty when he's been bad

C to show him there is nothing to be afraid of

D to tell him a bedtime story when he is sleepy

Look at how the poet describes his feelings about the wind in stanzas 2 and 3.

3 The theme of the poem is that nature can have a powerful effect on a person. What details from the poem help you understand the theme?

_____

_____

_____

_____

Read the poem. Then answer the questions.

The Arrow and the Song

by Henry Wadsworth Longfellow

I shot an arrow into the air,
It fell to earth, I knew not where;
For, so swiftly it flew, the sight
Could not follow it in its flight.

5   I breathed a song into the air,
It fell to earth, I knew not where;
For who has sight so keen and strong,
That it can follow the flight of song?

10   Long, long afterward, in an oak
I found the arrow, still unbroke;
And the song, from beginning to end,
I found again in the heart of a friend.

1   Part A

What is the same about the arrow and the song?

A   They both move quickly.

B   They both are gifts to a friend.

C   The poet finds them a long time after he sent them into the air.

D   The poet knows where they are going and how to find them again.

Part B

What do the arrow and the song symbolize in the poem?

_____

_____

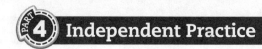
2 Why does the poet ask who can follow the flight of a song?

    A to show that songs are beautiful

    B to show that a song is really an arrow

    C to show that someone will find the song

    D to show that following the sound of a song is impossible

3 How does the poet feel when he finds the arrow and the song? Use two details from the poem to support your answer.

_____

_____

_____

_____

4 The theme of the poem is that what you give away is never really lost. What two details from the poem support this theme?

_____

_____

_____

_____

LESSON 3

Describing Characters in a Play

 **Introduction**

THEME: >>> **The Story Inside**

Characters are an important part of any story or play. Characters drive the action by what they do and say. You read stories to find out what happens to the characters and what they learn from their experiences. Characters are especially important in a play because a play tells its story mostly through the actions and words of its characters. In a play, some of a character's actions are described in **stage directions,** or text in italics or parentheses that is not spoken. Their words are conveyed through **dialogue,** or the words they speak out loud.

Read part of a play.

scene 1

The school lunchroom. BECCA, FRAN, *and* OLIVIA *are sitting together at one of the tables.* SARAH *is standing near them, holding her tray and looking nervous.*

BECCA: Hey, isn't that the new girl in our class?

FRAN: Yeah. It looks like she doesn't have anyone to sit with. Let's invite her to sit with us.

OLIVIA: *(rolling her eyes)* Do we have to? We don't even know her. Anyway, I wanted to talk about the slumber party I'm having this weekend.

BECCA: We can talk about that later.

FRAN: Yeah, don't be so mean, Olivia. (FRAN *waves at* SARAH, *who smiles and hurries over.)*

The characters in this play show what they are like through their words and actions.

Think about what each character says and does. Then fill in the boxes below with a word that describes each character.

Becca is	Fran is	Olivia is	Sarah is

Think about how the characters act and what they say. These details reveal what the characters are like. They are also important clues that help move the story along.

Read the first part of the play. Then answer the questions.

An Earth Day Celebration

CAST:

BOBBY, *9 years old*   **LILIA,** *8 years old*

JUAN, *9 years old*   **MRS. RUIZ,** *a teacher*

ABBY, *8 years old*

scene 1

MRS. RUIZ's *fourth-grade classroom. The school day is over, but a few students still remain working in the classroom.* MRS. RUIZ *is sitting behind her desk, grading papers.*

JUAN: *(staring intently at his computer screen and speaking to no one in particular)* Did you know that the first Earth Day was held in 1970?

ABBY: It's cool to think Earth Day has been celebrated for more than 40 years.

LILIA: We have to make this the best Earth Day parade ever!

BOBBY: *(looking up from his computer)* There are so many things we can do to help our planet. I want to make sure we show some of them in our parade.

JUAN: What were you thinking?

BOBBY: *(scratching his head)* One of us can carry a recycle bin around his neck with a rope—like a drummer in a marching band.

LILIA: Abby and I are working on the posters and banners. We are using recycled paper and materials to make them.

ABBY: We are going to include facts on them, too.

MRS. RUIZ: *(gets up from her chair and joins the students)* Abby, that is a wonderful idea. Can anyone think of a way to show others they should remember to turn off the lights when they leave the room?

JUAN: What about someone in the parade wearing a large light bulb cut out from poster board over his chest? And even better, with a lampshade on his head! *(Juan laughs to himself.)*

LILIA: Juan, since you came up with that idea, you can wear it! I am not wearing a lampshade on my head!

MRS. RUIZ: *(shaking her head)* That's a good idea, Juan. I'll expect you to do it yourself or find someone else.

ABBY: *(with excitement)* I know! Some of the people in the parade can ride their bikes or scooters. That will remind people to ride their bikes instead of driving their cars when they can.

BOBBY: That's an awesome idea, Abby. Maybe I can get my little brother, Mikey, to ride his little car in the parade. We can make a big circle with a line through it to tape to the back of the car.

LILIA: We could carry reusable water bottles and hand out some of the water bottles the local stores donated to us.

MRS. RUIZ: Good idea, Lilia! We can't forget about all the donations. We can carry the reusable shopping bags and put some of the information packets we made in them.

ABBY: I've finished the packets and brochures.

MRS. RUIZ: It sounds like everything is under control for a successful Earth Day parade. I'm so thankful to you four for your extra work on this project.

Think About It

What type of character is Mrs. Ruiz? You can find the answer by looking at how she speaks to the students.

What does Mrs. Ruiz say when Abby suggests that they include facts on the

posters and banners? _____

_____

Does she encourage the students or criticize them? Give an example. _____

_____

_____

_____

_____

Continue reading the play. Then answer the question.

A CLOSER LOOK
Circle phrases in this part of the play that show what Bobby is like.

scene 2

The grassy front lawn of the school near the flagpole. Posters and banners are scattered about. BOBBY, LILIA, JUAN, and MRS. RUIZ are busy putting finishing touches on the things needed for the parade.

BOBBY: *(pulling a red wagon behind him)* Here's the wagon we can use to move the compost bin through the parade route. Abby is finishing the sign that attaches to the side of it.

JUAN: *(looking at his watch)* Just to let you know, we have 15 minutes until the other fourth-grade classes and our own classmates will be here to line up. Let's go everyone; we can do this!

LILIA: *(looking frantic)* 15 minutes! No! We need to have more time than that!

MRS. RUIZ: I'm afraid not, my dear. You've worked hard for the past two weeks, and we are plenty ready.

ABBY: *(putting her arm around Lilia)* Mrs. Ruiz is right. We have done much more than the fourth graders last year! This parade is gonna rock!

BOBBY: *(pointing into the audience and waving)* Look, there's Mikey and my mom! It's show time, people!

What do the stage directions say about Lilia's actions?

Lilia is _____.

A confident that they are ready

B busy telling everyone what to do

C nervous that the parade will not go well

D upset because they have run out of time

DISCUSS IT
Think about how Mrs. Ruiz and the other characters speak to each other. What do their words tell you about these characters? Talk to another student about your ideas.

Read the play. Then answer the questions.

Partners

CAST:

KIM, *a fourth grader*

STEPHANIE, *her classmate*

MR. KINCHLEY, *their teacher*

TINA, *Kim's older sister*

act 1

KIM *and* STEPHANIE *are sitting in class.* MR. KINCHLEY *is in the front of the room.*

MR. KINCHLEY: Attention, class. It's time to choose a partner for your oral reports. Remember, your report must be about a fun place to go in our town. You'll have to create a poster and tell the class all about the area, what there is to do there, and why you think it is a great place to visit. You'll have to answer any questions from the class and me as well. Remember, this will be a big part of your grade, so you want to do a great job. Now, pair off. He or she will be your partner.

KIM: *(turning to her right)* Hey, Stephanie, it looks like we're partners.

STEPHANIE: That's great! I'm so excited about this project! I have so many good ideas.

KIM: Terrific! Do you want to come to my house after school?

STEPHANIE: I can't today, but let's walk home together and we can talk then.

End of act 1

act 2

A few days later. KIM *is sitting at her kitchen table, surrounded by pieces of paper. She looks upset. Her sister* TINA *enters.*

KIM: I can't believe Stephanie didn't show up today! The project is due on Monday, and I have to do all this work!

TINA: Isn't this the third or fourth time she's left you to do everything yourself? Stephanie is a terrible partner.

A CLOSER LOOK
Kim and Stephanie have very different ideas about how to work together. Underline details in the play that show how each character approaches the project.

KIM: Actually, she has lots of great ideas. It was her idea to write about the bike paths at the park, and she went to the visitors' center and got these great trail maps. But she hasn't been around to make the poster or write the report.

TINA: That doesn't seem fair. There's more to doing a project than just having ideas. Stephanie is going to get the same grade as you without doing the work. You two are supposed to be partners.

KIM: You're right. But I don't want to bug her.

TINA: Well, you'd better think of something.

KIM: *(smiling)* I think I just did.

End of act 2

act 3

Kim's kitchen, early that evening. KIM *and* STEPHANIE *enter the room.*

STEPHANIE: What's going on? You said it was urgent that I come over right away.

KIM: It is urgent. We're supposed to be working on this project together. I love your idea about writing about the bike paths. But you haven't done any work since then! I'm the one taking notes and making the poster, and I suppose I'll be the one to give the report.

STEPHANIE: I know I haven't been around much. It's just that—

KIM: Hold on, I'm not done. We're both getting a grade for this project, but I'm doing all the work. Does that seem fair to you?

STEPHANIE: Well, no, but—

KIM: So I had an idea. I'll make the poster and give the presentation. Your part will be to answer the questions—without any help from me.

STEPHANIE: How will I know the answers if I haven't seen the poster or done the research?

KIM: You'll have to do your own research. I'm just trying to be fair and give you half the responsibility.

STEPHANIE: You're right. I can't answer questions without working on the project. Let me text my mom and see if I can stay here to help you.

KIM: That would be great! Real partners have to work together to succeed.

STEPHANIE: *(looking at her phone)* My mom said to stay as long as I need to. Let's get to work and make this the best project in the class!

How does Kim make sure Stephanie does her share of the work?

1 Which answer *best* describes the character of Kim?

   A She likes to work by herself.

   B She doesn't want to do any work.

   C She lets others take advantage of her.

   D She is strong enough to stand up to Stephanie.

How does Stephanie react when Kim confronts her?

2 Which answer *best* describes the character of Stephanie?

   A She is selfish and refuses to help.

   B She takes on more than she can handle.

   C She does not realize that her work is important.

   D She does not care about getting good grades.

Problems are usually solved near the end of a story or play. Reread act 3 to see how Kim makes Stephanie see that she is not being fair.

3 How do Kim's feelings about Stephanie's contributions to the project change? Support your answer with details from the play.

_____

_____

_____

_____

_____

_____

Read the play. Then answer the questions.

excerpt from Cinderella

by Florence Holbrook

CAST:

   CINDERELLA

   MOTHER

   FATHER

   KATHERINE

   ELIZABETH

   PRINCE

scene 1

MOTHER: I am so glad we are all invited to the ball at the Prince's palace. You know, my dear, that it will be a great pleasure for our girls.

FATHER: Yes, and I suppose you will all have to buy new ball dresses.

KATHERINE: O Mamma! Isn't it lovely! May I have a blue silk dress?

ELIZABETH: May I have pink, dear mother? Shall we get them today?

MOTHER: Yes, my child, and you may both go with me to buy your dresses and slippers.

CINDERELLA: Dear Papa, may I go to the ball at the Prince's palace?

FATHER: You, my child! Aren't you too young for parties? Ask your mother.

CINDERELLA: May I go to the ball, Mother?

MOTHER: Nonsense, child! What are you thinking? A ball is no place for a child like you. You are better off at home by the kitchen fire.

CINDERELLA: But I'm 14. Sister Katherine, won't you coax Mamma to let me go?

KATHERINE: No, indeed, I'll not! What would you do at a ball? A silly thing like you!

ELIZABETH: Don't be a goose. Wait till you're older and better looking. There's no room in the carriage for you, and you are too young, anyway.

MOTHER: Come, girls, it is time for us to go downtown to buy our new gowns. Cinderella, go do your lessons. Don't think any more about the ball. You can't go, and so that's the end of it.

End of scene 1

scene 2

FATHER: Come, girls! Aren't you ready yet? Is your mother coming?

KATHERINE: Yes, Father, in just a minute.

MOTHER: Here we are, dear. Don't the girls look sweet?

FATHER: Yes, yes! But, come on, for we are late now.

MOTHER: Good night, Cinderella. Be a good girl and go to bed at nine o'clock.

All go out, leaving CINDERELLA alone.

CINDERELLA: Good-bye!—Now they have gone, and I am all alone. Oh, why couldn't I go, too! How pretty they all looked! I would not take up much room, and I don't like to be left here by myself when they are having such a good time. Oh, dear! I believe I'm going to cry, but I can't help it. *(cries)*

1 Part A

What word *best* describes the character of Cinderella in this excerpt?

A angry

B unhappy

C selfish

D excited

Part B

What detail from the play *best* supports the answer to Part A?

A Cinderella says "Good-bye!"

B Cinderella's parents say she is too young for parties.

C Cinderella asks her mother and father if she can go to the ball.

D Cinderella cries at the end of scene 2.

2 What kind of characters are Katherine and Elizabeth?

    A They are mean and selfish.

    B They are kind and generous.

    C They speak nice words.

    D They are afraid to disobey their parents.

3 How do you think Cinderella's family feels about her? Use two details from the play to support your answer.

_____

_____

_____

_____

_____

4 Think about what kind of character Cinderella is. Do you think she deserves something good to happen to her? Why, or why not? List at least two details from the play that support your answer.

_____

_____

_____

_____

_____

LESSON 4

Describing Settings and Events in a Story

Introduction

THEME: >>> The Story Inside

A story is made up of a sequence of **events,** called a **plot.** The plot is often about a conflict. The conflict may be between two characters. Or, it may be a struggle that one character has. A story's **setting** is also important. The setting is when the story takes place. It might be in a particular season or time period. The setting also tells where the story takes place. It may be on an island, another planet, or at school. The setting sets the **mood,** or feeling of a story. The setting provides a valuable background and is often an important part of the plot.

Look at the illustration. Then complete the chart with details about the setting and events.

Pay attention to details in the story and this will help you understand the setting and events of a story. Authors often appeal to the reader's senses in order to make the setting feel as real as possible. Details about where and when the events take place can give clues about what is happening in the story.

What event is happening?	
Where does the event take place?	
When does the event take place?	
What details help you know the setting and event?	
Describe the setting and what is happening.	

Read the first part of the story.

Marina's Garden

1   Marina looked out of her apartment window in the foggy morning and sighed. The city was all around her. Tall, gray buildings blocked her view, and the air was filled with the sounds of speeding cars and honking horns. There wasn't a speck of green to be found.

2   "If only we had a garden!" Marina sighed. Her grandmother's house had a big backyard and a beautiful garden. Marina loved to walk barefoot through the grass and feel the good garden earth between her toes. Every morning, she would fill a basket with plump red tomatoes or juicy strawberries. But her grandmother lived far away. Here in the city, there was no space for a garden. Her apartment did not even have a balcony where she could put a few flowerpots.

3   "Are you ready to go to the farmer's market, Marina?" her father asked. Marina jumped up. At least her family could still have fresh vegetables, thanks to the vendors at the market.

4   At the market, Marina walked up and down the rows of fresh vegetables and fruit. "Look at this squash, Papa!" she cried, holding the slim yellow fruit in her hands. "If only we had a garden, I could grow vegetables like these!"

Think About It

What is the setting of this story? To answer the question, look for phrases that describe where and when the story is happening.

Read the beginning of the story again. As you read, underline the lines that describe where and when the story takes place.

Where does the story take place?	When does the story take place?
•	•

A CLOSER LOOK

Events in this story happen over a few months. Circle phrases that show when key events take place.

Continue reading the story. Then answer the question.

5 "You want a garden?" said the vegetable vendor with a smile. "I hear that a community garden is going up on First Avenue."

6 Marina turned to her father. "We will definitely find out about that," he said.

7 A few days later, her father came home with some paperwork. "There is a garden starting in the neighborhood. Here is the registration form," he said.

8 "How does it work?" Marina asked.

9 "We pay a small fee and get a space called a plot. We can grow whatever we want there."

10 "Can we keep everything we grow?"

11 "Yes, although the garden organizers ask everyone to donate some of their vegetables and fruit to the community food bank."

12 Marina worked hard all summer. Together, she and her parents grew many beautiful plants. Their dinner table was full of fresh vegetables.

13 At last, fall arrived, and it was time to harvest the last of her plants. Marina packed a basket full of vegetables and headed to the farmer's market with her parents. "Are you going to set up a stand?" her mother joked.

14 "No," Marina said with a laugh. "I'm going to find the vendor who told us about this garden and give him a present as a thank you!"

What events move the story along and show what Marina does?

Marina gets her wish for a city garden when _____.

A she visits her grandmother once in a while

B her father comes home from the grocery store

C she joins a community garden in the summer

D she goes to thank the farmer's market vendor in the fall

 DISCUSS IT

Think about how the setting of the story affects the events that occur. Talk with another student about how the events in this story are connected to the setting.

Read the story. Then answer the questions.

adapted from Minnie's Pet Parrot

by Mrs. Madeline Leslie

A CLOSER LOOK
When do the events take place? Circle details that tell you.

Minnie and her pet parrot, Poll, were listening to a story told by Minnie's father when…

1 At this moment, Mrs. Lee opened the door to tell Minnie that Anne, the nurse, was waiting to put her to bed.

2 "It's too early," said the child, impatiently. "I don't want to go yet."

3 Her mother only answered by pointing to the little French timepiece on the mantel.

4 "I was having such a good time," sobbed Minnie. "I always have to go just when I'm enjoying myself the most."

5 Hearing this, Poll instantly began to whine, "I don't want to go." Then she put her claw up to her mouth and sobbed for all the world, just like her little mistress.

6 Minnie wanted to laugh, but she felt ashamed. She did not like to have her parents see her, so she said, "Keep still, Poll. You have nothing to do with it."

7 This reproof only excited the bird the more. In a loud, angry tone, she went on.

8 "Keep, still, Poll! Don't meddle! Don't meddle! Ah, Poll, what are you about? Take care, I see you!"

9 Mr. Lee watched his daughter anxiously to see whether she would recover her temper. He was pleased to see that she presently went over to the cage and held out her finger to say "Good night" to her pet as usual.

10 "Good night," repeated the bird, holding out her claw.

11 She then gave her parents their good-night kiss.

What detail in the story helps show where the story takes place?

1 Which answer *best* describes the setting?

   A a hospital

   B the living room in Minnie's home

   C a pet store

   D Minnie's bedroom

What does Minnie do just before Poll speaks in an angry tone?

2 Why does Poll speak in a loud, angry tone?

   A She does not like the nurse.

   B She does not want to go to bed.

   C She is imitating Minnie.

   D She wants to hear the rest of the story.

How do Minnie and Poll react to each other? Their interaction helps move the story along and solve the problem.

3 What event in the story makes Minnie calm down and agree to go to bed?

   _____

   _____

   _____

   _____

PART 4

Read the story. Then answer the questions.

adapted from Around the World in 80 Days

by Jules Verne

Chapter 3

1 "Well, Ralph," said Thomas Flanagan. "What about that robbery?"

2 "Oh," replied Stuart, "the Bank will lose the money."

3 "On the contrary," broke in Ralph. "I hope we may put our hands on the robber. Skillful detectives have been sent to all the principal ports of America and the Continent."

4 "But have you got the robber's description?" asked Stuart.

5 "In the first place, he is no robber at all," returned Ralph, positively.

6 "What! A fellow who makes off with 55 thousand pounds, no robber?"

7 "No."

8 "Perhaps he's a manufacturer, then."

9 "*The Daily Telegraph* says that he is a gentleman."

10 It was Phileas Fogg, whose head emerged from behind his newspapers, who made this remark. The affair had occurred three days before at the Bank of England. A package of banknotes, to the value of 55 thousand pounds, had been taken from the principal cashier's table. At that moment the cashier was registering the receipt of three shillings and sixpence. Of course, he could not have his eyes everywhere. Let it be observed that the Bank of England possesses a touching confidence in the honesty of the public. There are neither guards nor gratings to protect its treasures.

11 As soon as the robbery was discovered, picked detectives hastened off to Liverpool, Glasgow, Havre, New York, and other ports, inspired by the reward. Detectives were also charged with watching those who arrived at or left London by rail.

12 There were real grounds for supposing that the thief did not belong to a professional band. On the day of the robbery, a well-dressed gentleman had been observed going to and fro in the paying room where the crime was committed. A description of him was easily procured and sent to the detectives. Some hopeful spirits, of whom Ralph was one, did not despair of his being caught. The Reform Club was especially agitated, several of its members being Bank officials.

13 "I maintain," said Stuart, "that the chances are in favor of the thief."

14 "Well, but where can he fly to?" asked Ralph. "No country is safe for him."

15 "Oh, I don't know that. The world is big enough."

16 "It was once," said Phileas Fogg.

17 "What do you mean by 'once'? Has the world grown smaller?"

18 "Certainly," returned Ralph. "I agree with Mr. Fogg. The world has grown smaller, since a man can now go round it ten times more quickly than 100 years ago. And that is why the search for this thief will be more likely to succeed."

19 "And why he can get away more easily."

20 But the incredulous Stuart was not convinced, and said eagerly: "You have a strange way, Ralph, of proving that the world has grown smaller. So, because you can go round it in three months—"

21 "In 80 days," interrupted Phileas Fogg.

1 What event happens at the beginning of this passage?

   A A bank robbery occurs.

   B Some men are playing cards.

   C Phileas is reading the newspaper.

   D Phileas and his friends are talking about a robbery.

2 Where is this story set?

   A in England

   B in a bank

   C in New York

   D at a newspaper office

3 Why are the men so interested in the bank robbery?

_____

_____

_____

_____

4 How does the last line of the story connect to the title? What event do you think will happen next?

_____

_____

_____

_____

LESSON 5

Drawing Inferences from Literary Texts

 **Introduction**

THEME: >>> **The Story Inside**

Authors don't always tell everything they want readers to know. Often, readers have to make **inferences,** or educated guesses, from the text. When you make an inference, you use clues from the text and your own knowledge to figure out something the author does not tell you. As you read, it is important to pay attention to clues that help you figure out information that is not explained.

Look at the illustration.

Make an inference about why the boy asks his parents if they can leave.

Inference	Clue #1	Clue #2	Clue #3

It is important to pay attention to the details of a story. It would be boring if authors told everything that happened in a story, so readers must use inference to understand what is going on.

Read the first part of the poem. Then answer the questions.

The Hare and the Tortoise
by Jean de La Fontaine

Said the Tortoise one day to the Hare:
"I'll run you a race if you dare.
I'll bet you cannot
Arrive at that spot
5 As quickly as *I* can get there."

Quoth the Hare: "You are surely insane.
Pray, *what* has affected your brain?
You seem pretty sick.
Call a doctor in—quick,
10 And let him prescribe for your pain."

"Never mind," said the Tortoise. "Let's run!
Will you bet me?" "Why, certainly." "Done!"
While the slow Tortoise creeps
Mr. Hare makes four leaps,
15 And then loafs around in the sun.

Think About It

Why does the Hare agree to bet the Tortoise that the Hare will win? Think about why the Hare decides to run a race against the Tortoise.

Read the poem again. Underline clues that tell why Hare agrees to bet that he will win.

In the table below, explain why the Hare agrees to bet and run the race against the Tortoise. Use the details you underlined and what you already know about the two animals.

What the Text Says	What I Know	Inference
The poem says that "while the slow Tortoise creeps, _____ _____ _____.		

A CLOSER LOOK

Circle phrases in this part of the poem that tell what the Hare thinks about the race.

Continue reading the poem. Then answer the question.

It seemed such a one-sided race,
To win was almost a disgrace.
So he frolicked about
Then at last he set out—
20   As the Tortoise was as nearing the place.

Too late! Though he sped like a dart,
The Tortoise was first. She was smart:
"You can surely run fast,"
She remarked. "Yet you're last.
25   It is better to get a good start."

What does the Hare do during the race?

How does the Tortoise win the race?

A   The Hare stops to rest.

B   The Tortoise has longer legs.

C   The Tortoise gets a head start.

D   The Hare is not as fast as he thinks he is.

 DISCUSS IT

Based on the events in the story, what can you infer about the Tortoise and the Hare's personalities? Talk with another student about how the events in this story show what these characters are like.

42   UNIT 1 Key Ideas and Details in Literary Text

Read the passage. Then answer the questions.

Bruce and the Spider
by James H. Fassett

A CLOSER LOOK
Bruce's words and actions help you infer his feelings at the beginning of the story. Circle details that show how he feels.

Why does Bruce compare himself to the spider? Circle the part of the story that shows the reasons he thinks they are alike.

1   Robert Bruce, King of Scotland, was hiding in a hut in the forest. His enemies were seeking him far and wide.

2   Six times he had met them in battle, and six times he had failed. Hope and courage were gone.

3   Bruce had given up all as lost. He was about to run away from Scotland, and to leave the country in the hands of his enemies.

4   Full of sorrow, he lay stretched on a pile of straw in the poor woodchopper's hut. While he lay thinking, he noticed a spider spinning her web.

5   The spider was trying to spin a thread from one beam of the cottage to another. It was a long way between the beams, and Bruce saw how hard a thing it was for her to do.

6   "She can never do it," thought the king.

7   The little spider tried it once and failed. She tried it twice and failed. The king counted each time. At length she had tried it six times and had failed each time.

8   "She is like me," thought the king. "I have tried six battles and failed. She has tried six times to reach the beam and failed."

9   Then starting up from the straw, he cried, "I will hang my fate upon that little spider.

10 If she swings the seventh time and fails, then I will give up all for lost. If she swings the seventh time and wins, I will call my men together once more for a battle with the enemy."

11 The spider tried the seventh time, letting herself down upon her slender thread. She swung out bravely.

12 "Look! look!" shouted the king. "She has reached it. The thread hangs between the two beams. If the spider can do it, I can do it."

13 Bruce got up from the straw with new strength and sent his men from village to village, calling the people to arms.

14 The brave soldiers answered his call and came trooping in.

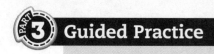
15 At length his army was ready to fight, and when the king led them in a great battle against the enemy, this time, like the spider, Bruce won.

> **What does Bruce do in the woodchopper's cottage?**

1 How does Bruce feel after he has lost six battles?

A angry

B brave

C defeated

D frightened

> **What does Bruce say about the spider?**

2 Why does Bruce let the spider decide if he will go back into battle?

A He dislikes making decisions.

B He believes that the spider is brave.

C He sees that the spider does not give up.

D He thinks the spider was sent to tell him what to do.

> **What does the spider do in the story? How do her efforts make Bruce feel?**

3 What can you infer about Bruce's attitude at the end of this story? Support your answer with at least one detail from the story.

_____

_____

_____

_____

Read the story. Then answer the questions.

The Class Trip

1   Ariana lay back on the couch and switched off the television. Last week, she'd been in the hospital for an operation. At first, she liked spending time with her mom, but now she was beginning to wish she was back in school. Ariana picked up her diary and a pen and began to write.

Dear Diary,

I never thought I would miss school so much! It seems like it's taking forever for me to get better. It's such a beautiful, sunny day outside, but I have to stay inside.

I can't believe I am stuck home today of all days. Today is the class trip to Marquette City. I looked forward to that trip all year. Let's see, it's 10:00 right now. I'll bet all of my friends are on the bus, singing songs and telling jokes. Pretty soon they'll get to the city, and then the fun will really start. And where am I? Home on the couch, watching television.

2   Ariana put her diary down and closed her eyes. Maybe taking a nap would make the day go faster. Sure enough, when Ariana woke up, it was lunchtime. Her mother helped her into the kitchen, where they shared a nice lunch. Still, all Ariana could think about were her friends and classmates.

3   Later that afternoon, Ariana turned on her computer. To her surprise, she had a video message from her best friend, Shauna. "Hi, Ariana," Shauna said, grinning into the camera. "I have a surprise for you." Ariana was puzzled. How could Shauna be sending her a video when she was on the class trip?

4   Shauna stepped back and turned the camera around. Ariana let out a yell. Her whole class was standing there, waving at her. "Hi, Ariana," they called. "We miss you!"

5   Shauna came back on the screen. "We decided that since you couldn't come on our trip, we'd bring the trip to you. Here's what we did today." The video went on to show her classmates on the bus and lining up for a special tour of the science museum. Shauna and Ariana's other classmates made sure to show her every detail of the museum. They even showed her the cool experiments they did there. After lunch at a seafood restaurant, the class got onto a special tour bus that traveled around Marquette City to visit all the historical places. Ariana laughed at the strange-looking buildings from long ago.

6 "Hey, Ariana, it's time to get on the bus to go home," Shauna said at the end of the video. "But we have one last surprise for you." Ariana noticed that all of her classmates were wearing yellow T-shirts with the school's name and *Marquette City Class Trip* on each of them. Shauna held up a shirt just like the one everyone was wearing. "This is for you, Ariana! I'll drop it off at your house tomorrow. We'll all wear our shirts on the day you come back to school. Meanwhile, we just want to say one more thing." She turned the camera around so everyone could crowd into the picture.

7 "Come back soon, Ariana!" everyone yelled.

8 Ariana grinned. She felt so much better than she had that morning. She grabbed a calendar and counted the days since her operation. It looked like it wouldn't be much longer before she could go back to school and join the fun!

1 Part A
How does Ariana feel at the beginning of the story?

A angry

B bored

C happy

D scared

Part B
What sentence from the passage *best* supports the answer to Part A?

A "Ariana was puzzled."

B "To her surprise, she had a video message from her best friend, Shauna."

C "Still, all Ariana could think about were her friends and classmates."

D *"Home on the couch, watching television."*

2 When can you infer that Ariana will go back to school?

 A the next day

 B in a few weeks

 C not for a long time

 D at the end of the school year

3 How do Ariana's classmates feel about her missing the trip? Be sure to include at least two details from the story to support your answer.

_____

_____

_____

_____

4 Think about the day Ariana returns to school. What can you infer about how she will feel on that day? Include two details from the story to support your answer.

_____

_____

_____

_____

_____

_____

LESSON 6

Summarizing Literary Texts

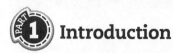

Introduction

THEME: >>> The Story Inside

When you read a story, play, or poem, it is important to **summarize** the text. When you summarize, you tell only the most important events and details. You leave out the unimportant ones. A good summary will tell about the setting, characters, events, problem and solution in your own words. As you read, pay attention to the important characters, events, and ideas of a story, play, or poem. This will help you to retell what you have read in your own words.

Read the story. Then answer the questions.

Mark threw back the covers and jumped out of bed. He couldn't believe it! He had slept through his alarm, and now he was late for school. Mark hurried to brush his teeth and comb his hair. He pulled on his pants and a shirt. "Oh no!" he yelled as a button popped off his shirt. Grumbling, he grabbed another shirt, not noticing that it did not match his pants at all.

Mark ran downstairs and made a cup of hot chocolate. He tried to gulp it down. "Ouch!" he said. "Too hot!" Then Mark grabbed a bowl of cereal, but it spilled all over him. Mark wiped up the mess as best as he could and ran out to the car where his mother was waiting. It was going to be a terrible day.

Who is the story about? _____

Where does it take place? _____

When does it take place? _____

What is the problem? _____

Use your answers to summarize the story. _____

_____

_____

_____

Read the first part of the poem. Then answer the questions.

from Sea Dreams

by Alfred, Lord Tennyson

What does little birdie say
In her nest at peep of day?
Let me fly, says little birdie,
Mother, let me fly away.
5 Birdie, rest a little longer,
Till the little wings are stronger.
So she rests a little longer,
Then she flies away.

Think About It

What is happening in the poem so far? The question asks about the events in this part of the poem. As you summarize the events, you will see how one event leads to another.

Who is the poem about? _____

Where do the events take place? _____

What happens in lines 1–4 of the poem? _____

_____

What happens in lines 5–8? _____

_____

On the lines below, summarize the first part of this poem.

_____

_____

_____

A CLOSER LOOK

Circle phrases in this part of the poem that tell what the baby wants to do.

Continue reading the poem. Then answer the question.

What does little baby say,
10   In her bed at peep of day?
Baby says, like little birdie,
Let me rise and fly away.
Baby, sleep a little longer,
Till the little limbs are stronger,
15   If she sleeps a little longer,
Baby too shall fly away.

How is the baby like the little birdie?

Which of the following is the *best* summary of this part of the poem?

A   The baby wants to learn to fly.

B   The baby wants to go away on her own.

C   The baby wants to watch the birdie fly away.

D   The baby wants to stay in her bed.

DISCUSS IT

Discuss with a partner what details should be included in a summary. Talk about what details should not be included.

Read the play. Then answer the questions.

Singing Idol

A CLOSER LOOK

What are the most important events that move the story along? Underline the main events in each act of the play.

CAST:

RACHEL, *a young musician*

SERGIO, *a singer*

ANDY, *an announcer*

JUDY, *another musician*

act 1

Backstage in an auditorium, RACHEL *is tuning her guitar. She is wearing a paper with the number 2 pinned to her shirt.* SERGIO *and other contestants are sitting alongside* RACHEL.

ANDY: *(entering)* Good evening! Is everyone ready to sing?

RACHEL and OTHERS: Yes!

ANDY: Great! Our "Singing Idol" contest is about to begin. When I call your number, come onstage and introduce yourself. Then you perform. Good luck! (ANDY *exits.)*

SERGIO: I'm so nervous!

RACHEL: Me too, but I'm excited. I've always wanted to be a singer. This could be my big chance.

ANDY: *(from offstage)* Please welcome, Number 1, Sergio Margonis!

SERGIO *exits. He returns a few minutes later, shaking his head.*

SERGIO: Those judges are tough, but I did my best.

ANDY: *(from offstage)* Next, welcome Number 2, Rachel Klein!

RACHEL *stands and carries her guitar offstage.*

act 2

Onstage, a short while later, the other contestants are lined up onstage.

ANDY: Congratulations to all our performers. For the next round, we'd like to hear contestants with these numbers: 3, 7, 10, 15, 20, and 25. To everyone else, thank you and best of luck!

SERGIO: Oh, well, we weren't chosen.

RACHEL: Oh no! I really thought… *(Her voice trails off, and she fights back tears.)*

SERGIO: Come on, let's go backstage.

RACHEL *follows* SERGIO, *wiping her eyes.* JUDY *is standing at the side of the stage, wearing the number 25 on her shirt.* JUDY *is looking around frantically.*

RACHEL: What's the matter? Andy called your number, didn't he? You get to move on to the finals.

JUDY: I'm supposed to, but the girl who was playing the guitar for me left. I can't sing without music. How am I supposed to go onstage?

RACHEL: Wow, that's terrible. *(She looks down at the guitar in her hands.)* Hey, I'm not busy. I mean, I'm not in the competition anymore. Maybe I could help you.

JUDY: *(looking hopeful)* Really? Do you know the song "Danny Boy"?

RACHEL: I do! It's one of my favorites. Come backstage with me. We can practice while the other contestants are having their turns. *(The two girls hurry backstage.)*

act 3

Onstage JUDY *and* RACHEL *have just finished performing and are walking back to line up with the other contestants.* ANDY *steps up to the microphone.*

ANDY: Nice job. Hey, wasn't that guitar player in the first round? (RACHEL *nods.*) Well, good for her for stepping up to help. Now I have the winning results. In fourth place, number 20, Ari Mendel. In third place, number 25, Judy Jackson. Second place goes to number 5, Alyssa Wilson. And our Singing Idol champion is number 10, Nivi Taylor!

RACHEL: You were great, Judy. I'm sorry you didn't win.

JUDY: *(shrugging)* It was my first year. I'm thrilled I won third place! I couldn't have done it without your help.

RACHEL: I was glad to help. I really like to perform. Performing is even better than winning—and so is making a new friend! Come on, let's go get some ice cream. *(The two girls exit, arm in arm.)*

> What does Rachel tell Sergio?

1 What does Rachel want in act 1?

   A to sing with Sergio

   B to win the contest

   C to play her guitar onstage

   D to help another performer

> What does Rachel do as she walks offstage in act 2?

2 How does Rachel feel when she is not picked for the final round?

   A She is upset.

   B She is relieved.

   C She is very angry.

   D She does not care.

> What does Rachel tell Judy at the end of the play?

3 Summarize how the events in the play show a change in the way Rachel feels. Include at least one detail from the play to support your answer.

_____

_____

_____

_____

_____

_____

Read the story. Then answer the questions.

The Fox and the Goat
by Aesop

1 A Fox fell into a well, and though it was not very deep, he found that he could not get out again. After he had been in the well a long time, a thirsty Goat came by. The Goat thought the Fox had gone down to drink, and so he asked if the water was good.

2 "The finest in the whole country," said the crafty Fox, "jump in and try it. There is more than enough for both of us."

3 The thirsty Goat immediately jumped in and began to drink. The Fox just as quickly jumped on the Goat's back and leaped from the tip of the Goat's horns out of the well.

4 The foolish Goat now saw what a plight he had gotten into, and begged the Fox to help him out. But the Fox was already on his way to the woods.

5 "If you had as much sense as you have beard, old fellow," he said as he ran, "you would have been more cautious about finding a way to get out again before you jumped in."

1 Part A

Why does the Goat jump into the well?

A He wants to help the Fox.

B He feels sorry for the Fox.

C The Fox tells him the water is good.

D He wants someone to keep him company.

Part B

What line from the passage *best* supports the answer to Part A?

A "jump in and try it"

B "what a plight he had gotten into"

C "it was not very deep"

D "the Fox had gone down to drink"

2 What happens immediately after the Goat jumps into the well?

   A The Goat gets stuck in the well.

   B The Goat begs the Fox to help him.

   C Fox says the Goat doesn't have any sense.

   D The Fox jumps on the Goat's back to get out of the well.

3 Why does the Fox refuse to help the Goat out of the well?

_____

_____

_____

_____

4 Write a summary of the fable on the lines below. Support your answer with a detail from the fable.

_____

_____

_____

_____

_____

_____

Key Ideas and Details in Literary Text

Read the poem. Then answer the questions.

Friends

by Abbie Farwell Brown

How good to lie a little while
And look up through the tree!
The Sky is like a kind big smile
Bent sweetly over me.

5   The Sunshine flickers through the lace
Of leaves above my head,
And kisses me upon the face
Like Mother, before bed.

The Wind comes stealing o'er the grass
10 To whisper pretty things;
And though I cannot see him pass,
I feel his careful wings.

So many gentle Friends are near
Whom one can scarcely see,
15 A child should never feel a fear,
Wherever he may be.

1 What is the setting of the poem?

   A inside looking out a window

   B outside under a tree

   C inside with gentle friends

   D outside on a very windy day

2 Part A

What can you infer about how the narrator feels in the poem?

A unhappy

B safe

C scared

D tired

Part B

What line from the poem *best* supports the answer to Part A?

A "So many gentle Friends are near"

B "How good to lie a little while"

C "The Sunshine flickers through the lace"

D "The Wind comes stealing o'er the grass"

3 What is the theme of this poem? Support your answer with details from the poem.

_____

_____

_____

_____

_____

Read the story. Then answer the questions.

Searching for Aunt Marie

1   Tina curled up on the couch, a cup of hot chocolate on the table beside her and a big box on her lap. Carefully, she opened the lid, and then pulled out the contents of the box. Dozens of old photographs spilled out across the couch.

2   Tina loved looking at old family photos. It was fun to see family and friends. Tina had never met some of these people, but she enjoyed looking at them and thinking about how she was related to them. It was funny to see them dressed in old-fashioned clothes, too!

3   Tina flipped through the photos until suddenly, she came across a photo she had never seen before. The photo showed a young woman standing on a trail in the woods wearing jeans, a heavy sweater, hiking boots, and a baseball cap.

4   "Hey, Mom, can you come here for a second?" Tina called. Her mother came out of the bedroom. "Who is this?" Tina asked her.

5   Her mother studied the photo. "Oh, that's Aunt Marie! Marie Horan. She was my mother's sister. I haven't seen her since I was your age."

6   "Why not?" Tina wondered.

7   "She was older than my mother, so they didn't really grow up together. Marie moved to another state—Colorado, I think—and lost touch with the family. I have no idea where she is now."

8   *A mystery relative!* Tina was fascinated. "Do you remember anything about her?"

9   Tina's mother frowned in thought. "I remember that she loved hiking and rock climbing. That photo looks like it was taken in the national park near where we grew up. I remember that Aunt Marie and her friends used to climb there all the time."

10   Tina stared at the photo while she drank her hot chocolate. Finally, she put the photos away and put the box back on the shelf where it belonged. Still, she couldn't stop thinking about Aunt Marie.

11   "Mom, I'm going on the computer," she called. Tina clicked on the Internet and typed "Marie Horan" into the search engine. A lot of names came up, but none of them seemed to be Aunt Marie. Tina frowned. Then she had an idea. Her fingers flew over the keys, typing, "Marie Horan rock climbing." She looked through the results, and then she began to smile.

12   "Mom, come look!" Tina yelled excitedly. When her mother hurried into the room, Tina pointed at the screen. "Here's a membership list for a rock-climbing club in Boulder, Colorado." She pointed at one name: Marie Horan Cullen. "Could that be Aunt Marie?"

13   "It could be. There's an email address, so I could always email her and ask." Tina's mother shook her head in disbelief. "Wouldn't that be amazing if it really was her? I haven't thought about Aunt Marie in 20 years, and you found her in just a few minutes."

14   "Well, you gave me all the clues I needed to find her," Tina said proudly. "Maybe I should be a detective!"

4 What is the setting of this story?

    A on a hiking trip

    B in a national park

    C Boulder, Colorado

    D inside a home

5 What can you infer about Tina?

    A She enjoys hiking outdoors.

    B She likes to solve mysteries.

    C She would rather live in the past.

    D She loves spending time on the computer.

6 Why does Tina enjoy looking at old photographs? Include two details from the story to support your answer.

_____

_____

_____

_____

_____

7 Write a summary of the story.

_____

_____

_____

_____

_____

_____

Read the play. Then answer the questions.

excerpt from Time and the Seasons

by Florence Holbrook

In this play, FATHER TIME *has asked his daughter* AUTUMN *what she has to offer children.*

CAST:

FATHER TIME

AUTUMN

FATHER TIME: Children are so fond of play and the long summer days out-of-doors that I wonder what they think of you, my older daughter, Autumn?

AUTUMN: Children do like to play, and I am glad they get so well and strong with the vacation my sister, Summer, gives them. Yet all children like to learn, too. We must not forget that. What joy it is to read the beautiful stories that great men and women have written for them. What delight they have in learning to write, to sing, to draw, and to make pretty objects of paper, clay, and wood.

FATHER TIME: Yes, that is true, but have you no pleasures out-of-doors for them?

AUTUMN: Some people say my days are the most pleasant of the year. The gardens have many beautiful flowers, and the fruits are ripening in the orchards and vineyards. The apples hang red on the boughs, and children like to pick them and eat them, too! I have the harvest moon, the time when the farmers bring home the crops ripened by August suns, and the earth seems to gather the results of the year's work, the riches of field, orchard, and meadow. The squirrels gather their hoard of nuts and hide them away for their winter's food. Gay voices of nutting parties are heard in the woods, and all the air is filled with songs of praise and thanksgiving for the bounty of the year.

FATHER TIME: Your work is surely one of worth, and I rejoice with you, my daughter, in your happiness. You are a true friend of men, showing them that honest effort and its work will always bring proper reward.

8 What word *best* describes Father Time?

A kind

B playful

C powerful

D uncaring

9 Part A

How does Autumn feel about her time of the year?

A She does not like it.

B She does not care about it.

C She thinks it is the best time.

D She thinks Summer is more fun.

Part B

What detail from the text *best* supports the answer in Part A?

A Autumn says children like to learn.

B Autumn thanks her sister, Summer.

C Autumn believes children like to be inside.

D Autumn says people say her days are the most pleasant.

10 What is the theme of this play? Use details from the play to support your answer.

_____

_____

_____

_____

_____

_____

Informational texts are different from stories, plays, and poems. Informational texts can be news articles, speeches, biographies, letters to the editor, or directions. Their purpose is in their name: Informational texts provide information! When reading these texts, look for the main idea and details that support the main idea. Practice summarizing, ask yourself questions, and make inferences, too—and you can learn the most you can from a text!

LESSON 7 Determining Main Ideas and Details will help you find the main idea in an informational text by thinking about the most important thing the author wants you to remember. You will also look for the important details that support the main idea.

LESSON 8 Explaining Events and Concepts in Historical Texts is about asking questions while you read texts about the past. When you pay close attention and ask yourself questions like *What happened?* and *Why?* you can better understand events and concepts and how they are connected.

LESSON 9 Explaining Events and Concepts in Scientific Texts will help you understand and explain the ideas and events you might find in science texts. Continue to ask yourself questions, think about the main ideas, and note the important details.

LESSON 10 Explaining Events and Concepts in Technical Texts will help you read technical texts, passages that can tell you how things work or how they are made. You will look at key details to understand concepts and events.

LESSON 11 Drawing Inferences in Informational Texts is about using clues from the text to make an educated guess, or inference. Look for the important details that support your inference, and use these details to explain what the text says directly.

LESSON 12 Summarizing Informational Texts will help you find the important ideas in a text. You will learn what belongs in a good summary of an informational text. You will also practice retelling the important points in informational texts in your own words.

LESSON 7

Determining Main Ideas and Details

Introduction

THEME: >>> **Making a Difference**

When you look for the **main idea** of a text, you identify the author's most important point. Sometimes, the main idea is stated explicitly in the text. Other times, you have to make an inference about the main idea. **Key details** provide information that supports the main idea.

When you summarize an article, you include the main idea and the most important details supporting that main idea. You summarize using your own words. A summary should tell who, what, when, where, how, and why.

Read this paragraph. Think about the main idea.

Mountain gorillas live in groups of about 30 in the mountains of Central Africa. Each family group is led by an older male. The group includes younger males, females, and their babies. The leader protects his group. When the group is in danger, the leader might pound his huge chest. He might also release a loud, scary roar.

Complete the chart with three key details that support the main idea.

Main Idea: An older male mountain gorilla protects his family group.		
Detail:	**Detail:**	**Detail:**

Now summarize the paragraph.

_____

_____

_____

Read the first part of the passage. Then answer the questions.

The History of LEGO® Bricks

1 The history of LEGO products started in 1934 in Billund, Denmark. Ole Kirk Christiansen was a builder who made houses and furniture. He also made small models of his products. He used them to show customers what he could make for them.

2 In 1934, Christiansen decided to make wooden toys. For his company he chose the name *lego.* It is a combination of two Danish words, *leg* and *godt,* which mean "play well." However, *lego* in Latin means "I put together." Christiansen chose his company name well!

3 In 1949, the LEGO Group started making plastic blocks that locked together. The company started with six or seven workers. They included Christiansen's son. He began working in the family business when he was only 12.

4 It took five years for Christiansen and his workers to find a way to make the first plastic bricks. They made the first ones by hand. The workers poured melted plastic into a mold to make each brick. When the bricks cooled, they could be stacked on top of one another, and they could easily be pulled apart. Soon, the company designed machines to make the bricks.

Think About It

How can you identify the main idea of this part of the passage? To answer this question, think about what the author wants you to remember from the passage.

Complete the table with three details that support the main idea.

Main idea: LEGO products started as a small business in Denmark.		
Detail:	**Detail:**	**Detail:**

Continue reading the passage. Then answer the question.

5   By the 1960s, the LEGO Group was making and selling millions of the bricks. Then the company decided to make them from a different kind of plastic. This plastic made the bricks stronger, with brighter colors. Over the years, wheels, cars, and trains were added to the bricks. Next, more plastic parts were included in the sets so children could make cities, airports, parking garages, and other things. Then LEGO products began to create sets with themes.

6   In 1967, the company started making bigger bricks in sets called LEGO DUPLO®. Small children could easily play with them. By 1975, the company had 2,500 workers. In 1998, LEGO bricks were accepted into the National Toy Hall of Fame.

7   By 2011, the LEGO Group was the world's third largest toy manufacturer. But the company had even more ideas. In 2012, they started a new product, LEGO Friends. These sets were created especially for girls.

8   Today, the LEGO Group continues to add new LEGO sets to store shelves. The bricks are still carefully made so that even the oldest ones fit in the newest sets. However, the oldest sets are hard to find—and valuable to collectors. Yet the plastic bricks and sets are only part of the LEGO story. Now it includes movies, video games, online games, and working robots used in competitions. Today, children all over the world play with LEGO products, and LEGO bricks get more popular every year!

A CLOSER LOOK

How do you know that the bricks are carefully made? Underline the sentence that supports this idea.

Look for the most important details. A summary should be short.

Which sentence summarizes the important points in this part of the passage?

A   The LEGO Group decided to use a different plastic that is stronger and has brighter colors.

B   The bricks are carefully made so that the oldest ones fit in the newest sets.

C   The LEGO Group keeps growing as it offers new and popular products.

D   Now children all over the world play with LEGO products.

DISCUSS IT

Turn to another student. Discuss which details you would include in a summary of this part of the article. Do you agree with each other? Tell your partner how you would summarize the article in your own words.

Read the speech. Then answer the questions.

So You Want to Be a Chef?

a talk given by Chef Luke

A CLOSER LOOK

Circle words or phrases that tell the main idea. Draw boxes around three or four details that support the main idea.

1   Good morning. I am Chef Luke, and I am glad to talk to you today. If you like to cook, you might dream of becoming a chef. After all, chefs are in charge of the kitchen. Everyone looks up to them. They have fun creating tasty new dishes, and they get paid to do it!

2   Being a chef has many benefits, but it also has many demands. Most chefs work six days a week. Each day can be 14 hours long. A day goes something like this:

3   Between 8:00 and 9:30 a.m., I arrive at the restaurant and make sure that all the orders from the day before were delivered. I also check for missing items as well as spoiled vegetables and foods. If I find a problem, I must call the supplier or go to a market and get a replacement.

4   Soon, the kitchen staff begins to arrive. I give them their jobs for the morning. They must begin preparing soups, sauces, and other foods that will take a long time to cook. If we have a special dish that day, I tell the staff how to prepare it. Then I make that dish for the waiters to see and taste. Later, they will describe it for our diners.

5   Lunch starts between 11:00 a.m. and noon. I must check each dish before it's presented to our diners. It must look delicious! I also have to handle any problems that come up. That can be stressful, let me tell you!

6   After the lunch rush, the staff cleans up and gets ready for dinner. I plan menus and check to see what we need to order for the next day. I might attend a business meeting. I might even get to eat lunch!

7   Before dinner begins, I meet with the kitchen staff to talk about the evening specials. When we start serving, I will check all the meals before they reach our diners. If a cook is out sick, I might also take over his or her job.

8 My day usually ends about 10:30 or 11:30 p.m. I spend most of the day in the kitchen, but I don't do much cooking. This job does have long hours and many responsibilities. Still, I love it! I really like to see the smiles on our diners' faces when they taste a new dish I created.

What does this speaker want you to remember?

1 What is the main idea of this passage?

A "I plan menus and check to see what we need to order for the next day."

B "If a cook is out sick, I might also take over his or her job."

C "The job does have long hours and many responsibilities."

D "I like to see the smiles on our diners' faces when they taste a new dish I created."

The speaker organized this information this way so listeners would understand the main idea.

2 Why does this speaker describe his day hour by hour?

A He wants to show how long his day is.

B He has a tight schedule.

C He wants to tell what he does at noon.

D He does something different every hour.

Someone should be able to read your summary and understand the main points of the article.

3 Write a summary of this passages in two or three sentences.

_____

_____

_____

_____

Read the passage. Then answer the questions.

adapted from George Washington, Commander-in-Chief

1   As Commander-in-Chief of the Continental Army, George Washington was a daring leader. He used the element of surprise to win American victories. One of the most memorable surprise movements was when he secretly led his troops across the icy Delaware River in the early morning of December 26, 1776, and attacked the unsuspecting Hessian troops at Trenton, New Jersey. This forced the British troops to spend the winter in New York City. During this short three-week campaign, the entire cause of the American Revolution was saved by Washington's bold and skillful action. The Continental Army became more confident that it could win the war.

2   The road to victory, however, was not easy. Over the next long months, Washington's Continental Army grew weary. The soldiers marched into Valley Forge, Pennsylvania, on December 19, 1777, after several tough battles with the British. Washington and his men spent the winter at Valley Forge. They lived in a log hut city for six months. There, the men received expert training to improve their skills as soldiers. Washington was able to reorganize several military departments to improve services to the soldiers.

3   On June 19, 1778, the Continental Army marched out of Valley Forge with new spirit and determination. The troops pursued the British as they departed from Philadelphia, and defeated them at the Battle of Monmouth in New Jersey.

4   The Continental Army bravely fought for another five years under Washington's leadership. Finally, they defeated the larger and better-equipped British. Washington's courage and determination inspired his troops. He defeated General Cornwallis and his troops at Yorktown in October 1781, the last major battle of the Revolutionary War.

1   What is the main idea of the entire passage?

  A   The road to victory was not easy, and one shouldn't give up.

  B   General Washington's leadership allowed his troops to defeat the British.

  C   The Continental Army defeated the better-equipped British army.

  D   Washington used the element of surprise against the British.

2 **Part A**

What is the main idea of the last paragraph?

   A   The Continental Army left Valley Forge with new determination.

   B   The Continental Army fought for five more years.

   C   The troops pursued the British as they fled from Philadelphia.

   D   Washington led his army to defeat the larger, better-equipped British.

Part B

What key detail *best* supports your answer to Part A?

_____

_____

3 Which detail does *not* support the main idea from the first paragraph: "Washington used the element of surprise against the British"?

   A   His troops attacked the unsuspecting Hessian troops at Trenton.

   B   Washington secretly led his troops across the icy Delaware River.

   C   Washington and his men spent the winter at Valley Forge.

   D   The American Revolution was saved by Washington's bold action.

4 Write a summary of this passage in three or four sentences. Be sure to include the main idea and several key details.

_____

_____

_____

_____

_____

_____

LESSON 8

Explaining Events and Concepts in Historical Texts

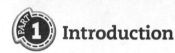 **Introduction**

THEME: >>> **Making a Difference**

You can better understand events, ideas, and concepts if you look for connections. Ask yourself questions as you read. For example, you might ask, "What happened? What caused that to happen? What was the result?" Then look for specific information in the text to answer your questions. Think about how events are connected.

> **Read this paragraph. Then answer the questions.**
>
> Elizabeth Cady Stanton set the stage for women to get the vote in the United States. Throughout her life, Stanton fought for equal rights for women. In 1848 at the Seneca Falls Convention, the first convention to advocate for women's rights, many participants signed Stanton's Declaration of Sentiments, which called for equal rights for women in many arenas. In championing the rights of women, Stanton worked closely with Susan B. Anthony. These two women formed the National Women Suffrage Association in 1869 and toured the United States to educate people about the issues. Stanton died in 1902. She didn't live to see the passage of the 19th amendment in 1920 that gave women the right to vote. But it is thanks to her legacy that this historical moment happened.

What happened at the Seneca Falls Convention in 1848? _____

_____

Why was the main concept of this passage important in history? _____

_____

_____

_____

_____

Read the first part of the passage.

The Great Plains, Then and Now

1   The middle of North America is called the prairie, or Great Plains. It covers all or part of ten states. This prairie land was once covered with grasses and colorful wildflowers. Very few trees grew there. The trees that did were small and grew along the streams or rivers.

2   Because the Great Plains covers millions of acres, the climate is not the same throughout. Areas near the Rocky Mountains are wetter, while the central area is drier. However, the amount of rainfall changes from year to year. The summers tend to be long and dry. Every 30 years or so, it barely rains at all for several years.

3   Long ago, herds of buffalo, elk, deer, and rabbits thrived on the Great Plains. However, in the late 1800s, people began to move west. Between 1878 and 1887, more rain fell on the prairie than usual. That made the Great Plains seem ideal for farming and ranching. Herds of cattle soon replaced the buffalo.

4   You might have heard about the "Dust Bowl" of the 1930s. By this time, farmers had plowed up much of the ground to plant crops. They did not realize that the native grasses had deep roots that were holding the soil in place. Because the grasses were gone, the next dry spell turned the soil into dust. Strong winds were able to pick up the dry soil. About 100 million acres of rich topsoil blew across the land. For months, great black storms covered the prairie with a layer of dust.

Think About It

What caused changes in the Great Plains? To answer the question, think about what events caused other events to happen.

How did events between 1878 and 1887 affect people? _____

_____

Why did farmers' actions affect the Great Plains in the 1930s? _____

_____

_____

_____

A CLOSER LOOK

What effect is the Nature Conservancy having on the prairie? Underline the sentences that tell about this connection.

Continue reading the passage. Then answer the question.

5   Since then, farmers have learned better ways to care for the land. Farmers in many parts of the Great Plains pipe water from a water source to the land. This helps irrigate the fields during periods when there is less rain.

6   Today, only one to two percent of the original prairies survive. Much of the land is used for farming or is occupied by busy towns and cities. The buffalo and other wildlife are nearly gone.

7   However, the US Environmental Protection Agency (EPA) has set aside ten percent of the Great Plains as wildlife habitat. Plants and animals in danger of disappearing from this habitat live there. Other plants and animals thrive there, too, such as ducks, quail, moose, and deer. Many other groups are also working to educate people about prairies. Several states are preserving what is left of their prairies and protecting native wildlife and plants.

8   The Nature Conservancy is working to put buffalo, also called bison, back on the prairie. About 30 years ago, this group set up its first herd on a South Dakota prairie. Now, that herd has 250 bison, with a goal of 300. A second herd lives on another ranch. Other herds are being set up in other prairie states. The bison graze all year, eating the grasses and leaving the wildflowers. That helps the prairie look more like it once did.

9   The Great Plains are still there, but they look much different than they did long ago. Still, many groups are working to make sure they do not disappear forever.

Think about cause-and-effect relationships.

Which statement describes something that happened on the Great Plains and explains why?

A   Farmers are selling farmland to create towns and cities.

B   The EPA is putting buffalo back on the Plains to preserve prairie wildlife.

C   The EPA set aside land to protect rare native plants and animals.

D   Many states are protecting what is left of the Plains because it is good farmland.

 DISCUSS IT

Turn to another student. Name something that happened in this article. Ask your partner to tell why it happened. Then switch roles.

Read the passage. Then answer the questions.

Dr. Martin Cooper, Inventor of the Cellphone

Way back in 1973, did you know that cellphones would become popular?

Dr. Cooper: I knew that people wanted to be able to talk from anywhere. People like the freedom to talk to other people anytime, not just at home or in the car. I knew that cellphones would be popular with people everywhere.

How did you invent the cellphone?

Dr. Cooper: I was the research manager at Motorola. Our engineers applied for a patent for a "radio telephone system." That was the beginning of the cellular phone.

What did the first cellphone look like?

Dr. Cooper: The first cell phone was made in 1973. It was named the Dyna-Tec. It was huge—almost the size of a shoebox. The battery lasted for only 20 minutes. However, that was fine because the phone weighed two and a half pounds. You couldn't hold it up to your ear that long because it was so heavy! It took ten hours to charge the battery.

Who got the first cellphone call?

Dr. Cooper: I made the first cellphone call from a sidewalk in New York City. I called Joe Engel, my rival in research, the general manager at AT&T. I wanted to let him know that we beat his team. We developed the cellphone first.

Did anyone around you notice what you were doing?

Dr. Cooper: The people standing around me were amazed. In 1973, no one had ever seen someone make a call from a sidewalk using a cellphone. Well, maybe they had seen one in a cartoon or on a funny TV show. Today, just about everyone has a cellphone. It took our company ten years to bring cellphones to market. Finally, cellphones could be sold in stores. Now, more people have cellphones than wired phones.

A CLOSER LOOK

Why did Dr. Cooper call Joe Engel? Circle the words that tell what happened. Draw a box around words that explain why.

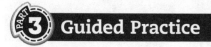

> Some choices resulted from his invention, but were they the real reason for it?

1 Why did Dr. Cooper want to invent a cellphone?

A to beat his rival in research at AT&T

B to become famous

C so people could talk to each other from anywhere

D so people would be amazed by his invention

> Think about why people could hold the phone up to their ears for only a short time.

2 Why was the first cellphone so heavy?

A because it was as big as a shoe box

B because the battery took ten hours to charge

C because the battery lasted only 20 minutes

D because it was the first one of its kind

> How has Dr. Cooper's invention affected people's lives today?

3 Using details from the passage, explain the results of Dr. Cooper inventing the first cellphone.

_____

_____

_____

_____

Read the passage. Then answer the questions.

adapted from How Baseball Began

1 No one is exactly sure how baseball began, but it seems to have its roots in the English game called "rounders" or "four-old-cat." Rounders had many of the same features as baseball has today. The one major difference was that in rounders the fielder put the batter out by hitting him with the ball.

2 This rule changed in 1845 when a group of men got together in New York City to regulate the rules of baseball. They decided that to get a player out an opposing player only needed to tag the base runner with the ball instead of hitting him with it. From then on, baseball was played using a hard ball.

3 Baseball became an organized sport in the 1840s and 1850s. People even played it during the Civil War. The first baseball teams were formed in New York City and Brooklyn.

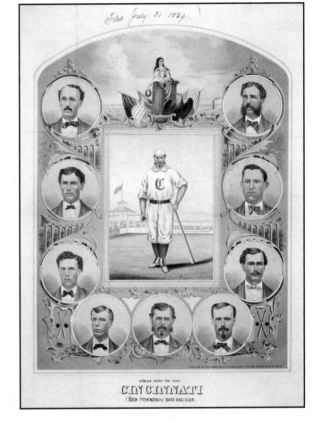

FIRST NINE OF THE
CINCINNATI
(RED STOCKINGS) BASE BALL CLUB.

By 1860, baseball had replaced the British game of cricket as America's most popular game. At this time, baseball was an amateur sport, which meant that players were not paid to play. The Brooklyn Atlantics were the leading team in early baseball. They won championships in 1861, 1864, and 1865.

4 Although New York had many amateur baseball teams, the first all-professional baseball team came from Cincinnati. Aaron B. Champion, the president of the Cincinnati Red Stockings, came up with the idea of paying players to play baseball. This was considered a bold move at the time. In 1869, the Reds' player-manager Harry Wright, known as the "Father of Professional Baseball," and his team toured the country, winning 60 games without a single loss. Although the National Association didn't want to support paying players in the professional baseball movement, they were overruled. Major League Baseball in America had begun.

1 What important event happened in 1845?

   A Baseball became an organized sport.

   B The Brooklyn Atlantics won a championship.

   C Players were now tagged with the ball to be considered out.

   D Baseball replaced cricket as America's most popular game.

2 Why was it surprising that the first professional team came from Cincinnati?

   A Most of the early baseball teams were from New York City and Brooklyn.

   B The National Association did not want to have professional teams.

   C Before professional baseball began, players were not allowed to be paid.

   D The Red Stockings toured the country and won 60 games without a single loss.

3 Why did the National Association not want to support professional baseball?

   A It thought the first pro team should have come from New York City or Brooklyn.

   B The National Association didn't want players to be paid.

   C President Aaron B. Champion was against professional baseball.

   D It was a bold move to pay baseball players.

4 Describe two ways that baseball changed between 1845 and 1869.

   _____

   _____

   _____

   _____

   _____

   _____

Explaining Events and Concepts in Scientific Texts

 Introduction

THEME: >>> **Making a Difference**

Scientific texts teach about the world around you. They tell you what happened as well as how and why it happened. They may explain a scientific concept or give more information about a natural process. These texts often use special vocabulary, or words, that are used regularly in science.

When reading a scientific text, read the details carefully. These will help you make connections to gain a deeper understanding of what you are reading.

Read the paragraph. Then complete the chart to tell why an event happened.

Emperor Penguins are amazing birds! Not only are they largest of their species; they are very social creatures. After a mother emperor lays an egg, she leaves it behind with the father penguin. She then embarks on a two-month hunting journey in a freezing environment. While the mother is away, the male emperor stands over the egg keeping it warm beneath its feathered skin. The male does not eat and must huddle close to other emperors to stay warm. When the females return, they provide food for the newly hatched penguins. Then the male emperors are free to hunt for their own food. They cannot fly like most birds, but they swim well and can survive in the difficult conditions of Antarctica.

What Happens	Why It Happens
Female leaves egg with male.	
Male stands over egg.	
Male is able to hunt.	

Read the first part of the passage. Then answer the questions.

The History of the Telescope

1   Have you ever stood on a beach and looked at a ship on the horizon? The ship probably looked very small from where you were standing. If you looked through a telescope, you would see the details of the ship. The ship would appear much closer to you. A telescope is a tube containing a magnifying lens that is used to view objects far away.

2   The Greeks used lenses and magnification tools as early as 5 B.C. Around 1300, people began wearing eyeglasses in Europe. By October 1608, a lens maker named Hans Lippershey had invented the first telescope in the Netherlands. Around this time, Jacob Metius built a small, hand-held telescope called a spyglass. Light entered one end of the tube and hit a curved, or convex, lens. The lens bent the light inward. A smaller image of the larger distant object was seen inside the tube. This first telescope made objects appear four times closer to the viewer than they actually were.

3   The telescope soon became the most important tool used by astronomers. Using this new instrument, they could now view clearly blurry distant objects in the sky, millions of planets, and billions of stars. Many astronomers noticed that certain objects seen only with the naked eye actually looked very different when viewed up close. Before the invention of the telescope, people thought that the moon was a perfectly smooth, round circle. In 1609, an Italian astronomer named Galileo, observed the moon through a telescope that he built. He saw that the moon's surface was actually rough and uneven, with deep holes, valleys, and mountain ranges.

4   Galileo built his telescopes from the spyglasses that were being sold in Europe. His telescopes were much longer than the spyglasses being sold and had higher magnifying abilities. With these telescopes, he was able to make a number of discoveries. He discovered that the planet Jupiter has four moons that rotate around, or orbit, the planet. He also discovered that Saturn has many rings around it. He observed multitudes of new stars in the Milky Way galaxy and noticed that there were an infinite number of stars reaching deep into space. Galileo helped confirm the theory that Earth and other planets orbit the sun at the center of our solar system.

Think About It

What events led to Galileo's new discoveries? This question asks you to think about the early history of the telescope and to describe how the telescope changed and improved since it was first invented.

What happened around 5 B.C.? _____

_____

What happened around 1300? _____

_____

Why was Hans Lippershey important? _____

_____

What did Jacob Metius invent? _____

How did Galileo improve upon existing inventions to discover more about the

universe? _____

_____

_____

_____

_____

Continue reading the passage. Then answer the question.

5 Other scientists began using Galileo's telescopes, known as refractors. These instruments had lenses that could bend or refract light. At first, Galileo had a hard time finding clear glass for the lenses. Over time, Galileo worked hard to improve his telescopes. Eventually, his instruments were 4 feet long and could magnify objects in space up to 30 times.

6 Telescope makers in the 1600s improved on Galileo's ideas and went on to make telescopes that were 15 to 20 feet long and that magnified objects up to 100 times. In 1847, American astronomer Maria Mitchell used the third largest refracting telescope to discover a comet. This telescope rotated along with Earth. It helped astronomers study the movement of stars and planets.

7 In 1990, the Hubble Space Telescope gave astronomers a new freedom. Previously, astronomers had to look through Earth's atmosphere, which can blur the view of objects in space. The Hubble Space Telescope floated in space just outside Earth's atmosphere. It photographed distant galaxies, planets, stars, and Earth, helping scientists learn about the history of the universe.

8 The Hubble Space Telescope is no longer in space. The National Aeronautics and Space Administration (NASA) is working on a telescope called the James Webb Space Telescope. It will orbit much farther from Earth than the Hubble. Astronomers hope to study the early formations of stars, solar systems, and galaxies when the new telescope launches into space.

A CLOSER LOOK
In paragraph 6, underline details that show how the telescope improved from when it was first invented.

What was the Hubble Telescope able to do that telescopes before it were not able to do?

Why did the Hubble Space Telescope give astronomers a "new freedom?"

A Maria Mitchell was able to discover a comet.

B The Hubble Space Telescope is no longer in space.

C The Hubble Space Telescope had a clearer view because it was outside Earth's atmosphere.

D This telescope rotated along with Earth to study the movement of stars and planets.

 DISCUSS IT
What main concept does this passage explain? With another student, find key details in the text that help explain this concept.

Read the passage. Then answer the questions.

The Coriolis Force

A CLOSER LOOK

Why are there no hurricanes at the equator? Circle words and sentences in the passage that help to answer this question.

1　The Coriolis force is caused by Earth's rotation. This force causes air to be pulled to the right, or counterclockwise, in the Northern Hemisphere and to the left, or clockwise, in the Southern Hemisphere. The Coriolis force is named for French engineer Gaspard Gustav de Coriolis (1792–1843) who first described this force.

2　The Coriolis effect is the curved path of moving objects relative to the surface of Earth. Hurricanes are good visual examples. As a result of the Earth's rotation, the air circulation, or winds, in a hurricane moves counterclockwise in the Northern Hemisphere and clockwise in the Southern Hemisphere. The Coriolis force helps set the air circulation of a hurricane into motion by producing a rightward (clockwise) deflection. This sets up a cyclonic (counterclockwise) circulation around the hurricane's low pressure.

3　What happens at the equator? The Coriolis force is too weak to operate on the moving air at the equator. This means that weather phenomena such as hurricanes are not observed at the equator, although they have been observed at 5 degrees above the equator. In fact, the Coriolis force pulls hurricanes away from the equator.

4　Some people have asked the question, "Does water go down the drain counterclockwise in the Northern Hemisphere and clockwise in the Southern Hemisphere?"

5　The answer is that it depends upon how the water was introduced and the geometric structure of the drain. You can find both counterclockwise and clockwise flowing drains in both hemispheres. Some people would like you to believe that the Coriolis force affects the flow of water down the drain in sinks, bathtubs, or toilet bowls. Don't believe them! The Coriolis force is simply too weak to affect such small bodies of water.

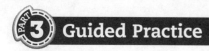

What do clockwise and counterclockwise mean?

1 Which explains why water might go down the drain clockwise in the Southern Hemisphere?

A The Coriolis force makes the water flow clockwise.

B There is a hurricane in the Northern Hemisphere.

C There is a hurricane in the Southern Hemisphere.

D The drain is angled in the clockwise direction.

Why does hurricane air flow counterclockwise in the Northern Hemisphere and clockwise in the Southern Hemisphere?

2 What causes the Coriolis effect?

A the equator

B Earth's rotation

C hurricanes

D the North and South Poles

How do hurricanes relate to water flowing down the drain when talking about the Coriolis effect?

3 Does the Coriolis force work the same on water as its does on wind?

_____

_____

_____

_____

_____

_____

Read the journal entries. Then answer the questions.

My First Tornado Chase!

May 14, 2013, 11:30 a.m. I love tornadoes! Even though they are dangerous, many scientists want to learn how and why these storms form. People have lost lives, loved ones, and possessions in these random and astonishing storms. I want to predict when a tornado will strike so that people have time to find safety.

May 15, 2013, 4:45 p.m. My first tornado chase is tomorrow! I saw twisters when I was growing up in Oklahoma. My family had a shelter in our backyard. It was a cold and windowless concrete basement. My family had to hide there when I was 11. Unfortunately, you only have a few minutes to find shelter after a tornado warning. We sat on pillows and listened to howling winds above. I was scared, but I wanted to know why and how these storms raged across the flat lands of America.

May 16, 2013, 8:00 a.m. Today, my partner Jim and I are chasing tornadoes! We spent the last two weeks preparing our weather-recording instruments. We will drive across Kansas tracking a tornado and recording data about it. This could help predict when more tornadoes might occur. We have probes packed into the back of Jim's van. These heavy metal containers were built to survive extremely high winds. We'll predict where the tornado will travel and place the probe in its path. We hope it won't get swept away. Inside the probes, we placed cameras and devices for measuring the temperature, humidity, air pressure, and wind speed inside a tornado. About 1,000 tornadoes touch down in the US each year. Most occur in the central plains of Tornado Alley. Tornadoes come in different shapes and sizes. The speed of the wind in most tornadoes is less than 100 miles per hour. Now and then, a severe tornado develops with wind speeds over 300 miles per hour. These tornadoes take lives and destroy buildings, houses, cars, and everything in their paths.

May 16, 2013, 9:45 a.m. Jim drives, while I check the radar. A thunderstorm is traveling across Barber County, Kansas. The weather report on the radio said that cold air is moving down from Canada and a warm front is blowing up from the south. If these winds come together during the storm, we may see a swirling funnel! I see dark clouds on the horizon. Paper, dust, and plastic bags float around us. The wind is picking up.

May 16, 2013, 10:15 a.m. Chunks of hail hit the car as lightning flashes and thunder roars. The blue sky from the morning is now a thick, dark gray ceiling of clouds. The radar shows that the storm is growing over Barber County. We are only a mile away from the center of the storm. Tornadoes usually travel a few miles before wearing themselves out. I think we can get ahead of this one. Our barometer is dropping. The lower the air pressure, the more likely there will be a storm.

May 16, 2013, 4:25 p.m. We chased a tornado across southern Kansas today! A warning was sent out to nearby residents. Cars drove quickly out of town, while we drove closer to the storm. "A twister's coming!" we shouted. We followed the storm on our GPS monitor and saw a twirling pole shoot down from mysterious clouds across a field. Jim drove faster to get ahead of it, but not too close. We passed the storm and stopped about a half a mile away. We quickly jumped out, grabbed the probe, and placed it in the road. Now, we had to get away as fast as we could. Tornadoes don't always move in a straight line. They can change direction at any moment. This one zigzagged across the fields. We hope it swept over our probe. Now, Jim and I are safe inside. We can hear faint thunder outside, but the tornado is probably gone. After a nice meal, we're heading back to see what is left of our weather instruments. We are hopeful that we recorded some good data!

1 Part A

Which event happens first?

A Chunks of hail hit the car.

B The writer and Jim quickly placed a probe in the path of a tornado.

C The writer and Jim put cameras and weather measuring instruments into probes.

D A warning is sent out to nearby residents of Barber County, Kansas.

Part B

What text evidence *best* supports your answer to Part A?

_____

_____

_____

_____

2 Which choice shows a weather effect that these storm chasers do *not* measure?

A air pressure

B snowfall

C temperature

D wind speed

3 Read these details from the passage.

> "People have lost lives, loved ones, and possessions in these random and astonishing storms."

> "Now and then, a severe tornado develops with wind speeds over 300 miles per hour."

> "Tornadoes don't always move in a straight line. They can change direction at any moment."

Which concept do these details support?

A "I saw twisters when I was growing up in Oklahoma."

B "We will drive across Kansas tracking a tornado and recording data."

C "After a nice meal, we're heading back to see what is left of our weather instruments."

D "Tornadoes are extremely dangerous storms."

4 Read this main idea from the passage.

> Tornado chasing is challenging and dangerous.

Write three details from the journal that support this main idea.

1. _____

_____

2. _____

_____

3. _____

_____

LESSON 10

Explaining Events and Concepts in Technical Texts

Introduction

THEME: >>> Making a Difference

Technical texts give readers information about how things work and how they are made. These how-to texts may explain the different steps involved in performing a task, such as building a birdhouse. These texts may have charts, instructions, and diagrams to support important ideas in the text. When reading a technical text, think about the order of events or instructions, how and why things happen, and the main idea.

Read the fruit salad recipe. Then answer the questions.

1. Choose 4 to 5 different fruits. It is best to choose fruits that are fresh and in season. Here is a list of seasonal fruits:
   Spring: melon, mangos, oranges
   Summer: peaches, plums, nectarines
   Fall: apples, pears, grapes
   Winter: pomegranate, figs, clementines

2. Wash fruits with edible skins well. Carefully cut the fruit into chunks. Place the fruit in a large bowl.

3. Peel fruits with nonedible skin. Cut into chunks (or separate pieces of citrus fruit). Place fruit in the bowl.

4. Pour 1 tablespoon of orange juice over fruit in the bowl.

5. Mix well, serve, and enjoy!

What is the first thing you do *before* cutting the fruit? _____

_____

What do you do *after* you put the fruit in the bowl? _____

_____

Understanding the order of steps or events is important in a technical text. If a step in a recipe is performed in the wrong order, the food might not taste good or be healthy.

Read the first part of the passage. Then answer the questions.

How Do Those Colors Appear in the Sky?

1   You often see a rainbow after it rains. When clouds move away, sunlight shines through the raindrops in the sky. Then you see a rainbow with the colors red, orange, yellow, green, blue, indigo, and violet. These colors come from the sun's light. Scientists call this light *white light*. When white light travels through a clear medium such as glass or water, it often breaks apart into different colors. These lights make up a spectrum, or range, of color.

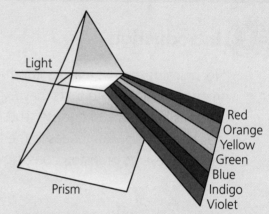
White light traveling through a prism.

2   In 1666, Sir Isaac Newton began experimenting with colors using a prism, which is a clear, crystal-like piece of glass with a three-dimensional shape. A prism has three flat rectangular sides and two triangular sides. Two of the rectangular sides bend inward, creating acute angles. Newton let a small amount of light shine into a dark room allowing the light to pass through a prism. The ray of light created a group of colors that appeared on the wall at the opposite side of the room. He did this experiment with many different prisms and all the prisms produced the same band of colors. Next, he experimented with two prisms. He placed a second prism in the path of the colors and noticed that a single white light shone through the other end. The light went through a change each time it traveled through the prisms.

Think About It

When sunlight appears after it rains, what makes a rainbow? To answer this question think about the colors of a rainbow and why they appear after a rainstorm.

After a rainstorm, what happens *after* clouds move away? _____

_____

How does this light from the sun become a band of colors? _____

_____

_____

Continue reading the passage. Then answer the question.

A CLOSER LOOK

Technical texts often explain why things happen. Circle details about how Newton explained why each color bent at a different angle.

3 Newton discovered the reason that white light disperses into different colors. The prisms actually bend, or refract, the white light. Each color refracts at a different angle. Newton was curious as to why each color bent at a different angle than the other colors. He found that each color travels through the medium at a different speed. All light travels extremely fast. White light is traveling so fast that you cannot see that it is actually made up of different colors. Mediums, such as a raindrop or prism, actually slow down the speed of light. The speed of each color depends on its wavelength. The color violet has the shortest wavelength and bends the most, while red has the longest wavelength and bends the least.

4 So, raindrops are one of nature's prisms. When sunlight travels through a raindrop, the speed of the light slows down and separates into the colors of a rainbow. Humans can only see a portion of the light that travels around the universe. Some other animals can see colored light that you cannot see. Many insects, for example, can see ultraviolet light (UV) light. This is light from the sun that travels faster than all of the colors on the visible spectrum. UV light is hotter than other colors and gives many people sunburns. Many people wear sunscreen to protect themselves from this kind of light.

Why do different colors bend at different angles when they pass through a prism?

What is true about the color violet?

A Violet has the shortest wavelength, and it bends the least.

B Violet has the longest wavelength, and it bends the least.

C Violet has the longest wavelength, and it bends the most.

D Violet has the shortest wavelength, and it bends the most.

 DISCUSS IT

Are there colors that humans cannot see but other living things can? With another student, think about why some creatures can see colors that humans cannot see. Discuss what you learned in the passage.

Read the passage. Then answer the questions.

Make Your Own Volcano!

A CLOSER LOOK
The first paragraph tells what a volcano is and how it behaves. This will help you understand how your own volcano models a real one. Circle words in the first paragraph that tell how a volcano acts.

Earth's surface has many openings that extend deep into the ground. Some openings appear on mountaintops, and some are cracks on Earth's surface. Others exist underground and below the ocean. The bottom layer of a volcano contains *magma,* which is hot liquid rock. Active volcanoes can erupt at any time. When a volcano erupts, the magma shoots up through the opening. Scientists call the magma *lava* after it has come out of a volcano. Sometimes, the magma shoots out so fast it creates an explosion. Lava, smoke, ash, and chunks of rock are blown all around the volcano. Some eruptions have been so extreme that ash was sent 17 miles up into the air.

You can create your own model volcano! With the right supplies, you can make your volcano erupt.

You will need these items:
- newspaper and paper towels
- empty plastic bottle
- aluminum pie tin or baking pan
- modeling clay or play dough
- funnel
- measuring spoon and measuring cup
- baking soda
- red food coloring
- vinegar

1. Lay down newspaper before you begin your project. Then place the aluminum pie tin or baking pan on top of the newspaper.

2. Put the empty bottle in the aluminum pie tin or baking pan. Place clay or play dough around the bottle to make it look like a volcano. You can add twigs to look like trees if you want.

3. Put the funnel on top of the bottle opening. Measure 3 to 4 tablespoons of baking soda. Use the funnel to add the baking soda into the bottle.

4. Add 3 drops of red food coloring to one-half cup of vinegar.

5. Place the funnel on top of the bottle opening.

6. Pour the vinegar into the funnel so that it slowly flows into the bottle. QUICKLY remove the funnel.

7. Your volcano will erupt! The baking soda and vinegar have a chemical reaction. When these two substances meet, a gas called carbon dioxide makes bubbles. You created lava! The gas bubbles force the "lava" out of the top.

Review the steps for making a volcano. Think about the order of the steps.

1 Which of these steps comes *before* the other steps?

  A Use the funnel to add the baking soda into the bottle.

  B Add 3 drops of red food coloring to one-half cup of vinegar.

  C Place clay or play dough around the bottle to make it look like a volcano.

  D Pour the vinegar into the funnel.

Find the sentence in the passage with the word *magma.*

2 What is *magma?*

  A an opening in the earth

  B hot liquid rock

  C an explosion

  D an active volcano

Put together details in the first paragraph to understand how a volcanic eruption might be dangerous.

3 Explain why a volcano can be dangerous to people.

_____

_____

_____

_____

Read the passage. Then answer the questions.

Gravity

1 Have you ever wondered how roller coasters stay on their tracks, and why people can hang upside down in them? It's all a matter of physics: energy, inertia, and gravity. Gravity is counteracted by the force of acceleration. Acceleration is the force that pushes you forward.

2 A roller coaster does not have an engine to generate energy. A lift or cable pulls the train up the first hill. This builds up a supply of potential energy that the train will use to go down the hill as the train is pulled by gravity. Then, all of that stored energy is released as kinetic energy, which is what will get the train to go up the next hill. So, as the train travels up and down hills, its motion is constantly shifting between potential and kinetic energy.

3 The higher the hill the coaster is coming down, the more kinetic energy that is available to push the cars up the next hill, and the faster the train will go. Plus, according to Newton's First Law of Motion, "an object in motion tends to stay in motion, unless another force acts against it." Wind resistance or the wheels along the track are forces that work to slow down the train. So toward the end of the ride, the hills are lower because the coaster has less energy to get up them.

4 The two major types of roller coasters are wooden and steel. Features in the wheel design prevent the cars from flipping off the track. Wooden tracks are more inflexible than steel. They usually don't have complex loops that might flip passengers upside down. In the 1950s, tubular steel tracks were introduced. The train's nylon or polyurethane wheels run along the top, bottom, and side of the tube. This secures the train to the track while it travels through intricate loops and twists.

5 When you go around a turn, you feel pushed against the outside of the car. This force is centripetal force, and it helps keep you in your seat.

6 In the loop-the-loop upside down design, inertia is the force keeping you in your seat. Inertia is the force that presses your body to the outside of the loop as the train spins around. Although gravity is pulling you toward the earth, at the very top the acceleration force is stronger than gravity. It pulls you upwards, thus counteracting gravity. The loop, however, must be elliptical, rather than a perfect circle. Otherwise, the centripetal, or g, force would be too strong for safety and comfort.

7 How do you know whether a roller coaster is safe? Engineers and designers follow industry standards and guidelines. The first "riders" are sandbags or dummies. Then engineers and park workers try out the ride. Would you want to be one of the first passengers on a new ride?

1 Part A

How does a roller coaster move without an engine?

A Wind pushes the train up and down hills.

B Roller coaster trains are powered by batteries.

C First, potential energy causes the train to go up the first hill. Next, gravity pulls the train up and down the hills.

D At first, a cable pulls the train up a hill. Then the train travels up and down hills due to shifting potential and kinetic energy.

Part B

What text evidence *best* supports your answer to Part A?

_____

_____

_____

_____

_____

_____

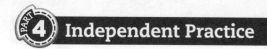

2 *Newton's First Law of Motion* says, "an object in motion tends to stay in motion, unless another force acts against it." What force acts against a roller coaster to slow it down?

   A   wind resistance or the wheels along the track

   B   gravity or potential energy

   C   kinetic energy or centripetal force

   D   lifts or cables

3 What does inertia do in the loop-the-loop?

   A   It counteracts the force of the train's acceleration.

   B   It keeps you going in an elliptical loop.

   C   It presses your body to the outside of the loop as the train spins around.

   D   It builds up a supply of potential energy.

4 What are the two types of roller coasters? How are they different? Use details from the passage to support your answer.

   _____

   _____

   _____

   _____

   _____

LESSON 11

Drawing Inferences in Informational Texts

Introduction

THEME: >>> Making a Difference

Good readers ask themselves questions as they read: Who or what is this informational text about? What happened? Why? Where and when do the events take place? The text may answer most of those questions. In these cases, the information is **explicit,** or stated clearly in the passage. Sometimes, though, the text just offers clues. You need to figure out the answers for yourself. You can use those clues, plus what you already know, to make an educated guess. This educated guess is called an **inference.**

Read this paragraph. Then answer the questions.

Frogs and toads are both amphibians, but they have several differences. For example, frogs must live near water to keep their skin moist. Toads, with their dry, bumpy skin, can live far from water. Frogs have longer back legs that allow them to jump higher and farther than toads. That's important because frogs have many predators trying to catch them. Toads run or take small hops, which would not prevent most predators from grabbing them. However, toad skin has a bitter taste and smell, much like a skunk. Predators have learned to leave toads alone.

The paragraph answers some questions explicitly. For example, why do frogs need to live near water? _____

The paragraph does not answer other questions directly. For example, why can toads live far from water? _____

_____

To answer the second question, use the details you read in the paragraph and what you already know. Put together details about frogs, toads, and water. The paragraph presents differences between frogs and toads. It gives details about frogs' skin and toads' skin as one of these differences. Then figure out why toads do not need to live near water.

In putting together these clues, you made an inference. You make inferences all day long. When a friend is smiling, you infer that he is happy. If you know that friend well, you might also infer what is making him happy. You can also make inferences as you read. They will help you better understand and enjoy what you read.

Read the first part of the passage. Then answer the questions.

An Unlikely Winner

1   Amy Van Dyken was born in Colorado, on February 15, 1973. When Amy was young, her doctor told her that she had asthma. This meant that sometimes she could not catch her breath. Being in gym class or running outside in the cold sometimes made her short of breath. People who have asthma need to stay on medication.

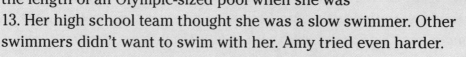

2   When Amy was 6, her doctor wanted her to try swimming, too. He said the warm water would help Amy's breathing. It would help her in daily tasks and allow her to play sports. Amy did not get better right away. She trained hard. She was finally able to swim the length of an Olympic-sized pool when she was 13. Her high school team thought she was a slow swimmer. Other swimmers didn't want to swim with her. Amy tried even harder.

3   She spent her first two years of college at the University of Arizona. She won a silver medal at the National Collegiate Athletic Association (NCAA) Championships in 1993. Amy knew she could do even better.

4   She left Arizona for Colorado State University. At the 1994 NCAA Championships, she won a gold medal. Amy was also named NCAA Swimmer of the Year. Amy decided to take time off from college to train for the 1996 Olympics.

Think About It

What are some inferences you could make about Amy? To answer the question, use details from the passage and what you already know.

Amy was _____ because she trained hard and kept trying even though other swimmers did not want to swim with her.

She was _____ because, even though she had asthma, she thought she could make the Olympic team.

Continue reading the passage. Then answer the question.

A CLOSER LOOK

Explicit details can help you learn more about a subject. Amy was very successful in her swimming career. Underline details about awards she won and honors she received.

5 At the 1996 Summer Olympics in Atlanta, Georgia, Amy won four gold medals. Two were for individual events. Two were for relays. She was the first female swimmer to win four gold medals in one Olympics.

6 What is so amazing about this? Amy's lungs could only take in 65% of a normal person's capacity because of her asthma. Fans loved Amy because of her likable personality and honesty. After she won gold in the 50-meter freestyle, Amy said, "This is a victory for all the nerds." She said this because many people with asthma cannot be in sports.

7 Amy graduated from college in 1997. Then she competed at the world championships. Here she won three gold medals. In 1998, while lifting weights, she hurt her shoulder. Surgery followed. Many people thought Amy would never swim again. Amy didn't have another plan.

8 She had overcome problems with asthma. She wasn't going to let an injury keep her from swimming again. Amy started training for the 2000 Summer Olympics in Sydney, Australia. She won two gold medals.

9 Amy was the only American swimmer to enter into the Swimming Hall of Fame in 2007. In 2008, she also became part of the Olympic Hall of Fame.

How do the details about swimming and asthma fit together?

What inference can you make, based on this passage?

A Being able to breathe deeply is very important when you swim in competitions.

B Many people with asthma cannot be in sports because they cannot swim as well as Amy.

C Amy began lifting weights because her asthma made swimming difficult.

D Amy was elected to the Olympic Hall of Fame because she has asthma.

 DISCUSS IT

Think about why Amy said, "This is a victory for all the nerds." Why would she talk about nerds? Make an inference, based on what you know about Amy and about young people. Turn to another student. Explain your inference and the reasons for it.

Read the passage. Then answer the questions.

excerpt from The Author of Little Women
by Edward Eggleston

1   Louisa May Alcott was a wild little girl. When she was very little, she would run away from home….

2   Louisa found it hard to be good and obedient. When she was 14 years old, she wrote some verses about being good.

3   The Alcott family was very poor. Louisa made up her mind to do something to make money when she got big. She did not like being so very poor.

4   One day she was sitting on the wheel of a cart thinking how poor her father was. There was a crow in the air over her head cawing. There was nobody to tell her thoughts to but the crow. She shook her fist at the big bird, and said, "I will do something by and by. Don't care what. I'll teach, sew, act, write, do anything to help the family. And I'll be rich and famous before I die. See if I don't."

5   The crow did not make any answer. But Louisa kept thinking about the work she was going to do. The other children got work to do that made money. But Louisa was left at home to do housework. She had to do the washing. She made a little poem about it. Here are some of the verses of this poem:

A SONG FROM THE SUDS

Queen of my tub, I merrily sing,
While the white foam rises high,
And sturdily wash and rinse and wring,
And fasten the clothes to dry;
5   Then out in the free fresh air they swing,
Under the sunny sky.

I am glad a task to me is given
To labor at day by day;
For it brings me health, and strength, and hope,
10   And I cheerfully learn to say—
"Head, you may think; Heart, you may feel;
But Hand, you shall work always!"

A CLOSER LOOK
Circle words in the poem that tell about Louisa's attitude toward life when she wrote the poem.

6 Louisa grew to be a woman at last. She went to nurse soldiers in the Civil War. She wrote books. When she wrote the book called *Little Women*, all the young people were delighted. What she had said to the crow came true at last. She became famous. She had money enough to make the family comfortable.

> What information is stated explicitly in the passage?

1 Why did Louisa want to be rich and famous?

   A She found it hard to follow rules, so she wanted to break them.

   B She wanted to do anything to help the family.

   C She was frustrated that she didn't earn money from doing housework.

   D She wanted to publish her poetry.

> Which answer choice hints that Louisa knew she would stay busy her whole life?

2 Which line from her poem "A Song from the Suds" supports the inference that Louisa accepted her life as it was?

   A "And sturdily wash and rinse and wring,"

   B "Then out in the free fresh air they swing,"

   C "To labor at day by day;"

   D "But Hand, you shall work always!"

> What did Louisa do as a child that helped her become successful later in life?

3 Think about what this author says about Louisa Alcott. Then make an inference about how her childhood experiences helped her become a famous author. Use examples from the text to explain the reasons for your inference.

_____

_____

_____

_____

_____

_____

Read the passage. Then answer the questions.

Beekeeping

1   Many people keep bees in their backyard as a hobby. Beekeeping does not require much money, time, or space. It does require blooming flowers. Still, how does honey get from a beehive to your toast?

2   First, let's review how bees make honey. Bees live in a colony. One queen lays all of the eggs. Thousands of worker bees gather food, keep the hive clean, and protect it from predators. They also use beeswax to create a honeycomb to store their food.

3   Some of the workers fly many miles to gather food for the queen, the workers, and the larvae that hatch from the queen's eggs. Other workers stay in the hive. To gather food, the flying workers use a tiny tube to suck nectar from flowers. Plants produce the nectar to attract bees and other insects. As bees suck up the nectar, pollen from the flower sticks to their legs and bodies. As the bees move from flower to flower, they spread this pollen. That allows the flowers to make seeds that will produce new plants.

4   We depend on pollination by bees for much of the fruits and vegetables we eat. In fact, some beekeepers rent their bees to farmers to pollinate crops. At least 90 of our crops depend, at least in part, on bees for pollination.

5   As the bees suck up the nectar, they store it in a special sac in their bodies. To fill this sac, a bee may visit more than a thousand flowers. When the workers return to the hive, they transfer the nectar to the bees that stay there. These bees "chew" the nectar for about 30 minutes. This chewing makes the nectar easier for the bees and larvae to digest. Next, the bees transfer the nectar to the cells of the honeycomb.

6   Then the workers fan the nectar with their wings. This helps the water evaporate from the nectar. At last, it is honey! The bees close each filled cell in the honeycomb with more beeswax. The honey is stored until the bees need it for food (or the beekeeper harvests it). A colony can produce 45 to 200 pounds of honey a year.

7   How do beekeepers help? They get the hives ready for spring and "put them to bed" in the fall. Beekeepers make sure the queen is alive and laying

eggs. They check to see whether the hive needs more storage space. The bees might need more food or medicine to keep them healthy. They also need to be protected from bears, raccoons, and other honey-lovers.

8   When all of the sacs in the honeycomb are closed, beekeepers know it is ready for harvest. They might sell the whole honeycomb. Or, they might take the honey out and bottle it. To collect the honey, beekeepers cut open the honeycomb with a knife. Then they use a special machine to spin the honey out. They also filter bits of wax out of the honey. Beekeepers are careful to leave enough honey to feed the colony.

9   The bees can use the honeycomb again. The honeycomb can also be used to make candles.

10   What equipment do beekeepers need? It includes a starter box with frames and a wax foundation for the hive. Beekeepers also need a bee veil and gloves to protect against stings. They need a hive tool, bee brush, smoker, and medication. They can rent the machine to spin honey out of the honeycomb. The total cost is $120 to $400. The bees can be ordered through the mail. One package holds about 11,000 bees and costs $50 to $70.

11   Learning more about bees makes honey taste even sweeter!

1 Part A

Which choice is an inference about bees?

A   Different bees have specific jobs.

B   If the queen dies, the hive will not survive.

C   Bees can get diseases.

D   Nectar contains water.

Part B

Which text evidence *best* supports your answer to Part A?

_____

_____

_____

_____

2 Based on this passage, you might infer that bees depend on their pollination of flowers as much as humans do. Which statement supports this inference?

   A The pollen sticks to their bodies as they move from flower to flower.

   B About 90 of our crops depend on bees for pollination.

   C Bees make their food from flowers' nectar.

   D Plants produce nectar to attract bees.

3 What is one thing that bees do in the process of producing honey?

   A They get the hives ready for spring.

   B Worker bees keep the hive clean and protect it from predators.

   C They filter bits of wax out of the honey.

   D Worker bees fan the nectar with their wings.

4 Do bees depend on beekeepers to survive? Make an inference based on this passage and what you already know about bees. Support your inference with details from the text.

_____

_____

_____

_____

LESSON 12

Summarizing Informational Texts

 **Introduction**

THEME: >>> **Making a Difference**

When you **summarize** something, you tell the most important ideas in your own words. For example, if your grandmother asks what you did today, you don't start with getting out of bed that morning. You tell the most important events of your day. Similarly, when summarizing an informational text, you won't tell every detail, only the important ones.

A summary is often short. The length of a summary depends on the length of what you are summarizing.

Read this passage.

Working dogs are trained in different ways to protect people and to make life easier for them. Some of these dogs act as eyes for blind people, ears for the hearing impaired, and helpers for the physically challenged. They also can help police with parts of their jobs. Some dogs find people who are buried under buildings by an earthquake or a hurricane.

Dogs are born knowing how to find things. A handler, the dog's human partner, teaches the dog what to search for. Dogs use most of their senses—hearing, seeing, and smelling—to find a specific person or thing. Handlers might hide things in a suitcase or in a closet. The dogs love to practice finding those things!

Identify important ideas in the passage. Then put these ideas together to write a summary.

Important Idea:	Important Idea:	Important Idea:
Working dogs help blind people, hearing impaired people, and physically challenged people.		
Summary:		

Read the first part of the passage. Then answer the questions.

Judy Blume, A Very Special Author

1   Judy Blume was born on February 12, 1938, in Elizabeth, New Jersey. Her father was a dentist. Her mother was a stay-at-home mom. Judy's mom taught her to love books.

2   Judy often went to the library growing up. Judy read many books there. She had a lovely imagination. Judy was always making up stories in her head! No matter if she was running around outside or playing quietly inside, she was making up new stories. However, she never wrote down her stories. This early storytelling would help Judy become the author we know today.

3   As a high school student, Judy was an editor for her school's newspaper. After high school, she studied education at New York University (NYU). There she met her husband. They had two children. While she stayed at home with them, she still wanted to be creative. Judy wanted to write, so she took classes at NYU. It was then that her career took off. She published her first book, *The One in the Middle Is the Green Kangaroo,* in 1969.

Think About It

What points should be included in a summary of Judy Blume's life? Sort the important ideas from the less important details.

What are three important ideas that should be included in a summary of this author's life?

1. _____

2. _____

3. _____

Summarize this part of the passage.

_____

_____

_____

A CLOSER LOOK
Underline the main ideas in these two paragraphs.

Continue reading the passage. Then answer the question.

4 In 1970, Judy wrote *Are You There, God? It's Me, Margaret.* This book was written for teens. Judy was recognized for writing about real events that teens face. Her next book, *Tales of a Fourth-Grade Nothing,* was published in 1972 and was the first in a series of five books. In this book, Judy tells of Peter's life with his younger brother Fudge. A book like this makes children laugh and want to read more!

5 Judy writes about what she knows. That is why her books take place in the cities where she has lived. She has sold more than 80 million books in 31 different languages. Some of her other books include *Freckle Juice, Superfudge, Blubber,* and *Iggie's House.* Judy is still writing for people of all ages and working to turn her books into movies. She lives in Key West, Florida, with her husband.

If a friend asked what these paragraphs are about, what would you say? What would you leave out?

Which sentence is the *best* summary of this part of the passage?

A Her books are popular because she writes about real events that her readers face.

B *Are You There, God? It's Me, Margaret* was written for teens.

C Her books include *Freckle Juice, Superfudge, Blubber,* and *Iggie's House.*

D Judy is working to turn her books into movies.

 DISCUSS IT
With a partner, take turns summarizing the entire passage. Discuss the details that each of you included and left out and why. Did your summaries have enough details?

Read the passage. Then answer the questions.

How Does Hail Form?

1   You have probably seen hail, tiny balls of ice that bounce a little when they land. Maybe you've seen much larger hail. Why does it hail during some storms and not others? How big can hail get? You're about to find out!

2   What causes hail? During thunderstorms, warm and cold air currents crash into each other. The warm air currents carry tiny drops of water, lifting them upward. They are like soap bubbles rising into the air. In a strong storm, the warm air currents can carry the raindrops high into the clouds. There, temperatures are below freezing. The raindrops instantly freeze into tiny balls of ice. Now, they are called hailstones.

3   Then a cold air current may pull the hailstones downward, where the air is warmer. If the hailstone melts completely, it will fall as rain. However, another warm air current may catch the hailstone before it melts and toss it back up into the freezing temperatures. There, the hailstone gains another thin layer of ice.

4   Each time the air currents toss the hailstone up and pull it down, it gets bigger. If the hailstone is tossed up and down for five to ten minutes, it can grow larger than a softball. In time, the hailstone gets too heavy for the air currents to carry it. It falls to the ground. The bigger hailstones do not have time to melt on the way down. Instead, they are still hail when they hit the ground.

5   A storm with few warm air currents creates only small, lightweight hail—or none at all. The currents are just not strong enough to keep the hailstones in the air. A strong superstorm, however, can produce hail weighing two pounds and measuring eight inches across. That is heavy enough to dent cars!

6   Hail falls mostly in the summer. What people call hail during a winter storm is actually sleet. In this case, raindrops fall through much colder air and freeze into sleet. They are not tossed up and down by the air currents. Pieces of sleet are quite small because they do not gain extra layers of ice, like hailstones. Sleet often melts quickly after it reaches the ground.

7   The next time you see hail, you will know it had an exciting journey before it reached the ground!

A CLOSER LOOK
How are hail and sleet different? Circle the sentence or sentences that tell you.

> Which detail explains a key step in how hail forms?

1 Which point is important enough to include in a summary of this passage?

  A The raindrops are like soap bubbles rising into the air.

  B The warm air currents carry tiny drops of water.

  C Some air currents are not strong enough to keep hailstones in the air.

  D Pieces of sleet are quite small.

> Summaries are short. Every sentence should help explain the main points of the article.

2 Which point is *not* important enough to include in a summary of this passage?

  A Why does it hail during some storms and not others?

  B A warm air current may toss the hailstone back up into freezing temperatures.

  C There, the hailstone gains another thin layer of ice.

  D Bigger hailstones do not have time to melt on the way down.

> What is the most important point discussed in paragraph 2?

3 Summarize the *most* important idea in paragraph 2 in one sentence.

_____

_____

_____

_____

Read the passage. Then answer the questions.

The Beauty of Bats

1 Have you heard that bats suck your blood and can give you a deadly disease called rabies? Are bats just "flying rats"?

2 No! Bats are beautiful—in their own way. There are more than 40 kinds of bats in the US, and all of them help people. For example, bats eat billions of insects, and they help pollinate plants. Their droppings are excellent fertilizer. In addition, scientists are studying bats to learn about using sound to find things.

3 Bats are the only mammals that can fly. The bones in their wings are much like the bones in your hand. Between the bat's bones are flaps of skin that form wings. They allow the bat to fly.

4 The smallest kind of bat in the US is about 2.5 inches long with a wingspan of 8 inches. It weighs about the same as a penny. The biggest kind of bat in the US is about 7 inches long with a wingspan of 21 to 23 inches. It weighs about two ounces. Still not much! However, the bats' lighter weight makes it easier for them to fly.

5 You might be wondering about vampire bats. Here's the good news: the closest ones are in Mexico. None live in the US. Vampire bats usually drink animals' blood and do not bother people. They do not turn animals—or people—into vampires!

6 You might be wondering about rabies, too. Like raccoons and some other wild animals, bats can carry rabies. However, the chance of getting rabies from a bat is extremely small. It is even smaller if you never touch a bat!

7 Most bats hunt at night and eat flying insects, including mosquitoes, beetles, and moths. For example, about 20 million bats live in Bracken Cave in central Texas. In one night, they eat more than 200 tons of bugs! One bat can gobble up 600 to 1,000 mosquitoes in an hour.

8 Other bats live on nectar and fruit. These are the bats that help pollinate plants.

9 Bats have long lives, as long as 20 years. They like almost any kind of habitat, so you can find bats in deserts, forests—and attics. Some live in caves in the mountains, while others live under bridges. In the summer, 1.5 million bats live under the Congress Avenue Bridge in Austin, Texas. Large crowds of people gather every night to watch the bats swarm out from the bridge, on the hunt for insects. During winter, some bats hibernate in caves and trees, while others migrate to warmer places.

10 To find insects, bats send out a high-pitched sound wave that you cannot hear. This sound wave bounces off objects, including insects. It's like an echo. When the sound wave bounces back to the bat, it can tell where the insect is located. The bat also knows how big the insect is and how fast it is flying. Then the bat quickly swoops in to grab it. These echoes, called sonar, work so well that scientists borrowed this idea. Ships now use sonar waves to locate objects in the water.

11 Now you can see why many people think bats are beautiful!

1 Which point is important enough to include in a summary of this passage?

A Between the bat's bones are flaps of skin that form wings.

B The smallest bat in the US is about 2.5 inches long with a wingspan of 8 inches.

C About 1.5 million bats live under the Congress Avenue Bridge in Austin, Texas.

D To find insects, bats send out a high-pitched sound wave that you cannot hear.

2 Which point is *not* important enough to include in a summary of this passage?

A Bats are beautiful—in their own way.

B One bat can gobble up 600 to 1,000 mosquitoes in an hour.

C Bats in the US range in size from 2.5 inches to 7 inches long.

D Bats live in many different habitats.

3 Part A

Which sentence is an accurate summary of paragraph 10?

A Bats use high-pitched sound waves that echo.

B Scientists learned how to use sound waves to help ships locate objects.

C Bats send out sound waves that bounce off insects, telling the bats where the insects are located.

D Sound waves tell bats how big the insect is and how fast it's flying.

Part B

Which two statements *best* support the answer to Part A?

A "This sound wave bounces off objects, including insects."

B "Then the bat quickly swoops in to grab it."

C "When the sound wave bounces back to the bat, it can tell where the insect is located."

D "These echoes, called sonar, work so well that scientists borrowed this idea."

E "It's like an echo."

F "Ships now use sonar waves to locate objects in the water."

4 Summarize paragraph 9 in one sentence.

_____

_____

_____

_____

Key Ideas and Details in Informational Text

Read the passage. Then answer the questions.

Global Positioning System

1   The Global Positioning System, or GPS, tells you where you are on Earth. It is the only system today that can show your exact position on Earth anytime, in any weather, no matter where you are! It is also one of the most popular technologies used today. Here are some of the different ways it is used:

- Scientists in Minnesota use GPS to study the movements and feeding habits of deer.
- Surveyors used GPS to measure how the buildings shifted after the bombing in Oklahoma City in 1995.
- GPS helps settle property disputes between landowners.
- Marine archaeologists use GPS to guide research vessels hunting for shipwrecks.
- GPS data has revealed that Mt. Everest is getting taller.
- GPS helps drivers by giving directions to places they want to go.

GPS answers five questions at the same time:

2   Where am I? Where am I going? Where are you? What's the best way to get there? When will I get there?

GPS has three parts:

1. The space part now has 28 satellites. Each satellite is in its own orbit about 11,000 nautical miles above Earth.

2. The user part is made up of receivers. These receivers can be held in your hand or mounted in your car.

3. The control part has five ground stations around the world that make sure the satellites are working properly.

Development

3   The US military designed GPS. The idea started in the late 1960s. However, the first satellite wasn't launched until February 1978. In 1989, the Magellan Corporation introduced the first hand-held GPS receiver. In 1992, GPS was used in Operation Desert Storm.

4   At first, the military did not want to let people outside the military use GPS. They feared that smugglers, terrorists, or hostile forces would use it. Finally, bowing to pressure from the companies that built the equipment, the Defense Department made GPS available for nonmilitary purposes, with some restrictions. On May 1, 2000, President Clinton lifted the restrictions. The federal government provides GPS technology for peaceful uses on a worldwide basis, free of charge.

1 Why was GPS invented?

    A to help people know where they are

    B to help the military

    C to track satellites as they orbit

    D to settle property disputes between landowners

2 Which statement is an accurate summary of this passage?

    A GPS can help locate shipwrecks and measure mountains.

    B GPS has three parts: satellites, receivers, and control stations.

    C GPS helps the military and civilians locate things and places.

    D GPS has many different uses and applications.

3 Many newer cars include GPS. The driver enters a location into the GPS device, and the device tells the driver how to get there. What can you infer about how using GPS is better than using a map? Support your answer with details from the passage.

_____

_____

_____

_____

Read the passage. Then answer the questions.

John Muir, a Man of Nature

"Everybody needs beauty as well as bread, places to play in and pray in,
where nature may heal and give strength to body and soul alike."

John Muir

1   John Muir worked to protect the natural beauty of the US. Muir was born in Scotland in 1838. His family moved to Wisconsin when he was 11. Even as a boy, Muir was creative. He invented a horse feeder, a wooden thermometer, and a device that pushed a child out of bed in the morning.

2   Muir attended the University of Wisconsin for a short time. Then he began exploring nature. He walked for hundreds of miles, doing odd jobs to support

himself. Working in a factory, he was blinded for a short time by an accident. When he recovered, he began walking again. He was eager to experience all that nature could offer.

3   Muir walked from Indiana to Florida. He made drawings not only of plants and animals, but also of the rivers, hills, and valleys he passed. In time, he sailed to Cuba and Panama. Muir first visited California's Yosemite Valley in 1868. He was one of the first people to realize that glaciers helped form this valley.

4   Working as a shepherd and at other jobs, he began writing articles about his surroundings. He wrote in poetic terms about the natural world. He tried to help readers understand their connection to that world—and their effect on it. For example, he described how grazing sheep and cattle were destroying mountain meadows.

5   Many people were eager to read Muir's articles. In 1890, his essays led to the creation of Yosemite National Park. The goal was to preserve the beauty there. He also helped establish Sequoia, Mount Rainier, and Petrified Forest National Parks.

6   To protect the parks from hunters, farmers, ranchers, and others, Muir and his supporters formed the Sierra Club in 1892. He served as its president for more than 20 years, until his death.

7   In 1903, President Theodore Roosevelt joined Muir on a three-night camping trip. This trip helped shape the president's ideas about conservation. He and Muir shared a love of nature. As president, Roosevelt added five national parks. He also created 18 national monuments, including the Grand Canyon. Roosevelt set aside 100 million acres of national forests.

8   At age 73, Muir was still traveling the world. He visited the Amazon to study its animals, and was amazed by the beauty of that region. In 1914, he died from pneumonia in Los Angeles. He was 76 years old. Muir is remembered not only for the parks he helped create. Another major contribution was the Sierra Club. This group still works every day to help preserve the natural beauty of our nation.

4   Why did John Muir walk so much?

   A   He didn't have enough money for a car.

   B   An accident blinded him for a time, so he could not drive a car.

   C   He was closer to nature when he walked.

   D   He was closer to people when he walked.

5 Based on this passage, how did John Muir learn so much about the environment?

   A   He learned about it at the University of Wisconsin.

   B   He learned from the many jobs he had.

   C   He taught himself by doing experiments.

   D   He taught himself mostly through observation.

6 Write a one- or two-sentence summary of paragraph 4.

   _____

   _____

7 John Muir helped to create the Sierra Club more than 120 years ago. That was long before most housing developments and shopping malls were built. What can you infer about why Muir thought the Sierra Club was needed? Include details from the passage in your answer.

   _____

   _____

   _____

   _____

   _____

   _____

   _____

   _____

Read the passage. Then answer the questions.

Medicine from Mold

1   Long ago, many children died in childhood. They caught diseases that had no cure at that time. Since then, two groups of discoveries have saved millions of lives. One group is the vaccines that prevent illnesses, including mumps, measles, and whooping cough. The other group of discoveries is antibiotics.

2   *Anti* means "against," and *bio* means "life." So *antibiotic* seems to mean "against life." What it really means is "against germs." Antibiotics cannot cure every disease, but they can heal many serious ones.

3   Before antibiotics were discovered, strep throat sometimes killed people. Ear infections spread to the brain. Other common diseases infected the whole body, sometimes causing death.

4   Then a British scientist named Alexander Fleming made an accidental discovery. In 1928, he noticed that a certain kind of mold could attack and kill certain kinds of bacteria. The mold produced a substance that dissolved, or melted, the bacteria. He called this substance penicillin. He named it for the *Penicillium* mold that produced it.

5   For years, Fleming and other scientists experimented with this penicillin. They developed ways to grow more of it. They tested it on animals and then on people. By 1941, they found that even a little bit of penicillin could cure serious infections. On World War II battlefields, it saved thousands of lives. Before penicillin, infected battle wounds caused about 15 percent of the total deaths. After penicillin, the number of deaths from infection dropped to nearly zero. By the late 1940s, people were calling penicillin a miracle drug.

6   Drug companies hurried to produce other antibiotics. The next to be developed was streptomycin. Streptomycin also began with organisms from soil. These organisms also produce a substance that kills bacteria. It cured tuberculosis, whooping cough, and other deadly diseases. Soon this drug was being produced in large amounts.

7   Scientists looked for more substances that could cure infections. By 1955, they had found about 3,000 chemicals that could kill bacteria. Only 15 of those were used in medicine. Currently, scientists have identified about 5,000 possible antibiotics. Only about 100 of them have produced effective drugs.

8   Today, doctors can choose from dozens of antibiotics. About 150 million prescriptions for antibiotics are written in the United States every year. However, they are not miracle drugs. Antibiotics help fight most—but not all—bacteria. They do not kill viruses.

9   At one time, if an antibiotic did not work, doctors tried another one, and maybe even a third one. Here's the problem: when an antibiotic is used to kill a certain bacteria, some of that bacteria may survive. (This can happen when the patient does not take all of the medication, too.) The stronger form of the bacteria can then grow and multiply. It can replace all of the bacteria killed by the antibiotic. The patient is still sick. Now, though, this new bacteria cannot be killed by the same antibiotic.

10   Or one kind of bacteria might change its form slightly. Then the usual antibiotic can no longer kill that bacteria. The new bacteria is able to resist that antibiotic. If the patient switches to another antibiotic, the same thing may happen. In time, few if any antibiotics may work against a certain bacteria.

11   To avoid this, doctors are much more careful when they prescribe antibiotics. They do not want bacteria to become able to resist these medicines. Still, used wisely, penicillin and other antibiotics have changed our lives and made the world a healthier place.

8 Part A

Why are antibiotics so important in our lives?

A They are miracle drugs, able to cure all infections.

B They are able to stop infections on the battlefield.

C They can cure many diseases that used to cause death.

D They are made from mold, which is easy to find.

Part B

What evidence from the passage *best* supports your answer to Part A?

A "This new bacteria cannot be killed by the same antibiotic."

B "Today, doctors can choose from dozens of antibiotics."

C "For years, Fleming and other scientists experimented with this penicillin."

D "Antibiotics cannot cure every disease, but they can heal many serious ones."

9 What inference can you make about what will happen if people continue to overuse antibiotics?

A Scientists will find ways to produce antibiotics in larger amounts.

B Strep throat may become a deadly disease again.

C Antibiotics will become harder to find, and the prices will go up.

D People will begin to use more vaccines to fight infections.

10 What is the main idea of the article? What key details support the main idea? Include examples from the article in your answer.

_____

_____

_____

_____

_____

_____

Do you know the difference between stories, poems, and plays? There are some important ways to tell them apart. In this unit, you will learn the different features of stories, poems, and plays, and practice comparing them. You will also use clues to define unfamiliar words and phrases and discover what point of view an author is using.

LESSON 13 Determining the Meaning of Words and Phrases in Literary Texts is about learning how to define unfamiliar words and phrases using context clues, or the sentences around the new word or phrase. You will read stories and poems looking for words and phrases you may not know.

LESSON 14 Explaining Structural Elements of Poems is about the different features of poems. Most poems have meter and are broken up in verses, and as you read them aloud, you will hear their rhythm.

LESSON 15 Explaining Structural Elements of Plays will help you become familiar with plays and learn about their features and how they are performed. After you read a play, you will look for details about the setting, characters, and events.

LESSON 16 Comparing and Contrasting Poems, Plays, and Prose will help you better understand the features of stories, poems, and plays. You will make a list of the parts that make up a story, poem, or play, and practice telling them apart.

LESSON 17 Comparing and Contrasting Points of View in Literary Texts explains the different points of view and looks at what point of view an author has chosen to use. Many stories, poems, and plays have first-person or third-person points of view.

LESSON 13

Determining the Meaning of Words and Phrases in Literary Texts

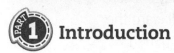

Introduction

THEME: >>> Words Carry the Story

Literary texts contain many words and phrases whose meanings you may not know. When you come across words or phrases you do not know, you can use **context clues** from the sentence or paragraph to help figure out the meaning. Look at the words or sentences that come before or after the unfamiliar word for help figuring out the meaning.

Examples of context clues include:

synonyms	words that have almost the same meaning.
examples	words that show what another word means.
definitions	words that tell what another word means.
descriptions	words that tell more about a word, such as by comparing or by explaining an action it causes.

Sometimes, words or phrases come from popular stories such as myths. **Myths** are stories with powerful themes and morals that have been passed down for many generations. The characters in them often have extraordinary powers. When an author uses a word or phrase from another story or myth, it is called an **allusion.** Mythological allusions can bring to mind the qualities of classic characters and scenes. Authors use allusions to make comparisons.

Read this paragraph.

Juan <u>jerked</u> awake from a sound sleep. His body shook as he sat up quickly to look around the room. What was that strange sound? He <u>yanked</u> the covers closer around his neck. Then he heard it again! "Aroo!" A spine-chilling <u>howl</u> was coming from the doorway. Was it a snake-haired <u>Medusa</u>? Juan peeked out, wondering what <u>unearthly</u> creature could be making that sound. Then his breath escaped in a rush of <u>relief</u> and laughter. Juan bent down and hugged his dog. "Prince," Juan said, "you don't have to howl like that just because you want me to take you outside! Can't you just bark like a normal dog would?"

Complete the table. The meaning of these words can be found using context clues.

Word or Phrase	Context Clue	Meaning
jerked	His body shook; he sat up quickly	
yanked	closer around his neck	
unearthly		
howl		
Medusa	snake-haired	Medusa was a monster in Greek mythology whose hair was made of snakes. One look from her turned people to stone.
relief		

As you read literary texts and come across unknown words or phrases, use context clues to help you determine definitions. Keep in mind that certain phrases could be allusions that come from myths or other stories. It is useful to look up these allusions to find where they come from. Think about how these allusions, or reminders of other texts, add layers of meaning to the story that you are reading. This will give you a richer understanding of literature.

Read the first part of the story. Then answer the questions.

The Red Badge of Courage

by Stephen Crane
an adaptation

1   When he woke from dozing, the young soldier struggled to see. He rubbed his eyes and squinted, trying to make out the shapes in the dark. The dying fire <u>silhouetted</u> the tall trees above them, and muddy grass carpeted the ground beneath. He could see small groups of men spread out, sleeping in the shadows. Their faces glowed in the low firelight, looking ghostlike. But the young soldier had no fear. After the long day's battle, the men slept hard. Arms and legs sprawled in every direction, but a few pairs of legs stuck out stiff and straight. Shoes were caked with mud and weeds, and trousers were torn from running through fields.

2   On the other side of the fire, the boy could see an exhausted officer knocked out. The man was sitting up straight, eyes closed, his back leaning against a tree, his body swaying back and forth like a <u>doddering</u> old man. His face was covered with dirt, and his jaw hung open. His uniform was frayed and stained. His once gleaming sword lay on the ground beside him.

Think About It

What context clues help you understand the meaning of the underlined words? Find words in the passage that help you understand the meaning.

Underline context clues that help you define these words.

What context clues help you figure out the meaning of *silhouetted?* What does the

word mean? _____

_____

_____

What context clues help you figure out the meaning *doddering?* What does the

word mean? _____

_____

_____

A CLOSER LOOK

Look at the underlined words in the text. Underline context clues that help you understand the meaning of *stir, grazed,* and *throbbed.*

Continue reading the story. Then answer the question.

3   Once in a while, a soldier would <u>stir</u>. He might turn his body to find a new position on the ground or suddenly sit up and look at the fire in confusion. He would glance over to his buddy and grunt. Then he would lie down to sleep again.

4   The young soldier's eyes grew heavy, and he began to nod. The place where the bullet had <u>grazed</u> his head still <u>throbbed</u> in pain. He picked up his blankets, spread one out on the ground, and wrapped the other around his shoulders. Then, at last, he stretched out on the ground. It felt as soft as a thick feather bed. The warmth and softness made him sigh as his head fell to his elbow. As his eyelids covered his eyes, with a sigh, he snuggled into his blankets. In seconds, he was sound asleep.

What is the soldier doing in paragraph 4?

What felt "as soft as a thick feather bed" to the soldier?

A   the trees

B   his head

C   his elbow

D   the ground

 DISCUSS IT

Discuss the meanings of *stir, grazed* and *throbbed* with a partner. Have you heard these words before? If not, how did the context clues help you understand the meanings? Did you think about the setting of the passage?

Read the poem. Then answer the questions.

Tenting Tonight

by Walter Kittredge, 1864

A CLOSER LOOK
The poem describes how soldiers feel as they camp after a battle. As you read the poem, circle words and phrases that are unknown. Think about the setting of the poem and find context clues to help you understand the unknown words.

We're tenting tonight on the old camp-ground
Give us a song to cheer
Our weary hearts, a song of home
And friends we love so dear.

Repeat chorus

5 We've been tenting tonight on the old camp-ground,
Thinking of days gone by
Of the loved ones at home that gave us the hand,
And the tear that said, "Good-by!"

Repeat chorus

We are tired of war on the old camp-ground;
10 Many are the dead and gone
Of the brave and true who've left their homes;
Others been wounded long.

Repeat chorus

We've been fighting today on the old camp-ground,
Many are lying near;
15 Some are dead, and some are dying,
Many are in tears.

Chorus

Many are the hearts that are weary tonight,
Wishing for the war to cease;
Many are the hearts looking for the light,
20 To see the dawn of peace.
Dying tonight, dying tonight,
Dying on the old camp-ground.

> What words describe the place where the soldiers are?

1 What does the word *tenting* mean?

A camping

B fighting

C singing

D sleeping

> Which detail is about the past?

2 **Part A**

Which word from the poem describes the soldiers as feeling tired, sad, and homesick?

A brave

B weary

C dear

D true

Part B

Which detail from the poem supports the answer to Part A?

A "Thinking of days gone by,"

B "We've been tenting tonight."

C "Give us a song to cheer."

D "We've been fighting today on the old camp-ground,"

> How are the soldiers feeling about the war?

3 What does the word *cease* mean in the poem? What two context clues helped you find the meaning of the word?

_____

_____

_____

_____

_____

_____

Read the story. Then answer the questions.

The Crazy Camping Trip

1   "Here we are!" Dad called as he inched the van into the campsite. "Let's get settled!" The van doors opened, and the whole family spilled out, grateful for the chance to stretch their legs after the long ride. "Everyone carry something!" Dad ordered.

2   Jayden grabbed the picnic basket and made a beeline for the nearest table. He wanted to set things up without delay. His big brother and sister, David and Laura, dragged out a box of sports equipment. "Who wants to play volleyball?" Laura called. "Come on, David, help me set this up."

3   "Great, kids, you take care of the sports and the food. Mom and I will set up the tent." Dad pulled the tent out of the back of the van, while Mom grabbed the instruction book. Dad added a word of caution. "David, please pay attention to where you hit that ball!"

4   "Okay, first we have to slide the poles together," Mom said. She grabbed two of the metal poles and tried to fit them together, but they fell to the ground with a clatter. "Whoops!"

5   "Let me try," said Dad. "Why don't these fit?" He jammed two poles together, but they stuck fast. He and Mom each grabbed an end and pulled mightily. Their herculean efforts did not quite pay off as the poles flew apart, and both grownups fell backward to the ground.

6   Meanwhile, Jayden spread out a tablecloth and laid sandwiches, water bottles, and napkins on the table. A gust of wind snatched the paper plates out of his hand. He ran to gather them up, almost tripping over the half-assembled tent poles.

7   "I don't like the look of those clouds," Dad said. He had finally figured out how to put the tent together, and a small forest of metal poles now stood in a big square. "Let's hurry up and get the canvas up." He and Mom grabbed the canvas and started sliding it over the poles. The wind grew stronger, flapping the canvas in the breeze.

8 "Watch me!" David yelled from the volleyball net. "This is the best serve ever!" He spiked the ball with Icarus-like excitement. Laura ducked, and the ball bounced into the picnic table, knocking water bottles and plastic containers in all directions. "Sorry!" David yelled. He hurried over to help Jayden retrieve the food.

9 Suddenly, there was a crash of thunder and the sky blazed with lightning. Screaming, Laura, David, and Jayden grabbed the picnic and ran for the van. Mom and Dad followed. The tent laid flat on the ground.

10 The sky opened and rain poured down. "I guess we'll eat lunch in the van," Dad said with a weary smile. He passed around a container of sandwiches while Mom opened a bag of chips. "This is not turning out to be a great trip."

11 Jayden snuggled into his mother's side. "This is nice," he said, as he munched a sandwich. Rain poured down outside, but the family was safe inside the van.

12 "It is pretty cozy," said Laura, leaning against her father's shoulder. "Maybe we could just camp in here."

13 David laughed. "Let's sing a campfire song," he suggested.

14 "It's a bit crowded," Mom said with a laugh. "Look, the sun is coming out. The storm is over."

15 The family stepped cautiously outside just as another van pulled up at the next spot. Jayden grinned as he saw several children his age jump out of the car. Their parents followed with a wave. "Need some help?" they asked Mom and Dad.

16 Jayden, Laura, and David exchanged high-fives. This was going to be a great camping trip!

1 Hercules was a hero who is described in ancient Greek myths. What does the word *Herculean* mean in this story?

A brave

B frightening

C otherworldly

D strong

2 Part A

In paragraph 2, what does the phrase *made a beeline* mean?

A   move slowly and carefully

B   take a rest

C   move in a straight and direct line

D   set something up

Part B

Which sentence in the story *best* supports the answer to Part A?

A   "He wanted to set things up without delay."

B   "'Everybody carry something!'"

C   "'Great, kids, you take care of the sports and food.'"

D   "He inched the van into the campsite."

3 In Greek mythology, Icarus was the son of an inventor who flew too close to the sun. His father had warned him that he would die if he flew too close to the sun with his new wings. Icarus did not obey his father. What does "He spiked the ball with Icarus-like excitement mean?"

_____

_____

_____

_____

4 In paragraph 6, what does the term, *half-assembled* mean? List at least two context clues from the story to support the meaning of the term.

_____

_____

_____

_____

CCLS RL.4.5: Explain major differences between poems, drama, and prose, and refer to the structural elements of poems (e.g., verse, rhythm, meter) and drama (e.g., casts of characters, settings, descriptions, dialogue, stage directions) when writing or speaking about a text.

Explaining Structural Elements of Poems

Introduction

THEME: >>> Words Carry the Story

Stories, poems, and plays have some things in common, but they also have features that are very different. A **poem** has several features that are very different from most stories and plays. Poems are usually written in sets of short lines called **verses.** A verse focuses on a particular event or idea. A group of verses that has space before and after it on the page is called a **stanza.** Poems have a **rhythm,** which is a pattern of beats. Beats are accented and unaccented, or stressed and unstressed, syllables. Poems also have **meter.** Meter is related to rhythm and describes the number and type of sounds in a line. Many poems rhyme. **Rhyme** is created when words end with similar sounds. A pattern of rhyming words is called a **rhyme scheme.**

> **Read the poem "The Little Elfman" by John Kendrick Bangs out loud. Then answer the questions.**
>
> I met a little elfman once,
> Down where the lilies blow.
> I asked him why he was so small,
> And why he didn't grow.
>
> 5 He slightly frowned, and with his eye
> He looked me through and through—
> "I'm just as big for me," said he,
> "As you are big for you!"

Based on the rhythm, which word in each line is emphasized? _____

_____

Which words in the poem rhyme or are close to rhyming? _____

_____

How many stanzas does this poem have? _____

When you read a poem, pay attention to the verse, rhythm, and meter. Also, take note of the language so you understand what the poem is about.

Read the first part of the poem. Then answer the questions.

Three Wise Old Women
by Elizabeth T. Corbett

Three wise old women were they, were they,
Who went to walk on a winter day:
One carried a basket to hold some berries,
One carried a ladder to climb for cherries,
5   The third, and she was the wisest one,
Carried a fan to keep off the sun.

But they went so far, and they went so fast,
They quite forgot their way at last,
So one of the wise women cried in a fright,
10   "Suppose we should meet a bear tonight!
Suppose he should eat me!" "And me!!" "And me!!!"
"What is to be done?" cried all the three.

Think About It

How do you know this is a poem? The question asks you to explain the features of a poem.

Make a list of the parts that show this is a poem.

1. It is written in lines or verses.

2. _____

3. _____

4. _____

Do any words rhyme in this poem? If so, what words rhyme? _____

_____

_____

Continue reading the poem. Then answer the question.

A CLOSER LOOK

This poem has a rhythm. Do you notice the beats? Remember that beats can be accented or unaccented, which means that a reader will say certain words louder or softer than the other words. Circle words that seem to be accented as you read along with the rhythm.

"Dear, dear!" said one, "we'll climb a tree,
There out of the way of the bears we'll be,"
15 But there wasn't a tree for miles around;
They were too frightened to stay on the ground,
So they climbed their ladder up to the top,
And sat there screaming "We'll drop! We'll drop!"

But the wind was strong as wind could be,
20 And blew their ladder right out to sea;
So the three wise women were all afloat
In a leaky ladder instead of a boat,
And every time the waves rolled in,
Of course the poor things were wet to the skin.

25 Then they took their basket, the water to bale,
They put up their fan instead of a sail:
But what became of the wise women then,
Whether they ever sailed home again,
Whether they saw any bears, or no,
30 You must find out, for I don't know.

What does the title tell you about the characters?

What is this poem about?

A   three wise women

B   three foolish women

C   three women chasing bears

D   three women who go sailing

 DISCUSS IT

Remember, a poem's meter describes the number and type of sounds in a line. Tap out the rhythm and meter of the poem with a partner. How many beats are in each line? Which words are stressed or unstressed? Discuss why the author created this meter for the reader.

Read the poem. Then answer the questions.

For Want of a Nail

A CLOSER LOOK

The repeated phrases create the rhythm of the poem. Underline the phrases that repeat.

For want of a nail, the shoe was lost;
For want of the shoe, the horse was lost;
For want of the horse, the rider was lost;
For want of the rider, the battle was lost;
5 For want of the battle, the kingdom was lost;
And all from the want of a horseshoe nail.

Tap out the rhythm of the poem as you read.

1 Based on the rhythm, which word or phrase is emphasized in line 6?

A "And"

B "from the"

C "of a"

D "horseshoe nail"

How is the meter different in these two sets of lines?

2 The meter of lines 4 and 5 is different from the meter of lines 1 and 2. How does this affect the overall feeling of the poem?

A Different words are repeated in the two sets of lines.

B The extra syllables in lines 4 and 5 create a rising feeling of desperation.

C The meter of lines 4 and 5 convey a renewed sense of hope.

D The meter of lines 4 and 5 show how the rider lost the battle.

Look at how the poem is printed and how it sounds when you read it. How is this different from a story?

3 What is one way this poem has a different structure than a story?

_____

_____

_____

_____

Read the poem. Then answer the questions.

The Reformation of Godfrey Gore
by William Brighty Rands

Godfrey Gordon Gustavus Gore—
No doubt you have heard the name before—
Was a boy who never would shut a door!
The wind might whistle, the wind might roar,
5   And teeth be aching and throats be sore,
But still he never would shut the door.

His father would beg, his mother implore,
"Godfrey Gordon Gustavus Gore,
We really do wish you would shut the door!"
10   Their hands they wrung, their hair they tore;
But Godfrey Gordon Gustavus Gore
Was deaf as the buoy out at the Nore.

When he walked forth the folks would roar,
"Godfrey Gordon Gustavus Gore,
15   Why don't you think to shut the door?"
They rigged out a Shutter with sail and oar,
And threatened to pack off Gustavus Gore
On a voyage of penance to Singapore.

But he begged for mercy, and said, "No more!
20   Pray do not send me to Singapore
On a Shutter, and then I will shut the door!"
"You will?" said his parents; "then keep on shore!
But mind you do! For the plague is sore
Of a fellow that never will shut the door,
25   Godfrey Gordon Gustavus Gore!"

1 What is the purpose of the first stanza of this poem?

_____

_____

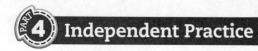

2 Part A

How does the number of beats in line 19 compare to the number of beats in line 20?

  A Line 19 has 8 beats; line 20 has 8 beats.

  B Line 19 has 10 beats; line 20 has 9 beats.

  C Line 19 has 9 beats; line 20 has 9 beats.

  D Line 19 has 11 beats; line 20 has 10 beats.

Part B

What other two lines in the poem match your answer to Part A?

  A lines 5 and 6

  B lines 13 and 14

  C lines 16 and 17

  D lines 22 and 23

3 What is the rhyme scheme of this poem? Give a specific example from the poem.

_____

_____

_____

_____

4 How does the repetition of the name Godfrey Gordon Gustavus Gore add to the rhythm and meaning of the poem? Give specific examples from the poem to support your answer.

_____

_____

_____

_____

_____

LESSON 15

Explaining Structural Elements of Plays

 **Introduction**

THEME: >>> **Words Carry the Story**

Like a story, a play has characters and a setting. A **play** is a dramatic work that can be performed on a stage. Because a play is meant to be acted out on a stage with actors, plays have features that are not found in stories or poems.

A play has **acts** and **scenes.** An act is a division in the text that is like a chapter. A scene is a shorter segment within an act. The **setting** of the play tells where or when the events happen. In a written **script,** or text of a play, the setting is described in detail, but when the play is performed, the setting is conveyed through **sets,** or what appears on the stage. Objects called **props** and backgrounds called **scenery** help create the set.

A play also has a list of characters, also called the **cast,** at the beginning.

Another feature of a play is **dialogue,** or the lines that each character says. **Stage directions** sometimes appear in parentheses when attached to a line of dialogue. They give information about what the characters do, expressions or gestures they make, or where they go on stage. Stage directions also appear between lines of dialogue and are sometimes set off in a different typeface.

Read this part of a play.

CAST:

    RABBIT   **THE FARMER**

    RABBIT'S MOTHER   **THE CAT**

                           act 1, scene 1

RABBIT *is hiding under a bush in the woods near a farm.* RABBIT'S MOTHER *hops up to him.*

Fill in the chart to tell more about this play.

Cast	
Act	
Setting	

Read the first part of the play. Then answer the questions.

A New Home

CAST:

LENA, *a young girl*

CHRISTINA, *her older sister*

MR. YALE, *an official*

scene 1

Below deck on a large ship. LENA and CHRISTINA are sitting on their bed, which is the lower bed in a bunk. Other women and girls are also crowded into the room.

LENA: Christina, have you seen my hairbrush?

CHRISTINA: *(spying the hairbrush and picking it up)* Yes, here it is. It slipped under the bed.

LENA: Thank you! I can't believe we have to sleep with our combs and brushes and just about everything else!

CHRISTINA: I know! It is so crowded here. I can barely stretch out my arms without touching someone.

LENA: *(brushing her hair dreamily)* I can't wait to get to New York City. Just imagine, Christina, how beautiful it will be! Papa's letter said the streets are paved, and there are tall buildings everywhere you look.

CHRISTINA: *(frowning)* I can't wait to see Mama and Papa again, but New York City sounds kind of scary. It will be very different than our farm back in Italy.

LENA: *(hugging her sister)* Things will be very different, that's for sure. But it will be wonderful to all be together again.

(A VOICE from offstage shouts): Everyone, come up to the deck! I can see New York City! We are almost there!

LENA and CHRISTINA jump off the bed, grinning with excitement. Around them, other women and girls start to hurry offstage.

LENA: Did you hear that? We are sailing into New York! Let's go see!

The girls rush offstage.

scene 2

The deck of the ship. The Statue of Liberty can be seen in the distance.

LENA: *(with excitement)* Christina, look! I can see New York City! How big it looks!

CHRISTINA: *(pointing)* What is that statue? It looks like a lady holding up a torch.

LENA: That must be the Statue of Liberty. Remember, Papa wrote about it in his last letter. He said when we saw the statue, we would know we were in New York.

CHRISTINA: *Liberty* means "freedom," doesn't it? I hope we will have freedom in our new home.

Think About It

What helps you know this is a play? To answer the question, think about how this play is different from a poem or a story.

Which part of the play tells who will be in the play? _____

_____

How do you know where the play takes place? _____

_____

How do you know who is speaking? _____

_____

How do you know what the characters are doing? _____

_____

The parts of a play are important because they _____

_____

_____.

A CLOSER LOOK

Focusing on the parts of a play will help you understand what is going on. Think about how the characters act and what they say. Underline the stage directions and descriptions that show how the characters act.

Continue reading the play. Then answer the question.

scene 3

LENA *and* CHRISTINA *are at the front of a long line.*

CHRISTINA: Whew! I feel like I have been standing for hours!

LENA: I'm tired of standing in line. First, we had to wait to get off the ship. Then we had to wait to put our baggage down. And then we had a medical exam! What are we waiting for now?

CHRISTINA: Those men are asking everyone questions. Oh, it's our turn now! Stay close to me, Lena.

MR. YALE: *(motioning to the girls to step forward)* Next! Hello, girls. What are your names?

LENA: I am Lena Martini, and this is my sister, Christina.

MR. YALE: You just came off the boat from Italy, am I right? *(The girls nod.)* Excellent. May I see your papers, please?

CHRISTINA: Of course. *(She hands Mr. Yale their papers.)*

MR. YALE: Do you have family in New York City?

CHRISTINA: Yes, our father and mother are here.

MR. YALE: *(smiling)* Your papers are all in order. Go that way, and you can find your parents. Welcome to America!

CHRISTINA: Thank you! *(LENA and CHRISTINA walk away.)* Just think, Lena, we will see Papa and Mama very soon. We are finally in America!

LENA: It certainly is different here. Maybe, a little scary, too. But when our family is all together again, we will be at home, no matter where we are.

Why are Lena and Christina excited?

How do Lena and Christina feel about being in New York?

A   They are unhappy.

B   They are frightened.

C   They are homesick for Italy.

D   They are eager to see their family.

 DISCUSS IT

What parts of the play show the reader what is happening and how the characters feel? Discuss with another student how these features help you understand the action of the play.

A CLOSER LOOK

Circle details in the play that show how the Queen feels about Raleigh's action.

Plays are mostly made up of dialogue. How does dialogue help you to understand what is happening in this play?

Read the play. Then answer the questions.

Sir Walter Raleigh

by Mary Ella Lyng

CAST:

WALTER RALEIGH

BLOUNT, *Raleigh's friend*

TRACY, *Raleigh's friend*

QUEEN ELIZABETH

COURTIER, *member of Queen Elizabeth's court*

WALTER RALEIGH *was the Englishman who checked the power of the Spanish in America. He was a friend of* QUEEN ELIZABETH, *and first gained her friendship, by an interesting incident. This act tells the story.*

act 1

WALTER RALEIGH, BLOUNT, *and* TRACY, *walking along shore to see the boat of the Queen.*

BLOUNT: See, the Queen's barge lies at the stairs. We had best put back and tell the Earl what we have seen.

RALEIGH: Tell the Earl what we have seen! Let us do his errand, and tell him what the Queen says in reply.

BLOUNT: Do, I pray you, my dear Walter, let us take the boat and return.

RALEIGH: Not till I see the Queen come forth.

QUEEN ELIZABETH *comes,* RALEIGH *removes his hat and stands close to* QUEEN *as she approaches with her court. She hesitates to pass the muddy spot.* RALEIGH *takes coat from shoulders and lays it on the ground.* QUEEN *looks at* RALEIGH *and passes on.*

BLOUNT: Come along, Sir Coxcomb, your gay mantle will need the brush today, I think.

RALEIGH: This cloak shall never be brushed while in my possession.

BLOUNT: That will not be long, if you learn not a little more economy.

Member of court comes after RALEIGH. QUEEN *and court at water's edge, waiting.*

COURTIER: I was sent to bring a gentleman who has no coat, you, sir, I think. Please follow me.

BLOUNT: He is in attendance on me, the noble Earl of Sussex, Master of Horse.

COURTIER: I have nothing to say to that. My orders are from her Majesty.

RALEIGH *and man walk toward* QUEEN.

BLOUNT: Who in the world would have thought it!

RALEIGH *is brought to* QUEEN, *who laughs, and talks to attendants.*

QUEEN: You have this day spoiled a gay mantle in our service. We thank you for your service, though the manner of offering was something bold.

RALEIGH: In a sovereign's need, it is each man's duty to be bold.

QUEEN: *(speaking to attendant)* That is well said, my lord. *(to* RALEIGH*)* Well, young man, your gallantry shall not go unrewarded. Thou shalt have a suit, and that of the newest cut.

RALEIGH: May it please Your Majesty, but if it became me to choose—

QUEEN: Thou wouldst have gold? Fie, young man. Yet, thou mayest be poor. It shall be gold. But thou shall answer to me for the use of it.

RALEIGH: I do not wish gold, your majesty.

QUEEN: How, boy, neither gold nor garment! What then?

RALEIGH: Only permission to wear the cloak which did this trifling service.

QUEEN: Permission to wear thine own cloak, thou silly boy?

RALEIGH: It is no longer mine. When your majesty's foot touched it, it became a fit mantle for a prince.

QUEEN: Heard you ever the like, my Lords? What is thy name and birth?

RALEIGH: Raleigh is my name.

QUEEN: Raleigh? We have heard of you. You may wear thy muddy cloak, and here, I give thee this, to wear at the collar.

Gives him a jewel of gold, RALEIGH *kneels, and kisses hand of* QUEEN.

1 Part A

What does Raleigh's dialogue tell you about him?

A   He is bold.

B   He is selfish.

C   He is embarrassed.

D   He is disrespectful.

What does Raleigh say to the Queen?

Part B

What detail from the play *best* supports the answer to Part A?

_____

_____

_____

Look at the beginning of the play. Where does it say the characters are located?

2 What is the setting of this play?

A   a ship

B   the shore

C   a battlefield

D   the royal court

What action does the Queen take at the end of the act?

3 What detail shows the Queen's feelings about Raleigh at the end of the act?

_____

_____

_____

Read the play. Then answer the questions that follow.

adapted from Mother Goose's Party

by Florence Holbrook

CAST:

MOTHER GOOSE MOTHER HUBBARD

JACK GOOSE   DOG

scene 1

Home of MOTHER GOOSE.

MOTHER GOOSE: I really think I must give a party. All my friends have been so good to me, and I have been entertained in so many homes! Let me see! Whom shall I invite? I think I'll ask Old Mother Hubbard to take tea with me, and we'll talk about the party together. Jack, Jack!

JACK: *(enters)* Yes, mother dear, what is it?

MOTHER GOOSE: Jack Goose, I wish you to run over to Mother Hubbard's house and ask her to take tea with me this afternoon. Now be nimble, Jack,—be quick!

JACK: Yes, Mother dear. See me jump over the candlestick! Isn't that fine jumping?

MOTHER GOOSE: Very fine indeed, Jack. Now do your errand.

JACK: Yes, Mother, I will. Good-bye.

MOTHER GOOSE: Good-bye.

scene 2

House of MOTHER HUBBARD.

JACK: *(knocking)* I wonder if Old Mother Hubbard is at home. Hark! I hear her dog barking. Yes, and I hear her step. Here she is!

MOTHER HUBBARD: *(opening the door)* Who is this knocking so loud? Oh, it's you, little nimble Jack! Will you come in?

JACK: No, thank you, Mrs. Hubbard. My mother wishes you to come over to our house for tea this afternoon. Will you come?

MOTHER HUBBARD: Yes, thank you, Jack, I will. Tell your mother that I'm just going to market to buy my poor doggie a bone.

JACK: O Mother Hubbard! Please let me play with your dog. He's such a dear old doggie! Do you remember how he danced a jig the other day?

MOTHER HUBBARD: Yes, Jack, I do; and I think you danced with him. You are both nimble young things and both like to dance. Well, good-bye, now. Have a good time together, and I'll bring you something little boys like.

JACK: Thank you! Good-bye, good-bye! Now, doggie, let's dance.
> Old Mother Hubbard, she went to the cupboard,
>> To get the poor doggie a bone;
> But when she got there, the cupboard was bare,
>> And so the poor doggie had none.

DOG: *(sadly)* Bow-wow, bow-wow, bow-wow!

JACK: Oh! You don't like that song! Never mind, old fellow! Mother Hubbard has gone to the butcher's, and she'll get you a bone, I'm sure. Wait till she comes back.

DOG: *(gayly)* Bow-wow, bow-wow, bow-wow!

JACK: I thought you would like that. Here she comes now. We've had a lovely dance, Mother Hubbard, and now I must hurry home.

MOTHER HUBBARD: Thank you for staying and taking good care of my dog. Here are some fresh Banbury buns for you.

JACK: Oh, thank you. I'm very fond of Banbury buns. Good-bye!

MOTHER HUBBARD: Good-bye, Jack. Tell your mother I'll be over soon.

JACK: Bring your dog with you, and we'll have another dance. Good-bye.

1 Which of the following is a stage direction?

A **Mother Goose's Party**

B **JACK:** *(enters)*

C **CAST:**

D *Home of* MOTHER GOOSE.

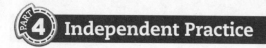

2 Part A

What do Jack's dialogue and actions tell you about him?

A Jack likes to stay home.

B Jack is happy and excited.

C Jack knows a lot of people.

D Jack does not want to run errands.

Part B

Which line from the play *best* supports the answer to Part A?

A "Yes, mother dear, what is it?

B "Now, doggie, let's dance."

C "I'm very fond of Banbury buns."

D "Yes, and I hear her step. Here she is!"

3 What element of a play is *most* important in showing what happens?

A action

B description

C dialogue

D setting

4 What would be different if this were told in the form of a poem? Include at least two examples to support your answer.

_____

_____

_____

_____

_____

_____

_____

LESSON 16

Comparing and Contrasting Poems, Plays, and Prose

Introduction

THEME: ⫸ Words Carry the Story

Stories, poems, and plays have some elements in common, but they also have elements that are very different. Stories and plays both have plots, but each develops the plot in different ways. Stories, also called prose, are usually written in paragraphs that contain description, as well as dialogue that may be one or several lines long. A narrator outside the story or a character in the story often describes the events. Plays are meant to be performed on a stage, and the story is told through the actors' dialogue and actions. Stage directions tell how the words should be spoken and how the performers should act. The play includes a cast list of characters and specific details about the settings. It is broken into scenes and acts. Poems might have a plot, but they might also just be a description of a person, place, or event. Or, they may just describe how the poet feels about an idea. Poems use rhythm and rhyme, and are broken into verses and stanzas. Knowing the elements of poems, plays, and stories will help you understand each type of literature.

Read the descriptions in the chart. Then identify whether it is a poem, play, or story.

	• dialogue • stage directions	• characters • action
	• dialogue • action	• characters • paragraphs
	• verses • rhythm	• characters • rhyme

When you read, pay attention to the elements and content you are reading. Look for clues that tell you what type of literature it is.

Read the first part of the story. Then answer the questions.

excerpt from Honey at the Phone
by Mrs. A. E. C. Maskell

1 Honey's mama had gone to market, leaving her home with nurse. Nurse was upstairs making beds, while little Honey, with hands behind her, was trudging about the sitting-room looking for something to do.

2 There was a phone in the house, which was a great mystery to Honey when it first came. She could hear voices talking back to mama, yet could not see a person. Was someone hidden away in the horn her mother put to her ear, or was it in the machine itself?

3 Honey never failed to be on hand when the bell rang, and found that her mother generally talked to her best and dearest friends, ladies who were such frequent callers that Honey knew them all by name.

4 Her mama wrote down the names of her friends, with the number of their phones, and, because the child was so inquisitive about it, she very carefully explained to her just how the whole thing worked, never thinking that Honey would sometime try it for herself; and, indeed, for a while Honey satisfied herself by playing phone. She would roll up a piece of paper, and call out through it, "Hullo!" asking and answering all the questions herself.

Think About It

How can you tell this is a story? The question asks you to think about what elements indicate that this is a story.

Make a list of the elements that show this is a story.

This story has:

1.
2.
3.
4.

Fill in the blank: The author uses mostly _____ to tell this story.

A CLOSER LOOK
This part tells the story through dialogue. Underline the dialogue that shows what is happening.

Continue reading the story. Then answer the question.

5 One day, finding herself alone, she took the receiver and tried to talk to one of her mama's friends, but it was a failure. She watched mama more closely after that. One morning, while mama was at market, she tried again.

6 Taking the receiver, she called out, "Hullo!"

7 "Hullo!" "I want A 215," said Honey.

8 "Yes," came the reply.

9 "Are you Miss Samor?" asked Honey.

10 "Yes," was the reply.

11 "We want you to come tonight to supper, mama and me."

12 "Who's mama and me?" asked the voice.

13 "Honey," was the reply.

14 "Honey, through the phone, eh?" laughed the voice. "Tell mama I will come with pleasure."

15 Honey was not only delighted, but greatly excited. She used every number on her mother's list, inviting them all to supper.

16 About four o'clock the guests began to arrive, much to mama's consternation, especially when they divested themselves of their wraps, and proceeded to make themselves comfortable. What could it mean? She would think she was having a surprise party if every one had not come empty-handed. Perhaps, it was a joke. If so, they would find she would take it pleasantly.

What does Honey say to her mother's friends?

Why is Honey's mother surprised when the guests show up?

A She did not expect them so early.

B She does not want to have a party.

C She did not want to invite those guests.

D She does not know Honey invited them.

DISCUSS IT
How does the author build suspense in the story? Discuss with another student how the elements of fiction provided clues that helped you understand what was going to happen.

PART 3

Read the poem. Then answer the questions.

A CLOSER LOOK
Circle details in the poem that compare the rainbow to a bridge.

The Rainbow
by Christina Rossetti

Boats sail on the rivers,
And ships sail on the seas;
But clouds that sail across the sky
Are prettier far than these.
5 There are bridges on the rivers,
As pretty as you please;
But the bow that bridges heaven,
And overtops the trees,
And builds a road from earth to sky,
10 Is prettier far than these.

What element is found in poems that is not usually found in stories or plays?

1 Which element *best* shows that this is a poem?

A description

B narration

C rhyme

D setting

What elements are never found in poems?

2 Which element is *not* found in this poem?

A a list of characters

B meter

C rhyming lines

D verses

What does the poet compare to the rainbow?

3 How does the author use comparison to describe the rainbow?

_____

_____

_____

_____

Read the play. Then answer the questions.

Jenna's Jobs

CAST:

JENNA

TONY, *Jenna's brother*

MR. NGUYEN, *a neighbor*

SERENA, *Jenna's friend*

TARA, *Jenna's friend*

act 1

Tony's bedroom. TONY *is lying on his bed, reading.* JENNA *knocks on the door.*

TONY: Hey, Jenna, what's up? Why the long face?

JENNA: I just feel so discouraged. I need money, but I spent everything I had on Grandma's birthday present. Now I have nothing left and no way to earn anything. Do you have any ideas?

TONY: *(laughing)* Well, I'd pay you to clean my room.

JENNA: *(looking excited)* Really? How much?

TONY: How about five dollars?

JENNA: That sounds great! Can I start now?

TONY: Why not? I'll go get a snack. (TONY *leaves.*)

JENNA: *(approaching Tony's desk)* Wow, there sure is a lot of junk to clean up. Eww! *(She holds up a dirty sock.)* That's disgusting! (JENNA *throws the sock into the laundry basket.*) Oh no, what's this? *(She picks up a plate with crusted food on it.)* Oh, this is so gross! Why should I have to clean up Tony's mess? I'm out of here!

end of act 1

act 2

Mr. Nguyen's driveway. MR. NGUYEN *is washing his car.* JENNA *approaches him.*

JENNA: Hi, Mr. Nguyen! What are you doing?

MR. NGUYEN: Washing my car. I'd much rather be watching the baseball game, though, but this has to get done today.

JENNA: I'm looking to earn some money. Can I wash your car for you?

MR. NGUYEN: That's a great idea! Ring the doorbell when you're done. (MR. NGUYEN *hurries inside.*)

JENNA: (*picking up the hose*) Hmm, I've never washed a car before. How hard could it be? (*She aims the hose at the car and sprays it at full force. The water splashes back, drenching her.*) Ahh! Yuck! I'm all wet! This is a terrible job!

JENNA *turns off the hose and goes to sit on the curb. Her friends* SERENA *and* TARA *come down the street. They are both eating ice cream cones.*)

JENNA: Hi! Wow, those ice creams look good. Where did you get them?

SERENA: At the store.

TARA: We cleaned our neighbor's yard to earn money. Since it's a hot day, we decided to buy some ice cream. See you later! (*They leave.*)

JENNA: I wish I had money for ice cream. I suppose I would if I had done the jobs I promised for Tony and Mr. Nguyen. If I want money, I have to work, and a promise is a promise. (*She jumps to her feet and picks up the hose.*) Clean car, here we come!

1 What element *best* shows that this is a play?

A action

B characters

C dialogue

D stage directions

2 Part A

How does Jenna feel after she starts cleaning Tony's room and washing Mr. Nguyen's car?

A determined

B disgusted

C excited

D frustrated

Part B

Which line from the text *best* supports the answer to Part A?

A **JENNA:** Oh, this is so gross!

B **JENNA:** I just feel so discouraged.

C **JENNA:** I'm looking to earn some money.

D **JENNA:** I wish I had money for ice cream.

3 What element tells you who is in the play?

A description

B dialogue

C cast list

D stage directions

4 What would be different if this were told in the form of a story? Include at least two examples from the text.

_____

_____

_____

_____

_____

_____

LESSON 17
Comparing and Contrasting Points of View in Literary Texts

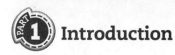 **Introduction**

THEME: >>> Words Carry the Story

Every literary work has a **point of view.** The point of view refers to who is telling the story and the relationship between the narrator and the events or ideas being described. Some stories are told in the **first-person point of view.** In first-person point of view, the narrator tells the story in his or her own words, using the pronouns *I, me,* and *we.* In **third-person point of view,** the story is told by an outside voice. The narrator is not involved in the action of the story. A third-person voice refers to the characters by name and uses words such as *he, she,* and *they* in the narrative.

> **Read two passages.**
>
> Smiling, Mrs. Miller told Justin to open the garage door. Justin did as he was told. He could not believe his eyes. Sitting in the garage was the dirt bike of his dreams, with a big bow tied around the handlebars. "Wow!" Justin yelled. "This is the best birthday ever!"
>
> ―――――――――――――――――――――――――――――――――――――
>
> I slammed the door and threw my books down on the kitchen table. "Practice was terrible!" I complained to my father. "We had to do push-ups and run laps, and I struck out three times. And then things got worse." I buried my head in my hands.

Think about the point of view in each paragraph. Then circle the correct answer in each sentence and answer the question below.

The first paragraph is told from a $\begin{matrix}\text{first-person}\\\text{third-person}\end{matrix}$ point of view.

What words help you know the point of view in the first paragraph?

_____

The second paragraph is told from a $\begin{matrix}\text{first-person}\\\text{third-person}\end{matrix}$ point of view.

What words help you know the point of view in the second paragraph?

_____

Read the first story. Then answer the questions.

Ana's Surprise Party

1 "Ana, I'm home!" my mother called as she walked through the front door.

2 "Hi, Mama! I'm doing homework in my room," I replied. Quickly, I shoved the paper and colored pencils under my backpack because I didn't want my mother to see what I was working on when she came in to see me.

3 Mama peered into the room and smiled. "I had such a busy day at work today," she said, taking off her coat. "Abuela is heading home now, and I'm just going to put my feet up for a few minutes. Then I'll start dinner."

4 "Sounds great!" I said. As soon as my mother left, I pulled out the paper and pencils I'd hidden. Painstakingly, I traced the letters I'd written on the front of the homemade card and colored them in. "Happy Birthday, Mama!" it read. Inside, I wrote, "You are the best mother ever. I love you! Ana."

5 I looked up from my card and sighed. Mama's birthday was tomorrow. Her card was finished, but what gift could I give her for her birthday? I'd checked my piggy bank that morning, and it was almost empty.

6 Just then, the phone rang and I heard my mother say, "Hello, Aunt Rita! How are you? I'm fine, but I am exhausted. It's hard to be on my feet all day at work and then come home and make dinner. Sometimes, I'd just like to relax and leave the chore of making dinner for another day. If only I could!"

7 An idea flew into my head like a lightning bolt, and suddenly I knew just what to give Mama for her birthday! I called Abuela and asked if she could help me tomorrow after school, and she quickly agreed. I explained my plan and she thought it sounded like a splendid idea and the perfect gift for Mama.

8 The next afternoon, I hurried home from school. After a quick hello to Abuela who was in the kitchen washing dishes, I got to work. I set the table with our nicest tablecloth. Then I found the colorful dishes we used for parties and set the table for Mama, Abuela, and me. Next, I spread out everything we needed for sandwiches: meat, vegetables, cheese, and bread. I opened a bag of lettuce, washed it, and placed it

in a bowl, then set out some chips and salsa. Finally, I poured three glasses of water and set Mama's birthday card next to her plate. Abuela looked over the table smiling at me proudly.

9   Just as I finished, I heard Mama's key in the lock. "Surprise!" I yelled as she came into the kitchen. "Happy birthday!"

10   Mama looked at the table, baffled, and smiled. "What's all this?" she asked.

11   "I heard you telling Aunt Rita yesterday how tired you are when you get home from work," I explained. "I wanted to give you a break on your birthday, so I made dinner for us. I hope you like it."

12   "Like it? Ana, I love it!" Mama cried. With a beaming smile, she gave me a huge hug. "You gave me the perfect birthday present. Now, let's sit down and eat this scrumptious meal!"

Think About It

Who is telling this story? The question asks you to identify the story's point of view.

Underline clues that show the story's point of view. Then fill in the chart below.

1. What clue words does the narrator use?	
2. What other clues tell you who is telling the story?	
3. Who is telling the story?	

This story is told from the _____ point of view.

Read the second story. Then answer the question.

excerpt from The Jungle Book
by Rudyard Kipling

A CLOSER LOOK

What is the point of view of *The Jungle Book?* Underline words and phrases that help you identify who is telling the story.

1   The bushes rustled a little in the thicket, and Father Wolf dropped with his haunches under him, ready for his leap. Then, if you had been watching, you would have seen the most wonderful thing in the world—the wolf checked in mid-spring. He made his bound before he saw what it was he was jumping at, and then he tried to stop himself. The result was that he shot up straight into the air for four or five feet, landing almost where he left ground.

2   "Man!" he snapped. "A man's cub. Look!"

3   Directly in front of him, holding on by a low branch, stood a naked, brown baby who could just walk—as soft and as dimpled a little atom as ever came to a wolf's cave at night. He looked up into Father Wolf's face, and laughed.

4   "Is that a man's cub?" said Mother Wolf. "I have never seen one. Bring it here."

5   A wolf accustomed to moving his own cubs can, if necessary, mouth an egg without breaking it, and though Father Wolf's jaws closed right on the child's back, not a tooth even scratched the skin as he laid it down among the cubs.

6   "How little! How naked, and—how bold!" said Mother Wolf softly. The baby was pushing his way between the cubs to get close to the warm hide. "Ahai! He is taking his meal with the others. And so this is a man's cub. Now, was there ever a wolf that could boast of a man's cub among her children?"

7   "I have heard now and again of such a thing, but never in our pack or in my time," said Father Wolf. "He is altogether without hair, and I could kill him with a touch of my foot. But see, he looks up and is not afraid."

> What does the reader learn about the characters in both stories?

How are the narrative points of view in the two stories different?

A The first story uses the word *her.* The second story uses the word *I.*

B The first story tells a story that includes a mother and grandmother. The second story tells a story that includes a father and mother.

C The first story tells the thoughts of one character. The second story doesn't tell the thoughts of any characters.

D The first story doesn't show what Abuela says. The second story doesn't show what the baby says.

DISCUSS IT

With a partner, discuss the narrative points of view of both stories. How are they similar? How are they different? What is the effect of the narrative points of view on the reader?

Read the passages. Then answer the questions.

A CLOSER LOOK

The vocabulary in the story and the poem tells the point of view. Underline the words in both selections that are clues to whether each selection is told from the first-person or third-person point of view.

Writing a Book
by M. Clifford

1 "Let us write a book," they said, "but what shall it be about?"

2 "A fairy story," said the elder sister.

3 "A book about kings and queens," said the other.

4 "Oh, no," said the brother, "let's write about animals."

5 "We will write about them all," they cried together. So, they put the paper, and pens, and ink ready. The elder sister took up a fairy story, looked at it, and put it down again.

6 "I have never known any fairies," she said, "except in books, but, of course, it would not do to put one book inside another—anyone could do that."

7 "I shall not begin today," the little one said, "for I must know a few kings and queens before I write about them, or I may say something foolish."

8 "I shall write about the pig, and the pony, and the white rabbit," said the brother, "but first I must think a bit. It would never do to write a book without thinking."

9 Then the elder sister took up the fairy story again, to see how many things were left out, for those, she thought, would do to go into her book. The little one said to herself, "Really, it is no good thinking about kings and queens until I have known some, so I must wait," and while the brother was considering about the pig, and the pony, and the white rabbit, he fell asleep.

10 So the book is not written yet, but when it is we shall know a great deal.

The Land of Counterpane

by Robert Louis Stevenson

When I was sick and lay a-bed,
I had two pillows at my head,
And all my toys beside me lay
To keep me happy all the day.

5　And sometimes for an hour or so
I watched my leaden soldiers go,
With different uniforms and drills,
Among the bedclothes, through the hills.

And sometimes sent my ships in fleets
10　All up and down among the sheets;
Or brought my trees and houses out,
And planted cities all about.

I was the giant great and still
That sits upon the pillow-hill,
15　And sees before him, dale and plain
The pleasant Land of Counterpane.

> How do you feel about the narrator? What does his or her voice tell you about the characters?

1 Part A

"Writing a Book" is told from the _____ point of view.

Part B

Which answer *best* supports the answer to Part A?

A The narrator tells the story using *I*.

B There are few characters in the story.

C There are many characters in the story.

D The narrator tells the story using *they*.

> What vocabulary does the narrator use to refer to the characters?

2 From whose point of view is "The Land of Counterpane" told?

  A first person

  B second person

  C third person

  D the soldiers

> Whose voice is telling the narrative?

3 How are the narrative points of view in the story and the poem alike and different?

_____

_____

_____

_____

_____

_____

_____

_____

_____

_____

Read the passages. Then answer the questions.

The Lion and the Mouse

based on an Aesop fable
by Marmaduke Park

A lion, with the heat oppress'd,
One day composed himself to rest;
But whilst he dozed, as he intended,
A mouse his royal back ascended;
5 Nor thought of harm as Esop tells,
Mistaking him for something else,
And travelled over him, and round him,
And might have left him as he found him,
Had he not, tremble when you hear,
10 Tried to explore the monarch's ear!
Who straightway woke with wrath immense,
And shook his head to cast him thence.
"You rascal, what are you about,"
Said he, when he had turned him out.
15 "I'll teach you soon," the lion said,
"To make a mouse-hole in my head!"
So saying, he prepared his foot,
To crush the trembling tiny brute;
But he, the mouse, with tearful eye,
20 Implored the lion's clemency,
Who thought it best at least to give
His little pris'ner a reprieve.
'Twas nearly 12 months after this,
The lion chanced his way to miss;
25 When pressing forward: heedless yet,
He got entangled in a net.
With dreadful rage he stamp'd and tore,
And straight commenced a lordly roar;
When the poor mouse who heard the noise,
30 Attended, for she knew his voice.
Then what the lion's utmost strength
Could not effect, she did at length:
With patient labor she applied
Her teeth, the net-work to divide;
35 And so at last forth issued he,
A lion, by a mouse set free.

from Company Manners

1 "Well," said Bessie, very emphatically, "I think Russell Morton is the best boy there is, anyhow."

2 "Why so, pet?" I asked, settling myself in the midst of the busy group gathered around in the firelight.

3 "I can tell," interrupted Wilfred, "Bessie likes Russ because he is so polite."

4 "I don't care, you may laugh," said frank little Bess, "that *is* the reason—at least, one of them. He's nice. He don't stamp and hoot in the house, and he never says, 'Halloo Bess,' or laughs when I fall on the ice."

5 "Bessie wants company manners all of the time," said Wilfred. Bell added, "We should all act grown up, if we wanted to suit her."

6 Dauntless Bessie made haste to retort. "Well, if growing up would make some folks more agreeable, it's a pity we can't hurry about it."

7 "Wilfred, what are company manners?" I questioned from the depths of my easy chair.

8 "Why—why—they're—it's *behaving,* you know, when folks are here, or we go a visiting."

9 "Company manners are good manners;" said Horace.

10 "O yes," answered I, meditating on it. "I see, manners that are *too* good—for mamma—but just right for Mrs. Jones."

11 "That's it," cried Bess.

12 "But let us talk it over a bit. Seriously, why should you be more polite to Mrs. Jones than to mamma? Do you love her better?"

13 "O my! No indeed," chorused the voices.

14 "Well, then, I don't see why Mrs. Jones should have all that's agreeable, why the hats should come off and the tones soften, and 'please,' and 'thank you,' and 'excuse me,' should abound in her house, and not in mamma's."

15 "Oh! that's very different."

16 "Mamma knows we mean all right. Besides, you are not fair, cousin. We were talking about boys and girls—not grown-up people."

17 Thus, my little audience assailed me, and I was forced to a change of base.

18 "Well, about boys and girls, then. Can not a boy be just as happy, if, like our friend Russell, he is gentle to the little girls, doesn't pitch his little brother in the snow, and respects the rights of his cousins and intimate friends? It seems to me that politeness is just as suitable to the playground as the parlor."

19 "Oh, of course, if you'd have a fellow give up all fun," said Wilfred.

20 "My dear boy," said I, "that isn't what I want. Run, and jump, and shout as much as you please; skate, and slide, and snowball; but do it with politeness to other boys and girls, and I'll agree you shall find just as much fun in it."

1 Part A

"The Lion and the Mouse" is told from whose point of view?

A the King

B the Lion

C the Mouse

D the author

Part B

What details from the poem *best* support the answer to Part A? Include at least one detail from the poem to support your answer.

_____

_____

_____

_____

2 How are the narrative points of view in "The Lion and the Mouse" and "Company Manners" alike?

   A Both passages have morals and teach lessons for the reader to learn.

   B Both narrators express opinions about characters, such as the "poor mouse" and "frank little Bess."

   C Both passages give the internal thoughts of the narrator.

   D Both narrators tell about their own perspectives on the situations in which they are involved.

3 How are the narrative points of view in "The Lion and the Mouse" and "Company Manners" different?

   A The poem tells the lion's thoughts. The story tells the children's thoughts.

   B The poem is about characters helping each other in surprising ways. The story is about how to behave.

   C The poem's narrator uses *he* and *him.* The story uses *I.*

   D The poem is subjective. The story is objective.

4 How would "The Lion and the Mouse" and "Company Manners" be different if they were written from a different point of view? How would specific text details change? Use examples from the passages in your answer.

_____

_____

_____

_____

_____

_____

Read the passage. Then answer the questions.

adapted from The Handy Box

by Mira Jenks Stafford

1 "Grandmother, do you know where I can find a little bit of wire?" asked Marjorie, running from the shed, where an amateur circus was in preparation.

2 Grandmother went to a little closet in the room and disappeared a moment, coming out presently with the wire.

3 "O, yes! Fred wanted me to ask if you had a large safety-pin." Marjorie looked a little wistful, as if she did not quite like to bother grandmother.

4 There was another trip made to the closet, and the safety-pin was in Marjorie's hand.

5 "You are a pretty nice grandma," she said, over her shoulder, as she ran out.

6 Not very long after, Marjorie came into the kitchen again. This time she stood beside the sink, where grandmother was washing dishes, and twisted her little toes in her sandals, but seemed afraid to speak.

7 "Fred wants to know"—began grandmother, laughing.

8 "Yes'm," said Marjorie, blushing.

9 "If I can't find him a piece of strong string?" finished grandmother.

10 "O, no—it's a little brass tack!" declared Marjorie, soberly.

11 She was a patient, loving grandmother, and she went to the little closet again. Marjorie could hardly believe her eyes when she saw the tacks, for there were three!

12 "He—said—" she began slowly, and stopped.

13 "You ought to tell him to come and say it himself," and grandmother laughed; "but we will forgive him this time. Was it 'Thank you,' he said?"

14 "He feels 'Thank you' awfully, I'm sure," said Marjorie, politely, "but what he said was that if wasn't too much bother—well, he could use a kind of hook thing."

15 Her grandmother produced a long iron hook, and Marjorie looked at her wonderingly. "Are you a fairy?" she asked, timidly. "You must have a wand and just make things."

1 What is the point of view from which this story is told?

A Marjorie's

B first person

C third person

D grandmother's

2 What literary element shows this is a story?

A There is dialogue.

B There are several characters.

C It is written in paragraphs.

D Characters face and solve a problem.

3 Complete the table to tell the characteristics of a story.

Stories have:
1.
2.
3.
4.
5.

Read the poem. Then answer the questions.

The Ant Explorer

by C. J. Dennis

Once a little sugar ant made up his mind to roam—
To fare away far away, far away from home.
He had eaten all his breakfast, and he had his ma's consent
To see what he should chance to see and here's the way he went—
5   Up and down a fern frond, round and round a stone,
Down a gloomy gully where he loathed to be alone,
Up a mighty mountain range, seven inches high,
Through the fearful forest grass that nearly hid the sky,
Out along a bracken bridge, bending in the moss,
10 Till he reached a dreadful desert that was feet and feet across.

'Twas a dry, deserted desert, and a trackless land to tread,
He wished that he was home again and tucked-up tight in bed.
His little legs were wobbly, his strength was nearly spent,
And so he turned around again and here's the way he went—
15 Back away from desert lands feet and feet across,
Back along the bracken bridge bending in the moss,
Through the fearful forest grass shutting out the sky,
Up a mighty mountain range seven inches high,
Down a gloomy gully, where he loathed to be alone,
20 Up and down a fern frond and round and round a stone.
A dreary ant, a weary ant, resolved no more to roam,
He staggered up the garden path and popped back home.

4 What two structural elements show that this is a poem?

A   It is written in verses.

B   It has dialogue.

C   It has a main character.

D   It describes an adventure.

E   It has a regular rhyme pattern.

F   It has acts and scenes.

5 What is the meter of this poem?

  A No syllables are stressed in each line.

  B Only one syllable is stressed in each line.

  C Several syllables are stressed in each line.

  D Only the first and last syllables are stressed in each line.

Read the play. Then answer the questions.

A Day at the Museum

CAST:

  CLAIRE, *a young basketball player*

  DAD, *her father*

  DAVID, *a professional basketball player*

  LAYLA, *a professional basketball player*

act 1

The exhibit room of a basketball museum.

DAD: Well, we finally made it to the basketball museum, Claire. There sure is a lot to see here.

CLAIRE: There sure is! Look! It's Dave Ward's jersey from last year's championship game! I remember watching that on television.

DAD: Yes, that was a great game. Look over here. I found a basketball signed by lots of famous players.

CLAIRE: *(hurrying over to the display case)* Let me see! Wow, to think that all those players touched that ball, and now I'm looking at it.

DAD: That's the great thing about museums. They connect the past and present.

CLAIRE: I wonder if my ball or jersey will ever be in a museum.

DAD: Well, you're an excellent player, so you never know!

CLAIRE *and* DAD *wander around the museum, looking at the different exhibits. Claire's feet begin to drag.*

DAD: What's the matter, Claire? Are you getting tired?

CLAIRE: No, not really. It's just that…well…playing basketball is more fun than looking at things about basketball. I think I'll take a walk outside and get some fresh air.

DAD: Okay. I'll meet you here when you're ready.

end of act 1

act 2

A basketball court outside the museum. DAVID *and* LAYLA *are shooting hoops.* CLAIRE *walks up to the edge of the court and stares at them.*

CLAIRE: *(to herself)* It can't be! Those players look just like David Lyons and Layla Pierre. But they are big stars who play professional basketball. What would they be doing here?

LAYLA: *(looking over at Claire)* Hey, David, I think we have company. Hi! What's your name?

CLAIRE: *(shyly)* Um, I'm Claire Dawkins. Are you Layla Pierre?

LAYLA: I sure am! This is my friend David Lyons. We just finished doing a program at the museum. We don't have to be at our next appointment for a while, so we decided to shoot some hoops. Want to join us?

CLAIRE: Who, me? Well…sure, I guess. I do like to play basketball.

DAVID: Great! *(He passes her the ball.)* Let's see what you've got.

CLAIRE *dribbles the ball and shoots. The ball swishes through the net.*

DAVID: Nice shot! Now it's my turn.

DAVID, LAYLA, *and* CLAIRE *take turns shooting the ball.*

LAYLA: You're a good player, Claire. Do you play for a team?

CLAIRE: Yes, at school. We're hoping to be in the state championships this year.

LAYLA: That's great! David and I both played ball in school. You never know where sports will take you.

DAVID: *(looking at his watch)* Uh-oh, we'd better go. Our ride will be here any minute.

CLAIRE: Can I take a picture first? My friends will never believe this!

LAYLA: Sure! *(The three players crowd together and* CLAIRE *takes a photo with her phone.)* Nice to meet you, Claire!

CLAIRE: Nice to meet you, too! Thanks!

LAYLA *and* DAVID *leave the court, just as* DAD *enters.*

DAD: Hey, Claire, did I hear you talking?

CLAIRE: I just came out here to shoot some hoops. You'll never believe who I met! *(She shows* DAD *the picture on her phone.)* Museums sure have a lot of surprises to offer!

6 Which of the following from the play is a stage direction?

A "Let's see what you've got."

B Claire and Dad wander around the museum.

C "Museums sure have a lot of surprises to offer!"

D "Well, we finally made it to the basketball museum."

7 What is the meaning of the word *jersey?*

A pants

B towel

C shorts

D shirt

8 How does Claire feel after looking at the exhibits in the museum? What structural elements of the play support your answer?

_____

_____

_____

_____

9 How would this narrative be different if it were a story told from Layla's point of view? Be sure to include details from the story to support your answer.

_____

_____

_____

_____

_____

_____

_____

Do you remember the last time you ran into a word you didn't know while you were reading? You may have looked it up in the dictionary or skipped over it. By looking for clues in the text, you may have been able to figure out the word's meaning. Another clue you should look for when reading is how the text is organized. There are different ways an author might choose to organize a text. You should also look to see if a text is a firsthand account or secondhand account.

LESSON 18 Determining the Meaning of Academic Vocabulary is about looking for clues that help you understand new words. You will practice searching for information in the text that helps you learn the meaning of unknown words.

LESSON 19 Describing Text Structures: Cause and Effect, Comparing and Contrasting is about the different ways an author may organize their writing. Writers may use cause and effect, which shows how one event or idea causes another, or comparing and contrasting, which shows how things are alike and different.

LESSON 20 Describing Text Structures: Chronology, Problem and Solution looks at more ways an author may organize a text. One is chronology, which shows the order of events in a text. The other is problem and solution, which shows something that is wrong and then gives ideas on how to fix it.

LESSON 21 Comparing and Contrasting Points of View in Informational Texts helps you practice identifying perspective, or point of view, in different texts so that you can compare points of view. You will compare the thoughts, feelings, and experiences of different people in a text that is a firsthand account, which is written by a person who actually experienced an event, or a secondhand account, which is written by someone who is describing an event but wasn't present for it.

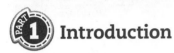

Determining the Meaning of Academic Vocabulary

Introduction

THEME: >>> **Putting the Information Together**

Informational texts almost always contain words that are common to the subject area of the text. Sometimes, these words may be unfamiliar to you. For example, a science passage might use words like *experiment, chemical,* or *species.* You can use a glossary, dictionary, or thesaurus to help you find the meanings. Often, you can use **context clues** to figure out the meanings of unknown words and phrases. Look at the words or sentences before and after the unfamiliar word. Perhaps you know the meaning of part of the word. This can help you figure out the word's meaning.

Look at the picture and read the paragraph.

Artists have been creating <u>mosaics</u> for many centuries. In ancient times, colored pebbles were used to create mosaics. Throughout history, most mosaics were made by putting small, square tiles close together to create an image, scene, pattern, or design. The tiles were glued or placed into wet cement or <u>plaster</u>. Mosaics are common decorations for walls and buildings. Artists have used shells, marble, hard stone, glass, clay, and other materials to create mosaics.

Complete the chart to find the meaning of these unknown words.

Unknown Word	What context clues does author provide?	What am I reading about?	What does this word mean?
mosaics			
plaster			

Read the first part of the passage. Then answer the questions.

The Bald Eagle

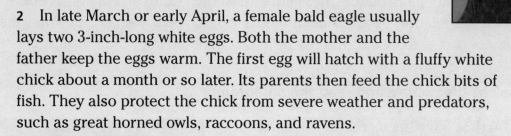

1   Our nation's symbol is a bald eagle. This adult eagle is immediately recognizable because of its bald white head, tail, and dark brown body. Adult bald eagles get their distinctive "bald" head and white tail when they are 4 or 5 years old. Younger birds are dark brown with just a touch of white underneath their wings and tail. These birds are harder to tell apart from large hawks or golden eagles.

2   In late March or early April, a female bald eagle usually lays two 3-inch-long white eggs. Both the mother and the father keep the eggs warm. The first egg will hatch with a fluffy white chick about a month or so later. Its parents then feed the chick bits of fish. They also protect the chick from severe weather and predators, such as great horned owls, raccoons, and ravens.

3   Eagles usually build their nests in tall trees. These nests are about four feet around and three feet deep. They have large sticks on the outside and are lined with a softer material. Sometimes, an eagle pair may just <u>refurbish</u> an old nest with new materials instead of building a new one. This is just like when people fix up an old house instead of building a new one.

Think About It

***What context clues help you find the meaning of* refurbish?** Find clues in the text that help you understand the meaning.

Reread the sentence in which *refurbish* appears. Then read the sentence that comes after that.

What is refurbishing an old nest compared to? _____

_____

Explain the meaning of *refurbish* and tell what clues helped you find the meaning.

_____

_____

_____

Continue reading the passage. Then answer the question.

A CLOSER LOOK
Read the text again carefully. Circle words that you do not understand. Underline words and phrases that provide context clues for these words.

4   The number of eagles was declining for many years. Then the Endangered Species Act protected the eagle and other birds by banning pesticides like DDT. Pesticides accidently affected eagles and other birds by causing their eggs to have thin shells that broke very easily. This kept the chicks from hatching. Today, the number of bald eagles has been increasing.

5   Wildlife biologists, scientists, and volunteers work to teach people about protecting eagles and their nesting sites. Government agencies and other groups have created educational materials to help people learn about protecting eagles. They also work with <u>loggers</u> and builders to protect nests. These nests could be on properties where people want to cut down trees to build homes and businesses. These different groups also help trappers, farmers, power companies, hunters, and schoolchildren learn more about eagles. It is hard work teaching everyone about the needs of eagles and keeping track of their nest sites and numbers.

What words, phrases, or sentences can help you find the meaning of the unknown word?

What are *loggers?*

A   people who protect nests

B   people who trap animals

C   people who cut down trees

D   people who build homes and businesses

 DISCUSS IT
Talk to a classmate about the words in the passage that were unfamiliar to you. Have you heard or read the word or words before? How did you find the meaning of the words? Talk about the strategies that help you figure out the meaning for unknown words.

Read the passage. Then answer the questions.

Black-Footed Ferrets

A CLOSER LOOK

This passage is about an animal called a black-footed ferret. Many readers may not know what a ferret is. Circle important words and phrases that help you learn about this animal.

1   Many people keep ferrets as pets. They are soft, easy to train, and playful. There are many types of ferrets, and many still live in the wild. There is one specific ferret that had not been seen since 1937. This is the black-footed ferret. The last time someone saw this kind of ferret was on a Canadian prairie. Scientists thought this ferret was <u>extinct</u>.

2   Yet, in 1981, scientists found a very small group of black-footed ferrets in Wyoming. This was an important <u>discovery</u>. Scientists wanted to increase the population of these ferrets. They believed the best way to do this was to keep them protected in zoos.

3   This plan worked well. There are now more than 300 black-footed ferrets in zoos. Many black-footed ferrets have been released into the wild. There will be many more released back into the <u>grasslands</u> in the coming years.

Reread paragraph 1. Did people see a lot of black-footed ferrets?

1 Which sentence from paragraph 1 helps you understand the meaning of *extinct?*

   A "Many people keep ferrets as pets."

   B "They are soft, easy to train, and playful."

   C "There is one specific ferret that had not been seen since 1937."

   D "There are many types of ferrets, and many still live in the wild."

Where do ferrets usually live?

2 Which other word from the passage has a similar meaning as *grasslands?*

   A "prairie"

   B "zoo"

   C "population"

   D "extinct"

Before 1981, did scientists see this type of ferret?

3 What does the word *discovery* mean?

_____

_____

Read the passage. Then answer the questions.

Rachel Carson

1 American biologist and writer Rachel Carson was a <u>pioneer</u> of the environmental movement. She inspired people all over the world to care about nature and treat wildlife with respect. Carson was born on May 27, 1907, in Springdale, Pennsylvania. Her passion for nature began at an early age. She was interested in wildlife and the sea. She studied and taught marine biology, the study of ocean life. She also taught zoology, the study of animals. Carson enjoyed writing about nature and how different animals and plants depend on one another to survive.

2 In 1936, Carson began working as a scientist and writer for the US Bureau of Fisheries. While there, she performed science experiments. She also worked as the editor-in-chief of the Fish and Wildlife Service's publications. During this time she wrote three books on sea life. Her most popular book, *Silent Spring,* was published in 1962. This was two years before she died in Silver Spring, Maryland, in 1964. Carson's books were not only full of scientific information. They were also full of poetic sentences and figurative language. Below is an excerpt from *Silent Spring:*

> "The town lay in the midst of a checkerboard of prosperous farms, with fields of grain and hillsides of orchards, where, in spring, white clouds of bloom drifted above the green fields. In autumn, oak and maple and birch set up a blaze of color that flamed and flickered across a backdrop of pines. Then foxes barked in the hills and deer silently crossed the fields, half hidden in the mists of the fall mornings."

3 In her book, she states that humans were causing serious harm to the environment, including wildlife, with their overuse of chemical <u>pesticides.</u> During the 18th and 19th centuries, farmers used mixtures of chemicals that killed insects and rodents that were harmful to crops. These mixtures were called pesticides. Over time, pesticides became stronger and deadlier. Farmers and scientists began to add dangerous materials like sulfur and cyanide. Carson told her readers that pesticides end up in the animal food chain when used on crops. She created awareness around the world about the dangers of pollution.

4 In 1945, people around the world were able to buy and use the most powerful pesticide, DDT. The DDT spray got rid of hundreds of different insects. Other, weaker pesticides only worked on a small number of pests. Not all insects are harmful to crops. Most insects help keep <u>ecosystems</u>

in balance. Carson performed research on the effects of DDT on the environment. She found out how DDT entered the food chain of plants, animals, and humans. It built up inside the fatty tissue of animals, including humans, and caused serious illnesses. Certain animal species became endangered. At first, many people rejected Carson's research, especially chemical companies. Shortly after Silent Spring was printed, many important scientists backed up Carson's research. Then-president John F. Kennedy ordered the Science Advisory Committee to inspect the effects of DDT that Carson talked about in her book. After this, the government checked the use of DDT and eventually banned its use altogether.

Carson writes,

"chemicals sprayed on croplands or forests or gardens lie long in soil, entering into living organisms, passing from one to another in a chain of poisoning and death. Or they pass mysteriously by underground streams until they emerge and, through the alchemy of air and sunlight, combine into new forms that kill vegetation, sicken cattle, and work unknown harm on those who drink from once pure wells."

5 Carson brought the importance of protecting our natural environment to the public. She encouraged many scientists, politicians, writers, and other people to pay attention to how they impact nature. She paved the way toward safer ways to grow food. She challenged people to act in ways that are respectful to the natural world.

1 Part A

What are *pesticides?*

A insects or rodents that harm plants

B substances put on plants that kill unwanted insects and rodents

C government workers who study chemicals and farming

D individuals who study science and write about it

Part B

What context clues *best* support your answer to Part A?

_____

_____

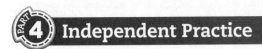

2 Rachel Carson uses the word *alchemy* in her passage about harmful chemicals. *Alchemy* means "a process that changes or transforms something in a mysterious way." Which context clue would help a reader understand the meaning of *alchemy?*

A "importance of protecting and respecting our natural environment"

B "the government checked the use of DDT"

C "sprayed on croplands or forests or gardens"

D "they (living things) emerge and…combine into new forms"

3 Which is another word for *ecosystem?*

A protecting

B balance

C natural environment

D research

4 The passage begins with this sentence: "American biologist and writer Rachel Carson was a <u>pioneer</u> of the environmental movement."

What does the word *pioneer* mean? Support your answer with at least two clues from the text that helped you understand the word's meaning.

_____

_____

_____

_____

_____

_____

_____

LESSON 19

Describing Text Structures: Cause and Effect, Comparing and Contrasting

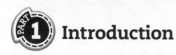 **Introduction**   THEME: **≫ Putting the Information Together**

Informational texts can be organized in a number of ways. A writer might compare and contrast events, ideas, or concepts. When using this **text structure,** the writer shows how one thing is similar to or different from another. For instance, the writer might compare and contrast horses and donkeys. Certain words and phrases can offer clues to the text structure the writer is using. Words and phrases that indicate a **comparison** are *like, as, similar,* and *alike.* Words that indicate a **contrast** are *different, differ,* and *in contrast.*

When authors use a cause-and-effect text structure, they describe an event, or a cause, and then they tell what happens as a result of that event. They show how one event causes another to happen. For instance, they might explain how a glass falls to the ground, and as a result, it shatters into many pieces. The cause is the glass falling. The effect is the glass breaking. Look for signal words that show a cause and an effect in the text. Verbs like *creates, makes,* and *happens* can tell about a cause. Examples of words and phrases that signal a **cause** are *because, since, reason for, due to,* and *on account of.* Words like *so, then, in order to, as a result, led to, happen,* and *effect* indicate an **effect.**

Read the paragraph. Then fill in the cause-and-effect chart.

Water on Earth is always moving and changing forms. Whether it is a solid, liquid, or gas, the amount of water on Earth stays about the same. One way to track water's movement is through rainfall. The sun heats up the water in Earth's oceans, rivers, lakes, puddles, and other water sources. Then the water reaches a certain temperature, and it becomes water vapor, which is a gas. It rises up into Earth's atmosphere. This is called evaporation. The vapor mixes with other tiny objects in the air like dust or salt. As a result, clouds are formed. Next, cool air causes the vapor to condense, which means it turns back into liquid. Raindrops build up in the clouds. Finally, the air cannot hold all of the liquid so it falls to Earth as rain.

Think about the things that happen and what causes them to happen. Then fill in the table with the cause and its effect.

Cause	Effect
The sun heats up water in the ocean.	The water becomes vapor and evaporates.
Water vapor mixes with dust and salt.	Clouds are formed.

Write any signal words from the paragraph.

_____

It is important to notice the structure of a text, or how a piece of writing is organized. When you come to recognize a cause-and-effect structure, you can better understand how one event makes another one happen. When you become familiar with a compare-and-contrast text structure, you can see how two things are alike and different.

Read the first part of the passage. Then answer the questions.

Why Do Leaves Change Color?

1 In the summer, when you are playing in the hot sun, the green trees in the parks and forests work to keep you cool. Trees use sunlight to convert water and carbon dioxide into sugar. This is called photosynthesis.

2 Then in autumn, the trees take a break. Photosynthesis no longer takes place, so the leaves change color from green to yellow, bright orange, or red. The effect is that you know the trees are beginning their long winter's rest.

Where do leaf colors come from?

3 Leaf color comes from pigments in the leaves. Pigments are natural substances produced by leaf cells. There are three pigments that color leaves. Green leaves come from chlorophyll. Carotenoid creates yellow, orange, and brown leaves. Red leaves are produced by anthocyanin.

4 Chlorophyll and carotenoid are in leaf cells all the time during the growing season. But the chlorophyll covers the carotenoid—that's why summer leaves are green, not yellow or orange. Most anthocyanins are produced only in autumn, and only under certain conditions. Not all trees can make anthocyanin.

Think About It

How do the leaves on trees stay shiny and green in the summer?

The effect is that the leaves on the trees stay shiny and green. What is the cause?

_____

_____

How do leaves on trees stay shiny and green in the summer? _____

_____

_____

The author also uses a compare-and-contrast text structure. What does the author

compare and contrast? _____

_____

Continue reading the passage. Then answer the question.

How do leaves change color?

5 As Earth travels around the sun, some places receive fewer hours of sunlight at certain times of the year. Here, the days become shorter and the nights get longer. The temperature slowly drops. Autumn comes, and then winter.

6 Since there is less sunlight, trees produce less chlorophyll. Soon, a tree stops producing chlorophyll. When that happens, the carotenoid already in the leaves finally shows through.

Do leaves change because of weather?

7 Temperature and cloud cover make a difference in a tree's red colors from year to year. When a number of warm, sunny, autumn days and cool but not freezing nights come one after the other, it will be a good year for reds. In the daytime, the leaves can produce lots of sugar, but the cool night temperatures prevent the sugar sap from flowing through the leaf veins and down into the branches and trunk. Some trees produce anthocyanins. These pigments are a form of protection that allow the tree to recover nutrients in the leaves before they fall. Anthocyanins give leaves their bright, brilliant shades of red, purple, and crimson.

8 The amount of rain in a year affects leaf color. A severe drought delays the arrival of fall colors by a few weeks. A warm, wet period during fall lowers the brightness of autumn colors. A severe frost kills the leaves, turning them brown and causing them to drop early.

> **A CLOSER LOOK**
> How does the amount of sunlight trees receive in autumn affect the color of their leaves? Circle phrases and sentences that tell you.

> How does temperature affect the color of fall leaves?

How is a severe drought different from a severe frost?

A   A severe drought produces red leaves, while a severe frost kills leaves.

B   A severe drought delays the arrival of fall colors, while a severe frost causes leaves to turn brown.

C   A severe drought and a severe frost both lower the brightness of autumn colors.

D   A severe drought and a severe frost both cause leaves to produce anthocyanins.

 DISCUSS IT

With a partner, identify at least two causes and two effects in the passage. Discuss whether this was an effective way for the author to present the information.

Read the passage. Then answer the questions.

A CLOSER LOOK
There are several text structures used in this passage. Underline one example of compare and contrast and one example of cause and effect.

Roll With It!

1   Have you ever touched a doorknob and felt a shock? The spark was created by static electricity (*static* means "nonmoving"). An electric charge built up on the doorknob. This happens when the air around an object is dry. If you live in a cold climate, you probably experience static electricity during the winter. Indoor heating creates dry air.

2   To explain how static electricity works, you need to think about atoms. Atoms are in everything! Atoms are very small, You can only view them with magnification. Atoms contain small particles, or specks, called protons, neutrons, and electrons. Protons produce positive electrical charges, while electrons produce negative electrical charges. Neutrons do not produce any charge.

3   Two particles with the same charge repel, or push each other away. Have you heard the phrase, "opposites attract?" Particles with opposite charges (one positive and one negative) attract each other. The diagram of an atom shows that protons and neutrons live in the nucleus, which is the center of an atom. Electrons bounce around the outer parts of the nucleus, and can jump from one atom to another one if they are attracted to other protons.

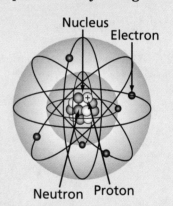

4   Sometimes electrons get rubbed off their atom. This leaves the atom with more protons than electrons. Now, another object (your shirt sleeve, for example) has extra electrons on it, so the proton will attract more electrons when something comes close to it as long as the air is dry. When there is moisture or humidity in the air, the charges flow through the dampness.

5   Try this experiment to see the attracting charges at work.

You will need:
- 1 empty soda can
- a table to work on
- your hair
- 1 inflated balloon

1. Put the soda can on its side on the table. Make sure that it is completely still and the table does not get bumped during the experiment.

2. Rub the balloon quickly on the hair on your head. (This process removes electrons from your hair and puts them on the balloon.)

3. Place the balloon as close to the can as possible without letting it touch the can.

4. Observe what happens! The can will roll toward the balloon. The extra electrons on the balloon will pull protons toward it!

Read paragraph 3 and look at the diagram. What happens when different kinds of particles meet?

1 What happens when protons and electrons are close together?

   A They attract each other and pull closer together.

   B They repel or push each other away.

   C Nothing happens when they are near each other.

   D They both become negative charges.

Why is rubbing a balloon on your hair important to the experiment?

2 What is the effect of rubbing a balloon quickly on your hair?

   A Protons move from your hair onto the balloon.

   B Protons move from the balloon onto your hair.

   C Electrons move from the balloon onto your hair.

   D Electrons move from your hair onto the balloon.

How are protons and neutrons alike? How are they different?

3 Compare and contrast protons and neutrons. Use details from the passage and the diagram to support your answer.

_____

_____

_____

_____

Read the passage. Then answer the questions.

How the Moon Affects Tides on Earth

1   Gravity attracts the moon and Earth to each other. In fact, all objects in the universe are attracted to one another by gravity. The closer objects are to each other in space, the stronger gravity pulls them together. The moon is the closest large object to Earth, so it has a greater pull on Earth than other planets or the sun.

2   The moon actually pulls the ocean closer to it. Water is flexible and can be pulled by the force of gravity. Land is not as flexible and is only pulled slightly. If part of Earth is positioned so that the sun shines directly on the moon, you see a full moon. This occurs about every 27 days. The opposite is also true. When the moon is directly between the sun and Earth, you only see a dark moon. When sunlight hits the moon, you see moonlight. If the moon is between the sun and Earth, the moon blocks the sunlight from viewers on Earth. This is called a new moon. During a full and new moon, gravity from the moon is the strongest. At high tide, the ocean covers more land than it usually covers. When the tide is lowest, the ocean moves away from land exposing more of it than usual. Tides are highest and lowest during these stages of the moon.

3   As objects move farther from each other, the strength of the force decreases. The side of Earth facing the moon experiences a stronger pull of gravity than the side that is facing away from the moon. The side of Earth facing away from the moon will experience a weaker pull of gravity on the tides.

1 What happens as a result of the moon being between the sun and Earth?

  A   the moon appears dark

  B   the ocean tides stay the same

  C   the air temperature cools

  D   a full moon appears

2 Part A

What force causes Earth and the moon to stay close?

A wind

B sunlight

C tides

D gravity

Part B

What evidence from the passage *best* supports your answer to Part A?

A "The moon is the closest large object to Earth,"

B "so it has a greater pull on Earth than other planets or the sun"

C "The closer objects are to each other in space, the stronger gravity pulls them together."

D "The moon actually pulls the ocean closer to it."

3 Which sentence from the passage describes one difference between the tides?

A "When sunlight hits the moon, you see moonlight."

B "At high tide, the ocean covers more land than it usually covers."

C "As objects move farther from each other, the strength of the force decreases."

D "This occurs about every 27 days."

4 The force of gravity between the moon and Earth changes depending on which side of Earth faces the moon. Explain these differences and why these changes happen. Support your answer with details from the passage.

_____

_____

_____

_____

LESSON 20

Describing Text Structures: Chronology, Problem and Solution

Part 1 Introduction

THEME: >>> Putting the Information Together

Informational texts are often organized in different ways depending on their subject. The way a passage is organized is called its **text structure.** One text structure organizes information in a sequence, or order. For example, a biography or diary is often organized according to when events happened. The text may describe a series of events from the earliest date to the latest date. This is called **chronological order.** Look for dates that signal the time period when each event occurs.

Writers also use sequence to tell how to do something. Each task is listed in steps from first to last. For example, a recipe will list the steps in order. Words such as *first, next, last, then, during,* and *finally* tell the order in which the tasks must be completed. If the steps appeared out of order, the text would not be as easy to understand.

Look at the illustrations. Write a number below each panel to show the correct order.

_____   _____   _____

How does numbering the steps help tell what is happening in the illustrations?

_____

_____

_____

Another text structure used to organize information is **problem and solution.** The writer tells about a problem or challenge in the text, and then explains how this problem is solved. You often see this type of structure used to explain problems in science and technology.

Look at the illustrations. Then answer the questions.

What is the problem in the first picture? _____

_____

What is the solution shown in the second picture? _____

_____

How does the solution help the boys? _____

_____

Read the first part of the instructions for an experiment.

Keeping Your House Cool

Shade trees help keep your house cool in the summer. This can help reduce your energy costs. Here is an experiment to see how planting shade trees near your house helps cool it in summer.

What do you need?

- 2 shoe boxes with covers
- Lamp with 100-watt bulb
- Different types of plants in pots
- 2 thermometers to measure air temperature
- Small can of black or dark-colored paint
- Small can of white paint

What to do?

You will do this experiment in two steps. First, you want to find out if shading your house keeps it cooler. Then you'll want to see if painting the outside of the house different colors affects the temperature inside.

Think About It

How is the passage organized? To answer the question, think about how the author presents information. Think about why this text structure might help the reader.

Why might one section appear before the other in the passage?

_____

_____

_____

What text structure does the passage use? _____

What are two problems that the experiment will explore?

1. _____

2. _____

Continue reading the passage. Then answer the question.

A CLOSER LOOK

Put numbers next to each part of Step 1, and Step 2 to show the order in which to do each part.

Step 1

- Place each box at an equal distance from the lamp so they both receive the same amount of direct light.
- Put one thermometer inside each box and close the lid.
- Place potted plants between the lamp and <u>one</u> of the boxes so that the shadows cast by the plants cover most of the entire box. The number of plants you will need depends on the size of the plants.
- Turn on the lamp.
- Record the temperature of the air in each box. Do this every day for 3 days.

Results

Which box has a higher temperature? Did the temperature change over time?

Step 2

- Paint one box white and the other box black.
- Put the thermometers inside the boxes.
- Return each box to the same position as in Step 1.
- Turn on the lamp.
- Record the temperature of the air in each box. Do this every day for 3 days.

Which box has a higher temperature? Did the temperature change over time?

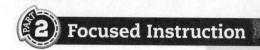

Step 3

- Subtract or add plants and measure again in a few days.

Results

Does the number of plants change the temperature of inside the box that is shaded?

What is the order of the steps?

Which step comes *before* putting the thermometers in the boxes?

A   "Place potted plants between the lamp and <u>one</u> of the boxes."

B   "Place each box at an equal distance from the lamp."

C   "Record the temperature of the air in each box."

D   "Turn on the lamp."

DISCUSS IT

With a partner, retell the sequence of instructions in Step 1 and discuss how changing the order might affect the results. Reverse roles so that your partner retells the sequence of instructions in Step 2. Then discuss differences in the sequence for that set of instructions.

Read the passage. Then answer the questions.

Johnny Clem

1   Did you know that boys under the age of 18 fought in war? During the Civil War, more than 10,000 boys served in the Union army. The youngest was John Lincoln "Johnny" Clem. Johnny was born in Newark, Ohio, in 1851. His parents named him John Joseph Klem. When Johnny was 9 years old, he ran away from home to join the army.

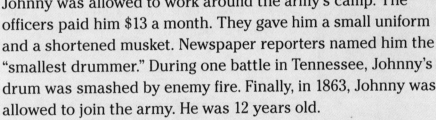

A CLOSER LOOK

In paragraph 2, underline words that signal the text structure.

2   First, Johnny tried to join the Ohio unit as the soldiers went through his hometown. They laughed at him because he was only 9 years old. He was turned down again when he tried to join the Michigan unit. Johnny would not give up. He followed them as their drummer boy. Finally, Johnny was allowed to work around the army's camp. The officers paid him $13 a month. They gave him a small uniform and a shortened musket. Newspaper reporters named him the "smallest drummer." During one battle in Tennessee, Johnny's drum was smashed by enemy fire. Finally, in 1863, Johnny was allowed to join the army. He was 12 years old.

3   Johnny entered the Battle of Chickamauga. He carried only his musket. A Confederate officer tried to capture him. Johnny got away. He was named the "Drummer Boy of Chickamauga." The newspapers loved to tell stories about him. Johnny soon became commander. Then he changed his name to John Lincoln Clem.

4   In October 1863, Johnny was captured. The enemy made an example of him. The Confederates said the Union army was poor. They said that they were sending "babies" out to fight. By late 1864, Johnny left the army.

5   Johnny tried to attend West Point. However, he had little education and was not accepted. In 1871, President Grant made him a lieutenant. Later, Johnny became a high-ranking officer. Johnny Clem lived to be 85 years old. He died in 1937 and was buried at Arlington National Cemetery. He is a true American hero.

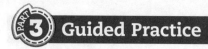
Think about what kind of clues dates give you.

1 What do the years listed in the passage tell you about the text structure?

  A The text structure is chronological.

  B The text structure is problem and solution.

  C The text structure is cause and effect.

  D The text structure is compare and contrast.

What did Johnny do first? What did he do next?

2 Which of the following *best* describes how paragraphs 2–5 are organized?

  A They tell the steps Johnny took to reach his goals.

  B They tell about when Johnny was born.

  C They focus on Johnny being captured.

  D They focus on the honors Johnny received.

What was unusual about Johnny's experience?

3 What was the problem with Johnny joining the army at age 9? What was the solution?

_____

_____

_____

_____

_____

_____

Read the passage. Then answer the questions.

The Story of Central Park, New York City

1   In the early part of the 19th century, most people in Manhattan lived at the southern tip of the island. With waves of immigration, the population there grew, and people began to move farther north—uptown. People wanted a place to get away from the noise and dirt of the city. The idea of putting a park in the middle of Manhattan was especially favored by some of the wealthy merchants. They had visited the grand parks and gardens of European cities. They thought New York should have something similar.

2   Politicians, merchants, and landowners argued about the park for several years. Finally, the state government purchased the land. To develop a proper park, a plan was needed. The first-ever landscape design contest was held. In 1858, Frederick Law Olmsted and Calvert Vaux won the contest.

3   One of the problems in building the park was that the land was full of rocky areas and swamps as well as pastures. In fact, the land that would become Central Park was home to some of the very poorest people in the city. It was dotted with small, run-down farms and little villages where immigrants and others seeking affordable shelter had taken up residence. One of these areas was Seneca Village, a settlement of free African Americans. Most of these residents began to leave when the plans for the park were announced. But the city paid the remaining 1,600 people for their homes so that construction could begin.

4   Building the park was the biggest project of its kind at the time. The job included creating countrylike landscapes and installing roads that carriages could drive through. One area of the park was designed as a meadow

where sheep could roam the pasture. This idea was part of the vision for the park as a country escape. Workers planted thousands of trees and shrubs. They built a reservoir and constructed lakes from the swamps. It required more than 20,000 workers, and it wasn't completed until 1873. However, the first area opened in the winter of 1858 with ice-skating on the lake at the south end of the park.

5   More attractions were added later, making the park more popular than ever. By the early part of the 20th century, adults and children came to enjoy the features of the park. They rode the carousel, which was built in 1871 and still stands today. They visited the zoo, which was one of the first in a city. This popular attraction also has been added to and changed over the years. Playgrounds, ball fields, and bicycle paths are a much-used part of the park, and have been changed and updated over the years. In 1934, the sheep were moved to Brooklyn, but that area of the park is still called the Sheep Meadow. An open-air theater, a skating rink, and a swimming pool are among the 20th-century additions. Today's Central Park is 843 acres and hosts more than 40 million visitors a year. City residents and visitors from all over the world come to see its beauty and enjoy the countrylike setting in the middle of a big city.

1 Part A

What is one problem the park was designed to solve?

A   People wanted a place to get away from the noise and dirt of the city.

B   The wealthy people in the city wanted a place where they could picnic.

C   Everyone wanted the city to be as grand as European cities.

D   People wanted to build better housing to replace the settlements that were in the park.

Part B

What is one solution that *best* supports your answer to Part A?

_____

_____

_____

_____

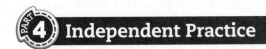
2 Which of the following tells you about the sequence of events in the essay?

A The idea for the park started before it was built and changes are still being made.

B Because of the size of the project, it took many years to build.

C Because of the size of the project, thousands of workers were needed to build the park.

D The park has been changed and updated over the years.

3 One of the problems with building the park was figuring out how to deal with the rocky landscape and swamps. What was one solution to this problem?

A The city paid 1,600 people living on the land to leave.

B Planners put an ice skating rink in part of the park.

C The city installed roads in the troublesome areas.

D Workers constructed lakes from the swamps.

4 Write a short paragraph that describes the changes to the park over time. Explain how the changes helped the park to reach its goal. Use examples from the passage.

_____

_____

_____

_____

_____

_____

LESSON 21

Comparing and Contrasting Points of View in Informational Texts

 **Introduction**

THEME: **»»** Putting the Information Together

Some informational texts are written by the person who experienced the event. This is a **firsthand account,** and uses the first-person point of view. Other informational texts are **secondhand accounts** written by others about the event or experiment. These are written in the third-person point of view.

Read two accounts about the Boston Tea Party.

A number of brave men, determined to do all in their power to save their country from the ruin which their enemies had plotted, in less than four hours, emptied every chest of tea on board the three ships commanded by the captains Hall, Bruce, and Coffin, amounting to 342 chests, into the sea!! Without the least damage done to the ships or any other property.

We then were ordered by our commander to open the hatches and take out all the chests of tea and throw them overboard, and we immediately proceeded to execute his orders, first cutting and splitting the chests with our tomahawks, so as thoroughly to expose them to the effects of the water.

In about three hours from the time we went on board, we had thus broken and thrown overboard every tea chest to be found in the ship, while those in the other ships were disposing of the tea in the same way, at the same time. We were surrounded by British armed ships, but no attempt was made to resist us.

What is the point of view of the first account? _____

_____

What is the point of view of the second account? _____

_____

Read the first passage. Then answer the questions.

excerpt from The Johnstown Flood
by Richard K. Fox

In 1889, the dam broke in Johnstown, Pennsylvania, and the entire town quickly became flooded, and fires broke out. Here is an account of the rescue of Rose Clarke and her mother.

1   "When the water rose, we were at home. It drove us from floor to floor, and we had just reached the roof when the house started. It went whirling toward the bridge, struck it, and went down. Mother, my little sister, and I caught on another roof that was just above the water. Then mother called out that she was going to drown. I got to her and raised her head out of the water. My head rested on a sawlog and a board protected me from the other timbers. Some rescuers came running down the bridge and saw us. I made them take mother out first, and meantime I struggled to get out of the timbers, but they closed in on me."

2   "The more I struggled the tighter they held me. The fire was just behind me, and I could feel its heat. By the time the men had carried mother to the bank, the fire was so fierce they could hardly get back. When they did reach me they could not get me out, for my foot was fast between a saw log and a piece of timber. Then they ran for tools. The fire kept sweeping on before the breeze from up stream. I had almost resigned myself to an awful death when some other men braved the fire and reached me. They began chopping and sawing. The men tied a rope around me. How they got me out finally I scarcely know."

Think About It

Is this a firsthand or secondhand account of events? To answer the question, look for clues that help you determine who is telling the story.

Who is telling the story? _____

How do you know? _____

_____

Is this a firsthand or secondhand account? _____

Now read the second passage. Then answer the question.

The Day the Dam Broke

1   Johnstown, Pennsylvania, is a small town in the western part of the state. It is located in an area that is often flooded. The town is in a valley, where the Conemaugh River and the Stony Creek meet. In the early part of the 19th century, canals were built to connect rivers so that goods could be shipped within the states. Toward the end of the century, the railroads stretched across the US. Most goods were shipped by train, and the canal system was not used much anymore. The Pennsylvania Railroad ran through Johnstown.

2   A dam had been built north of Johnstown as part of the canal system. The dam controlled the water in a large lake. Because the canals were not being used, the land around the dam and the lake was sold to a private club. Many club members were wealthy business owners. The club built a clubhouse and a road so members could get to the clubhouse. They built summer homes around the lake. They swam and fished in the lake. But downstream from the lake, there were problems.

3   The club had hired a man to manage the repairs to the dam. But the dam still leaked and always needed new repairs. People knew it could be a problem. Because the dam had always held, people laughed about it. But on May 31, 1889, no one was laughing.

4   The spring rains were heavy that year and at the end of the month, the rain lasted for days. The club members tried to prop up the sides of the dam, but it was too late. This time, the dam couldn't hold. It didn't take very long before the water came roaring down the river to the town 14 miles away. As the water rushed through the small river and overflowing creek, it gathered everything in its path. Trees, sides of buildings, wires, barns, rocks, and furniture, along with people and animals, were all pushed and dragged through the 30-foot high water. More than 2,000 people lost their lives. Some were trapped, but it was hard for rescue workers to get to people.

A CLOSER LOOK

Underline the text in paragraph 5 that shows that the passage is a secondhand account.

5 In less than a week, Clara Barton was in Johnstown to help. Barton was the founder of the American Red Cross. She had helped soldiers during the Civil War, but she did not want the Red Cross to only help people during a war. Barton and the Red Cross workers helped more than 25,000 people in Johnstown. The Red Cross built shelters and later hotels for people who were homeless from the flood. The flood was the first time that the American Red Cross gave so much aid after the Civil War.

6 The damage was not only in the town. The whole valley was in ruins. In addition, the people who survived the flood were at risk for disease. The town had no clean water system and no way to get rid of garbage and waste. It took more than five years before Johnstown recovered.

What tells you that the writer of the second passage was not there when the flood happened?

How is Rose Clarke's point of view different from the point of view expressed in the second passage?

A Rose was caught in the flood and tells her story directly. The second passage gives facts and information about the flood and why it happened.

B Rose tells her story as it is happening. The writer of the second passage tells the story about the flood right after it happened.

C Rose shows how the flood put her and her family in danger. The second passage doesn't discuss the dangers from the flood.

D Rose tells about her experience. The second passage tells about the experience of others who were caught in the flood.

 DISCUSS IT

Tell a partner about an experience you have had. The partner then should play the role of a reporter and use his or her own words to describe the experience. The partner should add more information to the story. Discuss the differences in the two accounts.

Read both passages. Then answer the questions.

adapted from Pack on My Back

recalled by Hyman Bernstein

In 1871, Chicago had a deadly fire. In 1937, the Federal Writer's Project collected firsthand stories about the fire. The speaker in this excerpt had immigrated from Russia in 1870. He was 18 years old.

1 It was the great fire of 1871 that made me a country peddler. It was in October. We used to go to bed early, because the two roomers had to go to work very early. We were getting ready to go to bed, when we heard the fire bells ringing. I asked the two men if they wanted to see where the fire was.

2 "Why should I care where the fire is?" one man asked. "As long as our house is not on fire, I don't care what house is burning. There is a fire every Monday and Thursday in Chicago."

3 But I wanted to see the fire. So I went out into the street. I saw the flames across the river. But I thought that since the river was between the fire and our house, there was nothing to worry about. I went into the house and went to bed.

4 The next thing I knew, my two bedfellows were shaking me. "Get up," they cried. "The whole city is on fire! Save your things! We are going to Lincoln Park."

5 I jumped out of bed. Everybody in the house was trying to save as much as possible. I tied my clothes in a sheet. With my clothes under my arm and my pack on my back, I left the house with the rest of the family. Everybody was running north.

6 People were carrying all kinds of crazy things. A woman was carrying a pot of soup, which was spilling all over her dress. People were carrying cats, dogs, and goats. In the great excitement, people saved worthless things and left behind good things.

7 When we came to Lake Street, I saw all the wagons of Marshall Field and Company lined up in front of their place of business…. Men and boys were carrying the goods out of the building and loading everything into the wagons. The merchandise was taken to the streetcar barns on State near 20th Street. I am sure that Marshall Field must have been one of the owners of the streetcar company. Otherwise, why would the

A CLOSER LOOK

Underline the pronouns in passage 1 that show that Hyman Bernstein is telling about his own experience. Underline the pronouns in passage 2 that show that this passage is a secondhand account of the same story.

streetcar people have allowed him to bring his goods there? A couple of weeks later, Marshall Field started doing business in the car-barns. I remember buying some goods there….

8 As many of the hopes were burned, many people left the city. Some went to live with relatives in other cities. A great many men became country peddlers. There were thousands of men walking from farm to farm with heavy packs on their backs. These peddlers carried all kinds of merchandise. Things that they thought the farmers and their families could use.

9 There was no rural mail delivery in those days. The farmers very seldom saw a newspaper. They were hungry for news. They were very glad to see a peddler from any large city. They wanted to hear all about the great fire. Then I told a farmer that I was from Chicago, he was very glad to see me. You see, I was a newspaper and a department store….

The Great Chicago Fire

1 A great fire hit Chicago in 1871. It burned for two full days before it finally died. The fire killed about 300 people, and it burned the entire downtown area of one of the biggest cities of the country at the time.

2 No one knows what started the fire, but it spread quickly for several reasons. There hadn't been much rain. Everything was very dry. Many of the buildings were made of wood. Wood burns quickly. The fire was also aided by the wind. The night the fire started, there were strong winds.

3 The city's fire trucks, called steam pumpers, were pulled by horses. The city had 17 steam pumpers. A large steam engine was taken to the fire. The engine pumped water from the water main in the street. The pump forced the water through the hose.

4 On the evening of October 9, 1871, the fire started. The Chicago Fire Department answered the call. However, because of a mistake, the firefighters went to the wrong place. This gave the fire more time to spread. When they did arrive, the fire had already spread and was on its way downtown.

5 Part of Chicago is on the river, where there were lumberyards and coal yards. Coal and wood are perfect materials for burning. As the winds got stronger, the fire blew across the river. From there, it kept going, headed downtown. People ran from burning buildings. The air was hot and sparks filled the sky. People jumped into the lake to try to escape.

6   The fire just kept going. When it was over, the fire had destroyed more than 17,000 buildings and millions of dollars worth of property. Because so many homes burned, thousands of people were homeless. Many fled the city and never returned.

7   Like other places that have experienced disasters, Chicago recovered from its worst fire. People started to rebuild immediately. The city wrote new laws to make new buildings safer. By the end of the decade, even taller buildings were going up in the downtown area. Today, the Chicago Fire Department is the largest in the Midwest. It was the first fire department in the country to use only motor-driven fire trucks.

> **What information do both accounts give?**

1 What do passage 1 and passage 2 have in common?

   A Both recognize that the fire was a great disaster.

   B Both show that people thought the fire would be put out quickly.

   C Both give information about the Chicago Fire Department.

   D Both discuss how the fire started.

> **Reread the last paragraph of passage 1 and passage 2.**

2 How did life in the city change after the fire compared to how Bernstein's life changed?

   A Marshall Field's department store was rebuilt. Bernstein got a job there.

   B Bernstein became a peddler who could tell people about the Great Chicago Fire. Chicago was rebuilt to become a great city.

   C The city built safer housing. Bernstein returned to his home.

   D Bernstein's life was difficult because he was poor. Chicago recovered.

> **What happened during the fire?**

3 Bernstein says that he became "a newspaper and a department store." What information in passage 2 might Bernstein have used while acting as a "newspaper"?

_____

_____

_____

Read the two passages. Then answer the questions.

excerpt from The Klondike Stampede
by Tappan Adney

North America has seen several gold rushes, or stampedes. The first one was California in 1849. Leadville, Colorado, was next in 1860. Then came 1884 and the Coeur d'Alene Salmon River "excitement" in Idaho. But in 1897, more goldseekers than ever before rushed to Alaska in the Klondike stampede. Many of them had absolutely no idea of what they were getting into. The magazine, Harper's Weekly, *sent Tappan Adney to report on the rush. In this excerpt, Adney asks an "old-timer" what he thought of the new arrivals.*

1   I asked one old-timer what he thought of it all. Said he, "I was in the Salmon River mining excitement in Idaho, but I have never seen anything like this. Ten thousand people went in that winter, over a single trail across the mountains; but it was nothing like this. There has never been anything on this coast like it."

2   Another, who is now the mayor of a town on the Pacific coast not far from the Strait of Fuca, said, in answer to the same question, "I saw the beginning of Leadville. But it was nothing like this. There has been nothing like this."

3   Still another, a mining engineer from California, said, "I have never seen people act as they do here. They have lost their heads and their senses. I have never seen men behave as they do here. They have no more idea of what they are going to than that horse has. There was one fellow in the tent alongside of mine—I saw him greasing his rubber boots. I said to him, "What are you doing that for?" "Why, isn't that all right?" he asked.

4   Another man came along and asked a fellow where [the] mining-pan was. The fellow said, "I haven't seen any mining-pan." Just then the man saw the pan lying alongside the tent, and said, "Here it is! Is that a mining-pan? I didn't know that was a mining-pan."

5   I have talked with many others, some who had been in the Coeur d'Alene excitement on Salmon River, Idaho, and have been miners since 1853 and 1854. Some, whose fathers were of the old '49's, say the same thing—that the country has gone mad over this Klondike business. And all agree as to the reason—nowadays, the news is carried by the telegraph and newspaper to all parts of the world, whereas formerly the excitement was all local, and had died away before word of it reached the rest of the world. No one pretends to follow the changes that are going on here. Those who

have been here a week are old-timers. When the next boat arrives people will ask questions of us in turn.

The Klondike Gold Rush

1   In August 1896, gold was found in a stream that feeds into the Klondike River in Canada's Yukon Territory. The men had no idea their discovery would set off one of the greatest gold rushes in history. Hearing the cries of "Gold! Gold! In the Klondike!" an army of hopeful gold seekers headed north. In the Yukon, they expected riches to be waiting for them. However, they didn't know that most of the good Klondike claims were already taken.

2   People came from all over the world to follow their dreams of getting rich. Though getting to the Klondike was not easy, the stampede had started, and the men didn't care. They had no idea of the hardships in store.

3   The most popular route was to go from Seattle by boat to the towns of Skagway and Dyea. From Skagway, a Stampeder could go over the White Pass Trail to Lake Bennett. If the Stampeder went to Dyea, he would hike over the Chilkoot Pass to Lake Bennett. From Lake Bennett, it was a 550-mile boat trip to Dawson City and the Klondike goldfields.

4   The great dangers didn't slow the stampede. All through the summer and into the winter of 1897–98, herds of people poured into the newly created Alaskan towns of Skagway and Dyea. There they had to collect a year's worth of supplies to take with them on their journey to the goldfields. They carried all of these supplies on their backs, up and down muddy mountain passes, in snow and bitter cold temperatures.

5   During the first year of the rush, 20,000 to 30,000 gold seekers spent an average of three months packing their supplies and taking them up the trails and over the passes to the lakes. The distance to the lakes was only about 35 miles. But the packs were so heavy they took them in stages. The men would walk with a lighter pack for miles. They would find a spot to hide their gear, and then return to get the rest of the supplies. They walked back and forth hundreds of miles. Once the gold seekers finally had all their gear at the lakes, they built or bought boats. The boats would take them downriver to Dawson City and the Klondike mining district.

6   By midsummer of 1898, there were 18,000 people at Dawson. More than 5,000 were working the diggings. By August, many of the Stampeders had started for home. Most of them were broke. The next year, still more miners left when gold was discovered at Nome, Alaska. The great Klondike gold rush ended as suddenly as it had begun. Towns such as Dawson City and

Skagway began to decay. Others, including Dyea, disappeared altogether. All that remained were memories of what many consider to be the last grand adventure of the 19th century.

1 Part A

Is passage 1 a firsthand or secondhand account?

_____

Part B

Which detail from the text *best* supports your answer to Part A?

A   "Some have been miners since 1853 and 1854."

B   "Another is now the mayor of a town on the Pacific coast."

C   "I have talked with many others, some who had been in the Coeur d'Alene excitement."

D   "Nowadays, the news is carried by the telegraph and newspaper to all parts of the world."

2 What is the perspective of the Klondike gold rush in passage 2?

A   It tells the events from the perspective of when it happened.

B   It tells the events from the point of view of a Stampeder.

C   It tells the events by giving the facts about what happened.

D   It tells the events by giving all points of view.

3 Which of the following describes what the two passages have in common?

A   They both use the first person to tell the story of the gold rush.

B   They both describe the events during the time that they are happening.

C   They both describe the dangers of the stampede.

D   They both describe the huge numbers of people who took part in the gold rush.

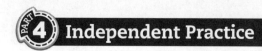

4 How is the focus of passage 1 different from the focus of passage 2? How does the point of view of each passage affect this focus? Support your answer with details from both passages.

_____

_____

_____

_____

_____

_____

_____

_____

_____

Read the passage. Then answer the questions.

Illusions

1   When what you see does not match the physical reality, it is an *illusion*. Illusions trick your eyes and brain so that you see something differently from the way it actually is.

2   Try this experiment to make your own illusion.

3   All you need for this is a piece of paper, a black marker, and a ruler.

4   On the paper, use a ruler to draw two straight lines that are the same length. Put them a couple of inches apart.

5   Now add short lines at the top and bottom of the lines to make the letter V. (See the example.) For the line on the right, add an arrow pointing up to the bottom end of the line. For the other line, add an arrow pointing up to the top end of the line.

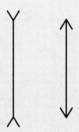

6   Look at what you have drawn. Even though **you know** the two long lines are the same length, one line looks shorter than the other. That's the illusion.

7   Now for the experiment. Find out how many people see that both lines are the same. Show the drawing to someone and ask, "Which line is longer?" Ask the same question to other people.

8   Here is a sample chart you can use to record your data.

How many people say:	Boys	Girls	Men	Women
the line on the left is longer				
the line on the right is longer				
both lines are the same length				

9   Look at your data. Are girls better than boys at this? Do more adults get it right, or are children better at this?

10   After people give their answers, use a ruler to show them that the lines are the same length.

1 Based on the passage text, what is an *illusion?*

    A a confusing picture

    B an experiment

    C a trick of the eyes and brain

    D physical reality

2 How does using the chart help compare your results?

    A It makes it easier to collect, sort, and review the data.

    B It shows the same results to everyone.

    C It helps you remember the information.

    D It puts the results in writing.

3 How is this experiment organized?

    A by time sequence

    B by date

    C by order of steps in experiment

    D by steps for solving a problem

4 What is an *experiment?* Why is this activity called an experiment?

_____

_____

_____

_____

Read the passages. Then answer the questions.

The assembly line used to make the Ford Model T started on December 1, 1913. Though the idea of the assembly line is credited to Henry Ford, Ford was one of several men who liked the idea and tinkered with it until it worked for his purpose.

The first passage was written by Charles Sorensen, a manager at the Ford plant in its early days. He was in charge of all production at the plant, and he helped Ford work out the details for mass production. Sorensen talks about the new process of mass production.

adapted from Birth of the Assembly Line
by Charles Sorenson

1   We worked out at the Ford plant the practice of moving the work from one worker to another until it became a complete unit. Then we arranged the flow of these units at the right time and the right place to a moving final assembly line. Then out came a finished product. Some of these ideas were already in use. However, mass production comes directly from what we worked out at Ford Motor Company between 1908 and 1913.

2   As may be imagined, the job of putting the car together was a simpler one than handling the materials. Charlie Lewis was the youngest and most eager of our assembly foremen. He and I dealt with this problem. We worked it out to bring up only what we decided were the fast-moving materials. The main bigger parts, like engines and axles, needed a lot of room. To give them that space, we left the smaller, more compact, light-handling material in a storage building on the northwest corner of the grounds. Then we arranged with the stock department to bring up the material we had marked out and packaged.

3 This simplification of handling cleaned things up a lot. But at best, I did not like it. It was then that I thought of the idea that assembly would be easier, simpler, and faster if we moved the chassis along. We would begin at one end of the plant with a frame. Then we would add the axles and the wheels. Then we would move it past the stockroom, instead of moving the stockroom to the chassis. I had Lewis put the materials on the floor. He arranged them so that what was needed at the start of assembly would be at that end of the building. Then the other parts would be along the line as we moved the chassis along.

4 We spent every Sunday during July planning this. Then one Sunday morning we laid out the stock in this fashion. Lewis and I and a couple of helpers put together the first car, I'm sure, that was ever built on a moving line. We first put the frame on skids. Then we hitched a towrope to the front end and pulled the frame along until axles and wheels were put on. Then we rolled the chassis along in notches to prove what could be done....

Henry Ford Changes the World

1 Henry Ford was the son of a farmer in Michigan. The young Henry was more interested in building things than in farming. He learned all about steam engines and for fun, he would take watches apart to try to fix them. By studying their inner parts, he learned how gears worked.

2 Henry worked for several companies, but he liked the idea of working for himself. Like other people of his day, he was trying to build a "horseless carriage." People used horse-drawn carriages for travel. There were trains for longer distances, but cars had not been invented yet. People wanted to replace the horses with an engine.

3 In 1896, with a few friends, Ford built something that looked like a four-wheel bicycle. But it had an engine. It could only move forward and could never go more than 20 miles per hour. However, it was a first, and it was what started the Henry Ford Company (later called the Ford Motor Company).

4 Ford's company improved the design of the horseless carriage and new models were built and sold. In 1908, Ford brought out his Model T car. It was easy to drive and maintain, and it didn't break down on the rough roads. Most importantly, the car was not very expensive. One of Henry's dreams was to build cars so that average people could own one. To make cars cheaply enough to do that, he would have to find a new way to make them.

5 Ford was always willing to try out new ideas, and he very much wanted to cut down on waste in his factory. He encouraged his workers to try out different methods. One idea was to have each worker stay in one place and do one job. Instead of many workers building one car, each worker would have a part in building many cars. As a car moved along in the factory, one worker would add a part. Each worker would add the same part to many cars. As cars came down the assembly line, parts were added in sequence. The assembly line saved workers' time because they didn't have to run back and forth between cars anymore. Making an automobile became a lot easier. With an assembly line, cars could be made faster and cheaper.

6 Ford was not the first businessman to use an assembly line. But he was the first to use an assembly line to make automobiles. When Ford's first cars were made, only the wealthy could afford to buy one. After a lot experimenting, by 1913 Ford's factory was rolling out cars from an assembly line. The company continued to build better and cheaper models. Cars became affordable for more and more people. As the price of an automobile came down, the number of car owners went up. Twenty years later, more than 40 percent of all households owned a car. That increase was largely a result of using an assembly line. Ford's dream had finally come true.

5   What is the text structure of the two passages?

   A   cause and effect

   B   compare and contrast

   C   chronology

   D   problem and a solution

6   What is the meaning of *mass production?*

   A   having each worker do one job

   B   making automobiles

   C   making many things at once

   D   inventing something new

7 Part A

How is Charles Sorenson's point of view in the first passage different from the point of view expressed in the second passage?

A Charles Sorenson tells his story as it is happening. The writer of passage 2 tells the story about the assembly line right after it happened.

B Charles Sorenson was involved in working on an assembly line and tells his story directly. Passage 2 gives facts and information about the assembly line and why it happened.

C Charles Sorenson shows how the assembly line made car production more efficient. Passage 2 doesn't discuss the efficiency of the assembly line.

D Charles Sorenson tells about his experience. Passage 2 tells about the experience of others who worked on the assembly line.

Part B

Which detail from the passages provides the *best* evidence for the answer to Part A?

A "Some of these ideas were already in use."

B "Then out came a finished product."

C "Lewis and I…put together the first car…that was ever built on a moving line."

D "The job of putting the car together was a simpler one than handling the materials."

8 Write a paragraph comparing how the two passages describe the assembly line. Discuss how the different points of view of the passages affect these descriptions.

_____

_____

_____

_____

_____

_____

Integration of Knowledge and Ideas in Literary Text

The illustrations you see in your books connect to the story. They help to show the mood and the theme of the story. Themes and topics are very important, too. Two stories can have the same theme or topic, but feature very different characters and events. Some stories might have the same pattern of events, or things that happen, but even then they most likely will not be exactly alike.

LESSON 22 Connecting Text and Visual Presentations of Literary Texts will help you think about how illustrations connect to stories. You will think about what an illustration shows and what mood is created with the story. You will also think about how an illustration can help you understand a story's main idea or theme.

LESSON 23 Comparing and Contrasting Themes and Topics in Literary Texts is about comparing themes and topics between different stories. You will read two passages and think about the differences in the characters and events.

LESSON 24 Comparing and Contrasting Patterns of Events in Literary Texts focuses on how stories from different parts of the world can still be alike by having similar pattern of events, or what actions occur over the course of the story. You will compare the themes in myths, folktales, and stories, as well as the characters.

LESSON 22
Connecting Text and Visual Presentations of Literary Texts

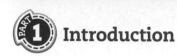

Introduction

THEME: >>> A World of Stories

Illustrations are often used in books to show important details in the text. Plays are acted out on a stage. Some stories and plays have been made into movies. These oral and visual presentations of a text often help you understand the author's message. Details that appear in an illustration may give clues to key ideas or the theme of the passage. An illustration can tell you more about the characters or the setting. It can also help set the mood of the story. Sometimes, there will be more in the illustration than what the author has described. Sometimes, the story will contain more information than what is seen in the illustration. When you read, you use your imagination to picture the setting, characters, and events. Artists do the same thing. Sometimes, their illustrations are very different from how you pictured the same scene or characters.

Look at the illustration. Then read the passage.

"Luz, it is your turn."

Coach Jackie smiled at me. But I could not grin back. My mom told Coach Jackie that I was scared of water. They both thought it was a good idea for me to overcome my fear.

I stood at the side of the pool. They were only asking me to jump into about two feet of water.

"Here, Luz. I will hold your hand, and you just jump." Coach Jackie was thoughtful, and holding his hand helped.

"Here goes nothing!" I yelled. After my jump, I noticed the water was only up to my waist. Why was I afraid to jump in? Thankfully, nobody else was around. They were all in the deep side of the pool, the side I dreamed to swim in.

Coach Jackie told me I was doing great. Soon, the lessons were getting better and better. I was not afraid of the water anymore. I knew that I could keep myself afloat in the deep end. On the last day of lessons, I still could not swim like the others. But I could join them in the deep end, and I knew that I would not sink.

Compare the details in the illustration with the details in the passage. Then answer the questions.

What does the illustration tell you about the setting? _____

_____

_____

What important scene from the story does this illustration show? _____

_____

_____

What does the illustration tell you about the main characters? _____

_____

_____

What details are in the illustration but not in the story? _____

_____

_____

Read the first part of the story.

The Sheep and the Pig
a Scandinavian folktale
adapted by Carolyn S. Bailey

1   One morning, bright and early, a sheep and a curly-tailed pig started out through the world to find a home. For the thing they both wanted more than anything was a house of their own.

2   "We will build us a house," said the sheep and the curly-tailed pig, "and there we will live together."

3   So they traveled a long, long way, over the fields, and down the lanes, and past the orchards, and through the woods, until they came, all at once, upon a rabbit.

4   "Where are you going?" asked the rabbit of the two.

5   "We are going to build us a house," said the sheep and the pig.

6   "May I live with you?" asked the rabbit.

7   "What can you do to help?" asked the sheep and the pig.

8   The rabbit scratched his leg with his left hind foot for a minute, and then he said: "I can gnaw pegs with my sharp teeth. I can put them in with my paws."

9   "Good!" said the sheep and the pig, "you may come with us."

Think About It

How do the details in the story and in the illustration help the reader know what the story is about? To answer this question, pay attention to the details in the illustration, and compare them to the story.

Read the passage again and underline the descriptive words. Then fill in the graphic organizer below using the descriptive words from the story in the first section. In the far right oval, make a list of what you see in the illustration. Be sure to use detailed descriptive words. In the center section, indicate which descriptions are in both places.

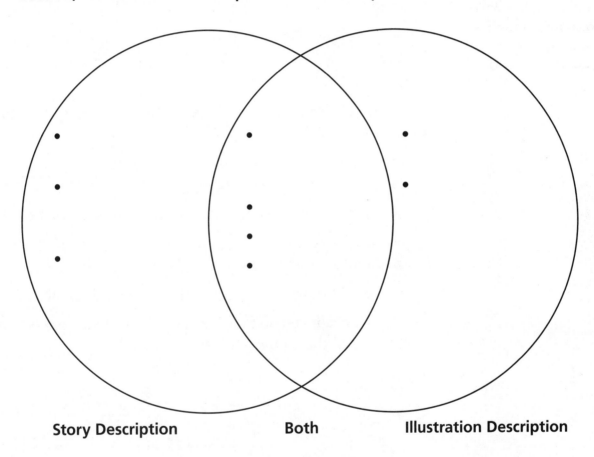

Story Description   **Both**   **Illustration Description**

Based on the illustration and the story, this passage is about animals wanting to

find _____.

A CLOSER LOOK

Think about the repetition in the dialogue throughout the story. Underline the similar questions from each animal and circle the similar responses from the other animals.

Continue reading the passage. Then answer the questions.

10 So the three went on a long, long way farther, and they came, all at once, upon a gray goose.

11 "Where are you going?" asked the gray goose of the three.

12 "We are going to build us a house," said the sheep, the pig, and the rabbit.

13 "May I live with you?" asked the gray goose.

14 "What can you do to help?" asked the sheep, the pig, and the rabbit.

15 The gray goose tucked one leg under her wing for a minute, and then she said: "I can pull moss, and stuff it in the cracks with my broad bill."

16 "Good!" said the sheep, the pig, and the rabbit, "you may come with us."

17 So the four went on a long, long way, and, all at once, they came upon a barnyard rooster.

18 "Where are you going?" asked the rooster of the four.

19 "We are going to build us a house," said the sheep, the pig, the rabbit, and the goose.

20 "May I live with you?" asked the barnyard rooster.

21 "What can you do to help?" asked the sheep, the pig, the rabbit, and the goose.

22 The rooster preened his feathers and strutted about for a minute, and then he said: "I can crow very early in the morning; I can awaken you all."

23 "Good!" said the sheep, the pig, the rabbit, and the goose, "you may come with us."

24 So the five went on a long, long way until they found a good place for a house. Then the sheep hewed logs and drew them. The pig made bricks for the cellar, and the rabbit gnawed pegs with his sharp teeth, and hammered them in with his paws. The goose pulled moss, and stuffed it in the cracks with her bill. The rooster crowed early every morning to tell them that it was time to rise, and they all lived happily together in their little house.

> **What are the animals doing in the illustration?**

How does the illustration show the central message of this folktale?

A   It shows that animals need homes.

B   It shows that sheep are good at cutting logs.

C   It shows that work is easier when everyone helps.

D   It shows that the farmers should have built a bigger barn.

> **What feeling do you get from the story?**

What mood do the illustrations create?

_____

_____

_____

DISCUSS IT

Working with a partner, look again at the two illustrations. Discuss which details in them help the reader understand more about the message of the story than the text does.

UNIT 5 Integration of Knowledge and Ideas in Literary Text **217**

A CLOSER LOOK

While trying to convey the key idea, the author tells the reader the main character's feelings. Underline all the words or phrases that support the idea that the stone baby is feeling lonely.

Read the passage. Then answer the questions.

The Stone Baby

by L. J. Bridgman
from The Youth's Companion

1   The stone baby was lonesome. He had looked forth over the city from his little round window on the side of the great building where the architect said he must forever stay, and had seen the homes of the other little ones.

2   Then he said to himself: "When it was summer I could see the children at their windows and in the street, but now they keep well inside. From here I cannot see the big boys and the girls skate and coast, even.

3   "I'd like to see the green grass in the square, and the boys sailing boats on the pond.

4   "Dear me, I believe it's snowing. I don't mind a cold nose and snow-powdered hair, but I can't see even the children's houses if it gets very thick."

5   Just then there was a "chirp, chirp" in the air, and something flew right under the stone baby's chin. It was a little sparrow coming for refuge from the storm. "Chirp, chirp," and another came, and another.

6   "Thank you, baby, for a little corner from the storm," said the sparrows.

7   "Oh, you're very welcome," said the stone child.

8   They nestled closer and closer.

9   "Isn't it pleasant to be of some use in the world!" said the stone baby—for stone babies are so much more serious than flesh and blood children, "and they wouldn't do this for a real, walking and running child."

Which choice states exactly what the stone baby says he wants to see?

1 What would the stone baby like to see?

A   the green grass and the boys sailing boats

B   the children's houses

C   the children in the street

D   the boys and girls coasting and skating

Which detail in the illustration helps you understand why the stone baby is lonely?

2 What is one detail in the illustration that is *not* in the story?

A   It shows that the sparrows huddle near the stone baby.

B   It shows how far the stone baby is from the rest of the town.

C   It shows that the stone baby is in a window.

D   It shows green grass in the square.

Read paragraph 9 to see how the sparrows make the stone baby feel.

3 What is the key idea of the story about the stone baby, and how does the illustration help you understand it?

_____

_____

_____

_____

_____

_____

Read the passage. Then answer the questions.

Little Owl

1   Little Owl sleeps during the day. After a night of flying around hunting for mice or other little creatures for her supper, she often visits with the other nighttime animals. Her best friends are Bat and Firefly. Bat hunts just like Little Owl, but Bat enjoys bugs like mosquitos for his supper. Firefly usually just floats around on the gentle breezes while bringing a bit of light to the dark woods.

2   One evening, Little Owl asks Firefly, "What happens in the woods when I'm asleep in the day?" "Why, I don't really know," answers Firefly. "I'm usually resting quietly in the grass during the day, and I don't see what is going on."

3   Later that night, Little Owl sees Bat hunting at the edge of the woods. Little Owl asks him, "Bat, what happens in the woods during the day when I am asleep?" This question makes Bat very curious, too. He tells Little Owl, "I don't know what happens during the day in the woods. I think you should stay awake one day and find out!" And that is just what Little Owl did!

4   The next day, Little Owl decides to stay awake to find out just what happens in the woods during the day. Little Owl looks all over for Bat and Firefly, but can't find them anywhere.

5   But she does see other animals she had never seen before. She meets Nutty the little gray squirrel, who is busy running up and down the big oak tree collecting the acorns. She meets Spot the fawn, and they both watch as a big black bear lumbers through the forest. They stay very still and quiet so they don't make the bear angry. But Bear,

mumbling and grumbling as he walks through the woods, keeps saying, "Where is the honey tree? Where is the honey tree?"

6   When Little Owl learns that Bear is hungry, she thinks that maybe she shouldn't be afraid of him. Instead, she calls, "You-whoooo! Mr. Bear, where are you going? Are you hungry?"

7   Bear is surprised to hear a new voice calling to him. He turns around quickly and sees Spot and Little Owl standing near some bushes. Bear says, "Who is that who called me?" Little Owl flies closer, and says to Bear, "If you follow me, I can show you a tree where there is a beehive that is full of honey."

8   Bear is surprised to hear Little Owl's offer. He knows he is hungry, though, so he eagerly follows Little Owl to the honey tree. "Thank you, Little Owl," says Bear. "If you ever need help, you let me know."

9   As it starts to get dark, Little Owl flies home to take a nap before her nighttime hunt. She thinks she may want to dream about her new friends. She wants to be sure to tell her nighttime friends, Bat and Firefly, all about her daytime adventures and Nutty, Spot, and Bear.

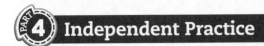

1 Why does Little Owl want to stay awake during the day?

   A She is bored with her nighttime friends.

   B She is afraid of the dark.

   C She doesn't know what happens during the day.

   D She doesn't have anywhere to sleep during the night.

2 What mood do the illustration and the story create together?

   A darkness and gloom

   B fun and laughter

   C fear

   D friendliness

3 What conclusion can you draw about Little Owl and Bear from the illustration?

   A Little Owl is afraid of Bear.

   B Little Owl is leading Bear to food.

   C Bear is trying to eat Little Owl.

   D Bear is afraid of Little Owl.

4 What is the theme of the story? List at least two details from the story and the illustration that support your answer.

_____

_____

_____

_____

_____

_____

LESSON 23

Comparing and Contrasting Themes and Topics in Literary Texts

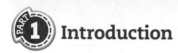 **Introduction**

THEME: ≫ **A World of Stories**

As you read, you may find that stories and myths have the same theme. The **theme** of two stories may be the same, but the events in the story may be different. Sometimes, the **topic,** or what the story is about, is the same, but the theme is different. For example, many stories have a theme of trying until you succeed or not giving up. However, the topic may be how the time a boy spent practicing paid off in a big game.

Read two passages with the same theme.

Passage 1:

The crow had flown a long way, and now he was very thirsty. He tried again to reach the water at the bottom of the jar. His beak was not long enough to reach it. "I am so thirsty," he thought. Then he put a pebble into the jug, and then another. Soon, the water in the jug began to rise. He tried one more time to reach the water in the jug. This time he was able to take a long, deep drink of water.

Passage 2:

DeShawn was dressed for the game. "Now, where is my cap?" He looked up at the display shelf above the window. "There it is!" he said. DeShawn reached up to take his hat from the shelf. To his surprise, he couldn't reach it. He tried again, but he still couldn't reach it. Then he saw his dad's umbrella. Carefully, he used the end of the umbrella to move the cap off the shelf. The cap moved, but now it was farther away from him. DeShawn moved, and tried again. This time he got the end of the umbrella beneath the cap. Slowly, he pulled it forward. Grinning, he grabbed his cap as it fell from the shelf. "Good thing I found this cap, or coach would have benched me," he said.

What is the theme in each story? _____

_____

How are the topics the same or different? _____

_____

Read the first passage. Then answer the questions.

How the Fox Got His Tail

1 Late one chilly night, Fox is getting ready to go to sleep. Winter is coming, and the nights seem darker and colder. As Fox curls himself up in a corner, he suddenly hears crying from outside. "Who could be outside on such a cold night?" he wonders. He doesn't really want to leave his cozy home. But he feels that he should go out into the freezing night and find out where the noise is coming from.

2 Fox carefully trots through the woods. He tries to follow the sound of the crying. At first, the sound comes from the left, then the right. It's hard for Fox to know where to look. Suddenly, he comes upon the baby son of the mountain spirit. The baby is lost in the dark woods and cannot find his way home. Fox quickly carries the baby to his own home. The baby is happy to have a friend and to get out of the cold. Fox snuggles next to the baby all night to keep him warm.

3 The next morning, Fox takes the baby to the home of the mountain spirit up near the top of the mountain. The mountain spirit is so happy to have the baby back home! Fox is happy to have helped and turns to leave. "Oh, no, Fox! Don't go yet," says the mountain spirit. "I must thank you for bringing my lost baby back home." Fox turns back around and is surprised by the gift. He has been rewarded with a new, thick, fluffy and bushy tail so that he will never be cold again.

Think About It

What is the theme of this fable? Look for the important things that Fox does.

Fill in the blanks to show Fox's actions.

Fox curls up to go to sleep. Then he hears _____. He trots through the

woods and _____. He _____.

The next day he takes _____ to the mountain spirit. He is surprised when

he is _____. The lesson the Fox learns is that being _____ can

bring _____.

Read the second passage. Then answer the questions.

The Fox Without a Tail

A CLOSER LOOK

Why does Fox Without a Tail make his speech? Underline details in paragraphs 1 and 2 that provide clues.

1   A handsome Fox was caught in a trap. He tried and tried to get out of that awful trap. Finally, he was free! But he had pulled so hard that his tail came off.

2   For a long time he stayed away from the other Foxes. He knew that they would laugh at him for having no tail. But he was lonely and missed his old friends. So he thought of a plan.

3   He called a meeting of all the Foxes. Then Fox Without a Tail made a long speech. He told of Foxes who had come to harm because of their tails. He described how hounds caught one Fox when his tail was caught in the bushes. Next, he talked about another Fox who had not been able to run fast enough because of the weight of his big, beautiful tail. He said these stories were proof of the danger of having a tail. Fox Without a Tail suggested that every Fox cut off his tail for safety reasons.

4   When he had finished, an old Fox said, "Master Fox, kindly turn around for a moment, and you shall have your answer."

5   When poor Fox Without a Tail turned around, all the other Foxes laughed and laughed. Fox Without a Tail saw it was useless to try to persuade the other Foxes to part with their tails.

The moral of the story is: *Do not listen to the advice of anyone who seeks to lower you to his own level.*

Are Fox Without a Tail's motives in the second fable very different from Fox's motives in the first fable?

What difference between the foxes gives each fable a different theme?

A   They treat other foxes differently.

B   They prefer different tails.

C   One fox lives in the woods, and the other fox lives in a field.

D   One fox thinks of himself, and the other fox helps others.

 DISCUSS IT

Working with a partner, take turns reading the last paragraph of the first fable and the moral of the second fable. Discuss how each lesson fits the theme of good versus evil.

Read two passages. Then answer the questions.

The Power of a Rumor

an Indian folktale

1   Once upon a time, a hare was resting under a banyan tree in the forest. He had a bad feeling and thought, "What would happen to me if the earth would break up?" Suddenly, he heard a loud, rumbling noise, and the earth shook violently. He said, "It's happened. The earth is breaking up!" He jumped up and ran crazily through the forest.

2   While he was running, another hare saw him and asked, "What happened? Where are you going in such a hurry?" The hare cried," The earth is breaking up. Run!" They yelled to everyone they passed to run, too. The other animals were terrified and started racing through the forest. It didn't take much time before all the animals joined the galloping herds. Reptiles, birds, insects, and four-footed animals—all tried to escape the earth breaking up.

3   A lion standing still saw all the animals running and wondered, "What is the matter?" He ran down the hill and positioned himself in front of the crowd. He shouted, "Stop!" The powerful presence of the lion made all the frightened animals stop. A parrot yelled, "The earth is breaking up!" The Lion asked, "Who said that it was?" The parrot replied, "I heard it from the monkeys." The monkeys said they had heard it from the tigers. The tigers heard it from the elephants. The elephants heard it from the buffaloes. Finally, they got to the hare who had started the story.

4   The lion asked the hare, "What made you think that the earth is breaking up?" The hare answered, "Your Majesty, I heard it cracking with my own ears." The lion investigated the matter and explored the sound that the hare had heard. He learned that the sound had been caused by a large coconut falling from a tree. The coconut fell on a pile of rocks, causing a landslide.

5   The Lion said to all the animals, "Go back to your homes. The earth is safe. Next time, check a rumor before acting on it." The animals, all feeling quite silly, went back to their homes.

Chicken Little

an American folktale

1   Chicken Little likes to walk in the woods. She likes to look at the trees. She likes to smell the flowers. She likes to listen to the birds singing.

2   One day, while walking through the woods, an acorn falls from a tree and hits the top of Chicken Little's head. "My, oh, my, the sky is falling!" she says. "I must run and tell the lion about it!" And off she runs.

3   She runs and runs. By and by, she meets the hen.

4   "Where are you going?" asks the hen. "Oh, Henny Penny, the sky is falling, and I am going to the lion to tell him about it."

5   "How do you know it?" asks Henny Penny.

6   "It hit me on the head, so I know it must be so," says Chicken Little.

7   "Let me go with you!" says Henny Penny. And they both continue running down the road. They run until they met Ducky Lucky.

8   "The sky is falling," says Henny Penny. "We are going to the lion to tell him about it."

9   "How do you know that?" asks Ducky Lucky.

10   "It hit Chicken Little on the head!" says Henny Penny.

11   "May I come with you?" asks Ducky Lucky.

12   "Of course! Come along," says Henny Penny.

13   So all three of them run on and on until they meet Foxy Loxy.

14   "Where are you going?" asks Foxy Loxy.

15   "The sky is falling, and we are going to the lion to tell him about it," says Ducky Lucky.

16   "Do you know where he lives?" asks Foxy Loxy.

17   "I don't," says Chicken Little.

18   "I don't," says Henny Penny.

19   "I don't," says Ducky Lucky.

20   "I do," says Foxy Loxy. "Come with me, and I can show you the way."

21   They all run on together until they reach Foxy Loxy's den.

22   "Come right in," says Foxy Loxy.

23   They all go in, but they never, ever come out again.

1 Part A

What is the moral of "Chicken Little"?

A   Chickens shouldn't walk in the woods.

B   Don't believe everything you hear.

C   Foxes shouldn't lead other animals.

D   Don't share gossip with your friends.

Part B

What sentence from the Indian folktale tells the moral of the story?

A   "The earth is breaking up!"

B   "I heard it from the monkeys."

C   "Go back to your homes."

D   "Next time, check a rumor before acting on it."

> Which of the choices in Parts A and B are similar?

2 How are the two folktales different?

A   One ends well; the other does not.

B   One is true; the other is a story.

C   One is about hares; the other is about lions.

D   One has a moral; the other does not.

> Which choice reflects the endings of the folktales?

3 Compare the two folktales by giving three examples of how they are similar.

_____

_____

_____

_____

_____

_____

> Who are the main characters? What do they do?

Read two passages. Then answer the questions.

Hofus the Stonecutter

a retelling of a Japanese folktale

1   There once lived a poor stonecutter named Hofus. Every day, Hofus went to work and worked very hard from morning until night.

2   One day, Hofus delivered stones to a very rich man. When Hofus saw this man's home, he wished to himself, "Oh, I wish I could be as rich as this man!" Much to his surprise, a voice responded to his request. "Hofus," the voice said, "Be as wealthy as this man!" Suddenly, Hofus was very rich.

3   When Hofus returned to his home, instead of his small, humble hut, there now stood a large palace of gold. Hofus decided he would not work anymore. He was happy at first, but the days started to bore him.

4   One day, when a golden carriage passed by his window, he thought, "How exciting it would be to be a prince, with an ornate carriage to ride in! Oh, I wish I could be a prince!" Again, the mysterious voice responded to Hofus. "Hofus," it said, "Be a prince!" And so it was.

5   Hofus enjoyed being a prince, but that, too, began to grow old. So he decided to make another transformation. When he looked out into the garden, he saw his flowers drooping, and he felt the sun burning him, in spite of his gorgeous, sheltering umbrellas. He realized the sun was very powerful. "Oh, I wish I could be the sun!" he said. That same, majestic voice replied. "Hofus," it said. "Be the sun!" And so it was.

6   But soon, a cloud got in his way, and Hofus realized he was not completely powerful!

"I wish," he said, "to be a cloud!" The voice responded, and Hofus was turned into a cloud. He poured rain down upon the land, but when he looked down upon his work, he realized that only the rocks stood unmoved by the flood he made. Hofus realized rocks were more powerful than he! "I wish," Hofus yelled, "to be a rock!" He heard that voice again, and then was turned into a mighty, strong rock.

7   Hofus stayed content as a rock for a while. One day, though, he felt a "tap! tap, tap!" at his feet. He looked down and saw a stonecutter. This stonecutter was slowly but surely breaking Hofus, the rock!

8   Hofus understood suddenly that there was something more powerful than a rock: a stonecutter. And so, Hofus made his last wish. "I wish to be a stonecutter. I want to be myself again!" The voice responded, "Hofus, be yourself!" And so it was. And Hofus never again wished to be anything but himself.

The Three Wishes

CAST:

NARRATOR   MYSTERIOUS WOMAN

HUSBAND   WIFE

act 1, scene 1

NARRATOR: One rainy day, a man was walking home when he saw a mysterious woman in a carriage. Her carriage was stuck in the mud, and it would not budge.

HUSBAND: Excuse me, may I assist you? Looks like you're pretty well stuck!

MYSTERIOUS WOMAN: Yes, thank you!

HUSBAND: Let me give your carriage a bit of a push, and you'll soon be rolling along on your way.

MYSTERIOUS WOMAN: Thank you for your assistance, and now, I'd like to return the favor. What can I do to help you?

NARRATOR: The man immediately thought of his wife at home. They did not have much money, and he wanted to give his wife something to show his love for her.

HUSBAND: I have a wife at home. I would love it if you could do something to help her.

MYSTERIOUS WOMAN: What if I could grant her three wishes?

HUSBAND: That would be perfect!

NARRATOR: The man was overjoyed. He ran the rest of the way home. His wife was in the kitchen, and he addressed her excitedly.

HUSBAND: You'll never guess what happened!

WIFE: What?

HUSBAND: I met a mysterious woman on my way home. I helped her, and she has granted us three wishes. I want to give those wishes to you!

WIFE: Oh, my goodness!

NARRATOR: The wife looked around their small, humble home and, then, she looked at the empty pan on their stove.

WIFE: There are many things I wish for, but right now, my wish is that we had some delicious sausage for dinner!

NARRATOR: Like magic, a sausage appeared in the pan, and they prepared to feast on it. The wife put the sausage on the plates, but, then, the husband clumsily knocked the plates over.

WIFE: Oh, no! Look what you've done! I wish that sausage were on your nose.

NARRATOR: The woman clapped her hand over her mouth to silence herself, but it was too late. The man now had a sausage instead of a nose!

HUSBAND: Look what you did! What in the world are we going to do now? We have wasted two wishes—and do I even need to mention my ridiculous new nose?

WIFE: Why don't you just remove it?

HUSBAND: I can't! It seems to be stuck!

WIFE: Well, we don't have any other choice, do we?

HUSBAND: No, we don't…I don't see any way to remove this sausage from my face except to wish it away.

WIFE: Well, then, here goes. I wish for the sausage to once again be back on our plates for supper!

NARRATOR: Well, she got her final wish, and the two had a wonderful meal…but nothing more. They had already exhausted their wishes. And, they learned a valuable lesson. They never fought again, and they were forever careful about what they wished for!

1 What do the husband and wife in the second passage learn after their second wish?

   A   They should have wished for a larger meal.

   B   They should have asked for more wishes.

   C   They had wasted their wishes.

   D   They had wasted their supper.

2 Which statement represents the theme for both passages?

   A Husbands and wives should not argue.

   B Be careful what you wish for.

   C Mysterious women should grant more than three wishes.

   D Being the most powerful is best.

3 Part A

What does Hofus learn at the end of the first story?

   A It is best to be himself.

   B He was happiest as a rock.

   C The wish granter was unkind to him.

   D It is fun to be rich.

Part B

What sentences from the story *best* support your answer to Part A?

_____

_____

_____

_____

4 Contrast the two passages by describing three differences between them.

_____

_____

_____

_____

_____

_____

LESSON 24

Comparing and Contrasting Patterns of Events in Literary Texts

Part 1 Introduction

THEME: >>> **A World of Stories**

Some stories tell the same events in a similar way. This is called a **pattern of events.** These stories may not be identical. However, the characters may be similar or the characters may take similar actions. One common pattern of events is the **quest.** In a quest, one or more characters travel to a special place or do something special to accomplish a challenge, reach a goal, or perform a superhuman feat. The Harry Potter stories are one example of a quest.

When you read, pay attention to how the events in stories are the same and different. For instance, in coming-of-age stories, the pattern of events might focus on what a young boy does that helps him mature. In myths, the pattern of events might show how gods interfere in the lives of humans. In other stories, the pattern of events might show how a character learns something or defeats a villain. When comparing and contrasting patterns of events across stories, look for what happens, how one event leads to the next, what happens as a result of the events, and who is at the center of the action.

Read the passages. Think about how the pattern of events is the same and different in each passage.

Passage 1:

Young Arthur was the son of King Uther of England. But he had been raised in secret by Ector. The wizard Merlin had stolen the baby boy to protect him from evil people. Later, Merlin placed a sword in a stone. He stated that whomever could draw the sword out of the stone would be king of England. Although many tried, they could not remove the sword. Arthur pulled the sword from the stone, and Merlin had him crowned king. Arthur fought many battles with his knights at first. He wanted to drive out the evil rulers from England. When everyone saw that he was a good king, the people of England lived in peace for many years.

Passage 2:

Along the banks of a great river in what would eventually become the US, there lived an old couple with a wonderful daughter. However, she married a mean man who took advantage of his kind in-laws. He went hunting with his father-in-law, but he kept all the buffalo meat to himself. One day, the father-in-law shot a buffalo, and when the son-in-law took all the meat, the father-in-law was upset. He kept the arrow that pierced the buffalo. When he got home, he put the arrow in a pot of boiling water to make soup. Out of that pot came a baby boy who could already speak. The old couple was very surprised. He told the couple to touch him to each lodge pole. When they did, the baby grew and became a man named Kutoyis. Kutoyis helped the old couple get food and get rid of their mean son-in-law. He then traveled from village to village solving any problems the people had so they were no longer hungry and could live in peace.

Each passage is from a different country, yet there are similarities. What do the main characters do at the end of each passage? _____

_____

What pattern of events is similar? _____

_____

_____

_____

What is one way the pattern of events is different in each story? _____

_____

_____

By comparing and contrasting the patterns of events in stories, you can better understand how authors construct plots. Two stories with similar events may have very different outcomes. Two stories with very different events may end up with similar conclusions. By paying attention to the patterns of events in more than one story, you can learn to think critically about why authors structure stories in a certain way.

Read the first passage. Then answer the questions.

Better Together

1   Anwar and Martin are neighbors and classmates, but they don't get along. When Martin first moved next door, Anwar thought it would be fun to have someone his age living so close. But Martin never wanted to do anything fun, like play soccer. He was always drawing. He never even drew anything cool—just comic book characters.

2   Martin liked living in his new neighborhood. Since he went to the same school, he didn't have to make new friends. He now lived next door to a classmate, but he didn't really get along with Anwar. Anwar always wanted to play something, and he didn't talk to Martin as much after Martin said he preferred drawing to sports.

3   One day at school, both boys were on the playground. They saw Eddie, a younger student, crying. When they asked him what happened, Eddie told them that other children were picking on him, and he felt scared. Martin and Anwar told Eddie that they would talk to the other children.

4   Anwar went to the children and told them to leave Eddie alone. "No one deserves to be picked on for any reason," he told them. Meanwhile, back in the classroom, Martin drew pictures of Eddie as a superhero to cheer him up. The other kids saw Martin's drawings and were impressed by the image of Eddie as a superhero.

5   Eddie was happy that no one was bothering him anymore. He thanked the boys for their help. Anwar and Martin realized they could work together toward a goal, even though they had their differences.

Think About It

What is the pattern of events in this story? To answer this question, look for details that tell you what happened and what the result was.

What happens at the beginning of the story? _____

_____

What happens that changes the boys' feelings about each other? _____

_____

Read the second passage. Then answer the question.

Two Birds in a Bush

1 Cardinal and Robin live in the same neighborhood. But they don't get along. They have their own friends, and they eat at different places every day. Cardinal likes to visit the backyard bird feeders to get different seeds. He always laughs because Robin has to eat yucky worms instead of seeds.

2 Robin is a very happy bird. He lives in a nice area with well-kept yards. It is a great place to hunt for yummy earthworms. He never pays much attention to the other birds, unless they are trying to catch some of the worms!

3 One day, the two birds are caught in a storm. They are both trapped under the same thorny bush. They cannot get out because the wind and rain have blown a branch across the opening. Robin wants to stay dry, so he pulls down some of the sticks to make a shelter. The bush is in a good area to find worms, so he shares his worms with Cardinal, who eats one because he is so hungry.

4 When the storm ends, the birds still cannot get out. Groundhog sees Cardinal's bright red feathers. He moves the branch to free the two birds. Cardinal and Robin are happy that they have worked together in spite of their differences.

How do the events of both stories help you understand the themes of the stories?

What is the theme in both stories?

A a hero's quest

B a response to disaster

C learning how to get along with someone

D understanding how to face a bully

 DISCUSS IT

How did the events at the beginning of each story lead to the events in the middle and end of the story? Talk with a partner about how these patterns of events helped the characters succeed in doing something.

Read the myths. Then answer the questions.

Demeter and Persephone

adapted from 'Round the Year in Myth and Song
by Florence Holbrook

A CLOSER LOOK
Think about how the patterns of events in the two myths are similar. Underline the sentence in each myth that describes the problem or challenge that must be solved or faced.

1   The king of all the gods was Zeus. He had two brothers and three sisters. Each had an important job. His sister, Demeter, was in charge of the harvest. Demeter had a little daughter, Persephone, who she loved very much. They played together every day.

2   You will wonder why Persephone is not always with her mother. This is the story the Greeks tell.

3   As Demeter takes care of the ripening grains and fruits all over Earth, she must visit every country. One day, she was seated in her chariot drawn by those wonderful winged dragons, ready to set forth on her travels. She kissed her little daughter, and warned her not to go far from home. She had never before felt so anxious about leaving her little girl, but she had to go.

4   Persephone threw a loving kiss to her mother, and then went to play with the sea nymphs. They are graceful, slender girls, with sea-green hair and eyes like opals. They are charming playmates, but cannot come out of the water. Persephone gathered flowers for them, and was obedient to her mother's command.

5   But Hades, the god of the palaces of gold and silver under Earth, looking out from one of the caverns, saw the pretty child, and wanted to carry her away to his home. So he caused a wonderful flower, all crimson and gold, to charm Persephone farther away. She stooped to pick it; and lo! it came up by the roots, a deep cavern yawned, and the chariot of King Hades appeared.

6   The driver, who was King Hades himself, caught the frightened Persephone in his arms. Whipping his coal-black steeds, he hurried away with her to his home in Hades.

7   When Demeter returned and could not find her little girl, she was frantic. Over the whole Earth she drove her chariot, calling upon all things to help her in her search—but in vain!

8   Then she became so sad that she refused to allow Earth to produce any food. The flowers and trees and harvests drooped

and faded. In vain did gods and men plead with her. She would not be comforted.

9   At last Zeus sent the swift-flying Hermes, messenger of the gods, to Hades, commanding him to release Persephone. When Demeter saw her daughter restored to her, what joy was hers! Yet she feared one thing.

10   "Have you eaten anything in Hades's kingdom, my child?"

11   "Yes, dear mother," Persephone replied, "six pomegranate seeds."

12   "Alas! Then you must remain with Hades six months of every year," said the sad Demeter.

13   Thus, it is that for six months Demeter and Persephone are together, Earth is covered with the blessed gifts of Demeter, and it is summer over the land. But when they are separated, the mother grieves, and winter is king.

Minerva and Daphne

by Florence Holbrook

1   The wonderful goddess Minerva is said to have come full-grown from the brain of her father, Jupiter, king of the gods. She is tall, and clad in full armor. Her name Minerva means "mind." She is called the goddess of wisdom.

2   A city in Greece was to be named, and Neptune, the god of the sea, and Minerva contended for the honor. The gods decided that the one who produced the object most valuable to man should name the city.

3   Neptune struck the ground with his trident, and there sprang forth a horse, strong and noble. All admired Neptune's gift, and did not believe that Minerva could surpass him.

4   When Minerva produced the olive tree, they laughed, and all thought that Neptune had won. But the goddess told them that the olive tree could furnish wood for fire, for building houses, and for making many useful articles; that food and oil could be obtained from it; and that even clothing could be made from its fiber.

5   The gods then said that, while men could live without horses, they could not live without food, warmth, and shelter, and Minerva had the honor of naming the city.

6 Minerva was called Pallas Athene by the Greeks, and so the city in Greece was named Athens. In this city was erected a beautiful temple in her honor, called the Parthenon. Its ruins are still standing.

What motivates the main characters to act?

1 How are the events of the two myths similar?

A They are both about the Underworld.

B They both have goddesses that are captured.

C They both are about the demands of gods.

D They both have contests between gods.

What happens at the end of each myth?

2 What is one way the events are different in the two myths?

A One myth describes how the weather on Earth came to be.

B One myth describes gods being kind to each other in the end.

C One myth shows that jealousy will not help you succeed.

D One myth shows that there's no good way to resolve a problem.

How do problems and solutions play a part in the patterns of events?

3 Give three examples of how the patterns of events are similar in the two myths.

_____

_____

_____

_____

Read the two passages. Then answer the questions.

The Endless Tale

1   There once lived an extraordinarily rich man who had a daughter who was an incredible storyteller. The daughter's father enjoyed her stories so much that he wished for her to never marry. He wanted to keep her around to tell him these fantastic stories. He wanted to listen to her tales forever.

2   "I wish your stories would go on forever," he said. "Or, at least, I wish they could each go on for a month!"

3   "Don't be silly, Father!" the daughter exclaimed. "Stories that go on for a month would be very boring."

4   "Surely, they would not!" said the father. "In fact, I believe that is so impossible, that if anyone could ever tell me a month-long story that bored me, I would let him marry you!"

5   This news quickly traveled throughout the daughter's small village. The young men in the village all worked tirelessly to invent fantastic, long stories to tell the rich man. The rich man's daughter, though, had fallen in love with one man. However, this man was poor. The daughter knew her father would not let her marry him. Therefore, she told him what to say when he told his story.

6   The man came to see the father to tell him the month-long story. The story was about a rich, wise man who harvested all his corn and hid it in a cave because he thought a famine might come. The man in the story did not see a tiny crack in the cave's wall, so he did not notice an ant that came in and began to steal the corn. "And then the ant came back and stole another grain of corn," the boy said. "And then, he stole another grain. And then, he stole another grain. And then he stole another grain…" the boy continued to say this, over and over.

7   Well, the man in the story had thousands upon thousands of grains of corn, so this story could go on forever! After three days of telling this story, the rich man spoke up. "You win!" he said. "This story is boring me to tears!"

8   The poor boy smiled. "But, sir, the story is not nearly over." The rich man laughed, in spite of the situation, and said, "I know when I am beat! You may have my daughter's hand in marriage. That is the most boring tale I have ever heard!"

The Flea

a traditional Mexican folktale

1   There once lived a brilliant magician. He had a daughter, whom he loved very much. Now, this daughter fell in love with a boy and asked her father if the two could be married. Her father, always protective of his daughter, said, "If he can outsmart me, you can marry him." Turning to the boy, the magician said, "If you can sleep for three nights where my spells cannot find you, then you can marry her."

2   The magician was smug. This was not the first time that someone had tried to outsmart him! What the father did not know was that this boy was also a magician!

3   The first night, the boy tried to sleep cradled on the moon. But the next day, the older magician said, "It cannot be comfortable to sleep on the moon." The boy was perplexed. He had always thought himself a mighty smart fellow! How had the older magician known where he was?

4   The next night, the boy tried to sleep inside a shell, hidden deep in the dark blue sea. But the magician found him yet again! It seemed like the boy might not win this contest.

5   The boy thought hard. What could he do? Then he had a fantastic idea! He snuck outside and turned himself into a tiny flea. Then he waited…and waited…and waited. Finally, just when he was about to give up on his plan, the magician came outside, and he jumped onto the rim of the magician's sombrero. Surely, he would not find the boy now!

6   The magician looked high and low for the boy. He looked absolutely everywhere! He couldn't understand how he could be tricked. (He certainly didn't realize that the boy was sitting on top of his hat!) Finally, he gave up looking, and decided to find the boy the next day. When the magician went inside, the flea hopped down from the hat onto the door jamb and settled down for a good night of much-needed rest. He repeated this for the next three nights, and each night, the magician wandered around, inside and out, searching for this very clever boy.

7   On the third day, the flea turned back into the boy. He walked through the door of the house and addressed the magician. The magician simply shook his head in wonder. "You have outsmarted me," he said.

1 Part A

Which choice is *not* a way in which the events of the two folktales are alike?

A   They both have contests.

B   They are both about fathers and daughters.

C   They are both about magicians.

D   They both have young men meeting a challenge.

Part B

What details from both folktales *best* support the answer to Part A?

_____

_____

_____

_____

2   How do the two young men's responses to events differ in the two folktales?

A   One knows how to tell stories. The other does not.

B   One needs help with the challenge. The other does not.

C   One marries the daughter. The other does not.

D   One is successful in the father's challenge. The other fails.

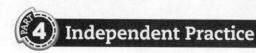
3 In both folktales, young men seek to prove themselves. Explain how the fathers' responses to these efforts are alike and different, and how these responses affect the pattern of events.

_____

_____

_____

_____

_____

_____

4 Describe how the similarities in the pattern of events affect the outcomes in both folktales.

_____

_____

_____

_____

_____

_____

Read the story. Then answer the questions.

adapted from A Tomato Story

from The Youth's Companion, *Issue 62, 1894*
by Brent

1 "Have another tomato, Johnny," said Grandma, as she saw the last red slice disappear from Johnny's plate. "I think you like tomatoes."

2 "I do," said Johnny. "I like them raw, and stewed, and baked. I like them 'most any way you can make them! Didn't you like tomatoes when you were little, Grandma?" Johnny asked. He had been watching Grandma look down at her plate with a smile in her eyes.

3 "No," Grandma said, "but that was because I was a big girl before I ever tasted one. I never saw any until I was 13 years old."

4 "I can remember it so well. A peddler came by our farm once a month. He would bring buttons and thread and other such little things to sell. He brought the seed to my mother.

5 "He used to carry seeds and cuttings of plants from one farmer's wife to the next. Everyone liked to see him come because he would always bring news, too. He'd bring news from town and from up one road and down another."

6 "One spring morning he came. After Mother had bought all she needed from his big, red wagon, he fed his horse and sat by the kitchen fire waiting for his dinner. He began fumbling about in his pockets in search of something. Finally, he drew out a very small package and handed it to Mother."

7 "'I've brought you some love-apple seeds,' he said. 'I got them in the city, and I gave my sister half and brought half to you.'"

8 "'Thank you, kindly,' Mother said, as she looked at the little yellow seeds. 'I'm right glad to get them. What kind of a plant is the love-apple?'"

9 "'Well,' said the peddler, 'the man who gave the seeds to me had his plants last year in a sunny fence corner. The flowers are small, but the fruit is bright red. The fruit looks real pretty among the dark-green leaves. You can't eat the fruit, though—it's poisonous. It's something new—the man who gave me the seeds got them from a captain of a ship from South America. They grow wild there.'"

10 "So Mother planted her love-apple seeds in a warm fence corner. They grew, and the little yellow blossoms came. After them came the pretty red fruit. We children would go out and look at it and talk about it. We would wonder if it would hurt us if we just tasted it.

11 "One day Mother heard us talking about it. She called us over and told us that if we could not be satisfied with the pretty red fruit to look at without wanting to eat it, she would have to pull up the love-apple vines and throw them away. She did not want us to get poisoned."

12 "We knew she would hate to do that, for no one else had them. So we kept away from the fence corner, and the vine grew and blossomed. The red showed in new places every day. The birds did not seem to be at all afraid of the poison fruit but ate all they wanted of it."

13 "One day, in the early fall, my uncle came from New York to pay us a visit. When he went out in the garden he stopped in surprise. 'Why, Mary,' he said, 'what fine tomato vines you have! Where did you get them?'"

14 "'We call them love-apples,' Mother said. Then she told him how the peddler brought the seed. But when my uncle found that we were afraid to eat them, he had a good laugh. He showed Mother how to get some ready for supper. And that was my first taste of tomato, Johnny," Grandma said. "You shall have some for supper fixed the same way— with cream and sugar."

1 What details in the story are shown in the second illustration?

   A the fruit of the love-apples

   B the peddler

   C Mother

   D the items Mother bought

2 **Part A**

How does the first illustration confirm story details about how Grandma has changed?

   A It shows that she is still afraid of tomatoes.

   B It shows that she is growing tomatoes herself.

   C It shows that she loves tomatoes now.

   D It shows that she tastes tomatoes for the first time.

Part B

What story details *best* support the answer to Part A?

_____

_____

_____

_____

3 Compare the illustrations with the details in the story. List at least five details in the story that are confirmed by the illustrations. Then, describe how the illustration helps you understand the story.

1. _____

   _____

   _____

2. _____

   _____

   _____

3. _____

   _____

   _____

4. _____

   _____

   _____

5. _____

   _____

   _____

Read the stories. Then answer the questions.

Making a Difference

1   Marta slowly walked out to the practice field after school. What if she didn't make the soccer team? It was already hard to come to a new country and a new school. She and her family had only been in the United States for a few months. She felt so awkward and out of place at school. She knew that she dressed differently, talked differently, and had had a very different life from all the other students. But she so wanted to fit in! If she could play on the soccer team, maybe she could make a friend and feel better about everything.

2 All of the other girls who came out for the tryouts seemed to be very good players. Marta was more worried than ever about getting onto the team. However, when Coach Hanson asked Marta to go through some of the drills, everyone else was impressed with her skills. Kaylee, Marta's classmate, congratulated Marta on her abilities. Kaylee asked Marta to walk home together after tryouts. That started a new friendship for both girls.

3 The next day at school, Marta and Kaylee were excited to learn that they both made the team. There would be practices two nights a week after school and games on Saturdays.

4 One day after practice, the girls noticed a skinny, dirty, sad-looking dog sitting just outside of the practice field. They walked over to see if the dog had a collar or tags so they could call its owner. There were none. After making friends with the dog, they decided to try getting it over to the animal shelter in case someone was looking for it. The woman at the shelter said that unfortunately, the shelter was full and had no more money to buy food for the animals that were currently there.

5 Marta and Kaylee talked about what they could do to help out the poor animals that needed shelter, food, and help finding good homes. They talked to Coach Hanson about charging admission for one Saturday's game and contributing those funds to the animal shelter. Coach Hanson offered to go with the girls to get permission from the school board for this project. Everything was approved, and the girls and their team were successful in raising money for the shelter.

6 Later, Marta thought back to her first days at the school and how fearful she was about trying out for the soccer team. She realized that she was wrong about being very different from everyone else. Yes, she did talk and dress differently, but deep down she and Kaylee and the other girls were pretty much the same. They wanted to be liked, to have fun and have friends, and to help others if the need arose.

adapted from Robin Hood and King Richard

in Stories of Robin Hood Told to the Children
by H. E. Marshall

The story of Robin Hood is an English legend, possibly based on an actual person. According to the legend, Robin Hood robbed from the rich and gave to the poor. In this story the king, Richard the Lionheart, wants to meet the outlaw secretly.

1   When King Richard Coeur de Lion came back from the Holy Land, he found England in a sad state. Prince John had ruled badly and had been cruel and unjust. He had made the people very unhappy. Everyone rejoiced when the king returned.

2   Because of Prince John's nasty treatment of the people, a man named Robin Hood started to take matters into his own hands. He and his followers would hide in Sherwood Forest. When anyone passed by on the road, they were stopped. Poor people were allowed to pass. Any abbots, priors, knights, or backers of Prince John would have to pay a toll for using the road.

3   When King Richard was back in England, he wanted to put things right again. He also wanted to go to Nottingham to find out the truth about Robin Hood.

4   With a dozen of his lords, King Richard rode to Nottingham. He went to the castle, where he stayed for many weeks. There were balls and parties in honor of the king.

5   The king would hunt in Sherwood Forest. Sometimes he would wander in there by himself. But never once did he meet Robin Hood. And Robin Hood was the very person he wanted to meet most.

6   Other people would talk about having met Robin. Robin still stopped all the abbots, priors, and bad knights. But try as he might, King Richard never met him.

7   Robin often saw the king, however. Whenever Richard came into the forest, Robin and his men would hide. They thought that Richard would be angry with them for killing his deer and for robbing the nobles and priests.

8   Because they honored and loved the king, Robin's men would never have stopped him or taken money from him. In fact, Robin gave orders to his men to follow the king in the forest. Robin wanted to keep him safe.

9   So, Robin continued to take money from the wealthy. He continued to give money to those who were poor. He helped those who were treated unfairly by Prince John and some of the nobles in the area.

4   How does the illustration in "Making a Difference" help you understand the events of the story?

   A   It shows that the team does not care about animals.

   B   It shows that there are many lost animals.

   C   It shows that the parents watching the game don't want to help.

   D   It shows one animal that needs help.

5   How is the theme of "Robin Hood and King Richard" similar to the theme of "Making a Difference"?

   A   Both emphasize the value of helping the less fortunate.

   B   Both have characters who honor the king and knights.

   C   Both show that stealing is okay if it's for a good cause.

   D   Both deal with the challenge of moving to a new home.

6   The illustration in "Robin Hood and King Richard" shows what story details?

   A   It shows how Robin Hood and his men get food.

   B   It shows how Robin Hood and his men collect tolls.

   C   It shows how King Richard is angry that he cannot find Robin Hood

   D   It shows how Robin Hood and his men help people in need.

7 Part A

What is one difference in how the topics are treated in the two stories?

   A Marta interacts only with animals. Robin Hood interacts only with nature.

   B Marta's team raises money for animals in need. Robin Hood raises money for people in need.

   C Marta makes friends. No one is Robin Hood's friend.

   D Marta works as part of a team. Robin Hood acts alone.

Part B

What evidence from both stories *best* supports the answer to Part A?

_____

_____

_____

_____

_____

_____

8 Write a paragraph comparing the patterns of events in the two stories. Explain how the events lead to a better understanding of the theme.

_____

_____

_____

_____

_____

_____

_____

UNIT 6
Integration of Knowledge and Ideas in Informational Text

In this unit, you will learn that authors create visuals such as illustrations, charts, and diagrams to give more information about their topics. You will practice looking at these graphic elements to understand what additional information they offer. You will also practice identifying reasons and evidence that support the main points in a text. Finally, when you are writing or talking about a topic, you will learn to look at two different texts, or resources, in order to get a more complete picture about the topic.

LESSON 25 Interpreting Visual Elements of a Text is about why authors include pictures, charts, or other visuals with their writing. You will learn to read these elements to learn more about a topic.

LESSON 26 Explaining an Author's Purpose focuses on identifying the main points of a text. You will then look for reasons and evidence in the text that support these important points.

LESSON 27 Integrating Information from Two Texts looks at how to understand and combine, or integrate, information from more than one resource. You will compare different sources on the same topic to evaluate new information that will help you learn more about a subject.

LESSON 25

Interpreting Visual Elements of a Text

 Introduction

THEME: ⟫ **Finding the Facts**

Authors often include visuals in informational text to help you better understand a subject. Visuals include photographs, drawings, graphs, charts, diagrams, or time lines. You should always look closely at these visuals and think about how they support the text. Many times, they include additional information that an author could not express with words.

Read the note. Look at the map and pictures. Then complete the Venn diagram on the next page.

Dear Juan,

Here are the directions to the restaurant. I drew a map and included a picture of the restaurant to help you find it. You and Dad can meet us there at 7:00 p.m. Have Dad make a **right** out of the driveway and make the **second right** onto Hickory Lane. Stay on Hickory for 3 miles. Turn **left** onto Ridge Avenue. The restaurant is called "Mickey's" and it is on Ridge Avenue. See you both tonight!

Love,
Mom

Maple Road

Hickory Lane

Ridge Avenue

Laundromat

Mickey's

Read the note again and look at the map. Think about what information you learn from just the text and just the map with pictures. The Venn diagram shows what you can learn from only reading the text, only looking at the map, and what you can learn from both. Fill in more information on the Venn diagram.

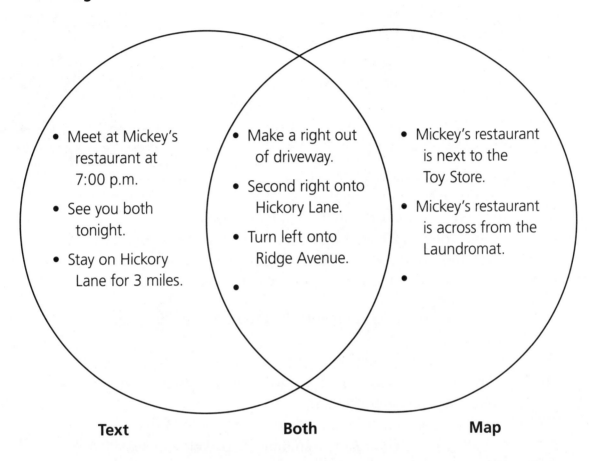

- Meet at Mickey's restaurant at 7:00 p.m.
- See you both tonight.
- Stay on Hickory Lane for 3 miles.

- Make a right out of driveway.
- Second right onto Hickory Lane.
- Turn left onto Ridge Avenue.
-

- Mickey's restaurant is next to the Toy Store.
- Mickey's restaurant is across from the Laundromat.
-

Text   **Both**   **Map**

When a text shows a visual like a map, photograph, chart, or drawing along with text, remember to look at the visuals carefully. The visuals give you extra information that the words alone do not.

Read the first part of the passage. Then answer the questions.

Climbing Mount Everest
by Catherine Bevard

1   The highest point in the world is Mount Everest. Its peak is 29,035 feet high. In the 1990s, people started using tools to track changes on it. The tools have shown that the mountain moves a little bit to the northeast every year. It also rises a fraction of an inch each year. So, the world's highest point keeps getting even higher.

Jordan Romero and Ang Pasang, a Sherpa guide, reach the summit of Mount Everest

2   It took a long time for anyone to climb to the summit, or top, of Mount Everest. In 1953, two men, made it to the top. In 1980, the first person climbed to the summit alone. In 2001, a blind man made it to the mountain's peak. In 2010, the world was shocked when Jordan Romero, age 13, made it to the top. He is the youngest person to climb the mountain.

1953	First people reach summit (Edmund Hilary and Tenzing Norgay)
1975	First woman reaches summit (Junko Tabei)
1978	First people reach summit without extra oxygen (Reinhold Messner and Peter Habeler)
1980	First person reaches summit alone (Reinhold Messner)
2001	First blind person reaches summit (Erik Weihenmayer)
2010	Youngest person (age 13) reaches summit (Jordan Romero)
2013	Oldest person (age 83) reaches summit (Yuichiro Miura)

Think About It

What information do the visuals give that the text does not?

The photo shows that the climbers wear _____ and use

extra _____. The time line tells that Junko Tabei was the first

_____ to reach the top. The oldest person reached the

summit in _____.

A CLOSER LOOK

Look at the map. Underline the words and phrases in the final paragraph that talk about the routes up the mountain.

Continue reading the passage. Then answer the question.

3   There is a reason that few people reach the top of the mountain. It is a challenge in many ways. First, the weather on the mountain is so harsh that it cannot support human life. The weather is not the only issue. The mountain is so high that a climber's pulse and heart rate go up as his body works harder to get enough oxygen. Many climbers bring extra oxygen with them for the climb. Some try to finish the climb without it.

4   There are a few routes to the top that people can take when they climb the mountain. The south route is the most common. The north path is used less, but people still climb it sometimes. People do not climb the East Face, the mountain's biggest side, very much. Whatever path these climbers take, trying to reach the top of Mount Everest is dangerous. Yet, many still make it one of their life goals to reach the mountain's summit.

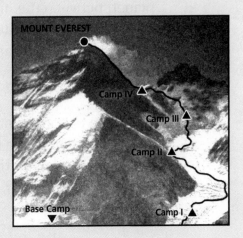

Which route would most likely be marked on the map—a route that is often climbed or less often climbed?

Which route is most likely *not* shown on the map of Mount Everest?

A   the south route

B   the north path

C   the East Face

D   base camp

 DISCUSS IT

Talk to a classmate about how the visuals helped you learn more about Mount Everest. What information did they provide that the text alone did not?

Read the passage. Then answer the questions.

How Was Mount Everest Formed?

by Catherine Bevard

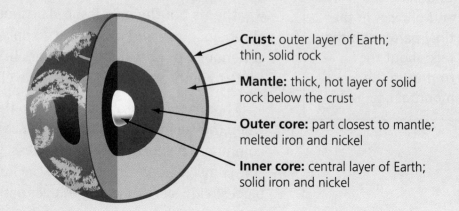

Crust: outer layer of Earth; thin, solid rock

Mantle: thick, hot layer of solid rock below the crust

Outer core: part closest to mantle; melted iron and nickel

Inner core: central layer of Earth; solid iron and nickel

A CLOSER LOOK

As you read, use the diagrams to help you understand what you are reading. Circle the words in the text that relate to the diagrams.

1   Earth is comprised of different layers. The outer part of the planet, between the mantle and the surface, is called the crust. The crust and the outer part of the mantle are broken into about a dozen large plates and many smaller ones. They are called tectonic plates. The continents and the ocean floor rest on these gigantic plates.

2   These tectonic plates move very slowly over Earth's surface. The places where the plates touch are called plate boundaries. At plate boundaries, the plates grind by, slide under, and buckle on top of one another.

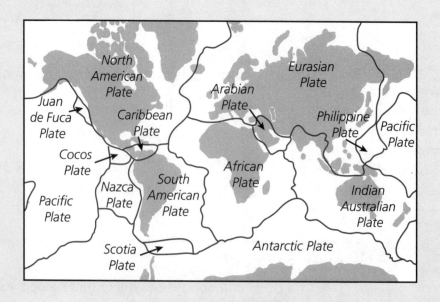

3 Mountains such as the Himalayan Mountains also form at plate boundaries. The Himalayans began forming about 40 to 50 million years ago. The plate containing India collided with the Eurasian plate. As the plates pushed together, Earth's crust folded and was pushed upward. Rocks that were previously buried were forced up to become mountains. The Himalayans are the biggest mountains in the world. They are growing taller every day as the plates continue to collide.

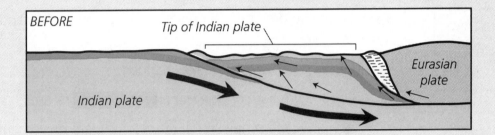

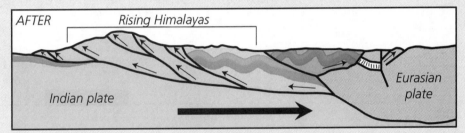

The Himalayan Mountains formed when the Indian plate pressed against the Eurasian plates. Then Earth's crust folded over another crust.

Reread the first paragraph and look at the diagram. How does this help you understand more about Earth?

1 What does the diagram of Earth show?

   A the mantle of the Earth

   B the Earth and its inner parts

   C the Earth's atmosphere

   D the Earth's oceans

What does the after diagram show?

2 How do the before and after diagrams help you understand concepts in the passage?

   A They show how earthquakes happen.

   B They show how high the Himalayan Mountains are.

   C They provide a simple visual of tectonic plate movement.

   D They show how Earth's lower mantle is involved in rock formation.

How does the map help you learn more about the location of the Himalayan Mountains?

3 How does the map of Earth's plates help you understand the passage?

_____

_____

_____

_____

_____

_____

Read the passage. Then answer the questions.

The First Woman to Climb Mount Everest

1   Twenty-two years after the first two men climbed to the top of Mount Everest, the first woman reached the summit. Junko Tabei was a Japanese mountain climber who led the first all-women journey to the top of the world's tallest mountain. Tabei was 35 years old. She felt relieved as she "gazed down from the icy, wind-swept roof of the world." Like most climbers, Junko was guided by a male Sherpa, who is someone who lives in the mountains of Nepal, India. Sherpas help many people from all over the world climb Mount Everest. The women reached the summit on May 16, 1975. There were 15 women in the climbing group.

Junko Tabei at the top of Mount Everest. May 16, 1975.

2   Climbing Everest is an extremely difficult and dangerous task. At one point during her climb, Junko Tabei was buried beneath an avalanche. She had her tent with her, so she set it up and slept there beneath the snow until a Sherpa rescued her. After surviving the cruel snow, Junko kept climbing for 12 days until she reached the summit. While on top of the world, Tabei knew that they had a difficult climb ahead—the climb down. This takes great physical and mental strength. "It was much harder than climbing up," Tabei stated. She kept telling herself, take "one more step…Eventually it must end."

3   The early climbers of Mount Everest were very focused on reaching the summit. They did not think about the equipment and trash that they left behind on the mountain. Over the next few decades, tons of trash gathered on the mountain as people from all over the world climbed the mountain. This was harmful to the natural environment and also dangerous for climbers.

4   Junko Tabei has become one of many climbers to speak up about the dangers of pollution on the mountain. She is a leader in the nonprofit organization Himalayan Adventure Trust Japan. Her organization works with Nepalese villagers near Everest to help clean up the mountain. They helped build an incinerator to get rid of the waste left by climbers. When

Junko first climbed Everest, there were very few cars in Kathmandu, the capital and largest city of Nepal. No cars meant no pollution. Today, there are many cars and tall buildings in the city. There are also more climbers than ever coming through the city. Junko Tabei teaches people about the dangers of water contamination and other environmental dangers. In 2011, Tabei acted as Nepal's goodwill ambassador for tourism. She worked hard to raise awareness about the environment around Mount Everest.

5 In 1992, Junko Tabei was the first woman to reach the summits of the highest peaks on each continent. These peaks are known as the "Seven Summits." Thirty-nine years after her famous climb, Tabei is a wife and mother of two children. One of her life goals is to reach the summit of the highest mountain in every country. She has climbed 60 of these peaks so far. She continues to climb and help others reach mountaintops.

1953 ┼─ The first two men climb to the top of Mount Everest.

1975 ┼─ Junko Tabei is the first woman to reach the top of Mount Everest.

1992 ┼─ Tabei is the first woman to reach the "Seven Summits."

2011 ┼─ Tabei acts as Nepal's goodwill ambassador for tourism.

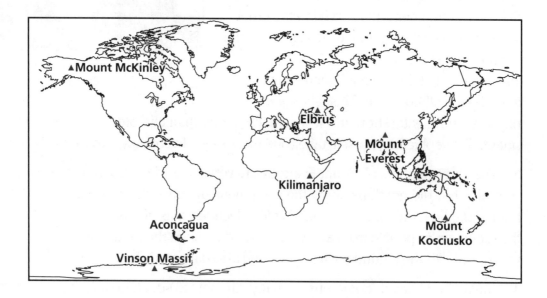

Seven Summits

Mountain	Country	Continent
Mount Everest	Nepal/Tibet	Asia
Aconcagua	Argentina	South America
Mount McKinley	Alaska	North America
Kilimanjaro	Tanzania	Africa
Ebrus	Russia	Europe
Vinson Massif	Ellsworth Range	Antarctica
Mount Kosciusko	Australia	Australia

1 How does the picture of Junko Tabei at the top of the passage support the statement, "Climbing Everest is an extremely difficult and dangerous task?"

A The weather in the picture looks dangerous.

B Junko Tabei is all alone.

C There is a Japanese flag in the picture.

D Junko is wearing heavy clothing and holds a heavy tank on her back.

2 Why did Junko Tabei speak about the dangers of pollution on Mount Everest?

A When Junko first climbed Everest, there were very few cars in Kathmandu.

B Climbers from all over the world leave trash and equipment on the mountain.

C Villagers helped build an incinerator to get rid of the waste left by climbers.

D Junko was the first woman to reach the summit of Mount Everest.

3 Part A

What information do you get from the chart that is *not* in the article?

_____

_____

Part B

Which sentence from the passage explains the map and the chart?

A "Twenty-two years after the first two men climbed to the top of Mount Everest, the first woman reached the summit."

B "There were 15 women in the climbing group."

C "Her organization works with Nepalese villagers near Everest to help clean up the mountain."

D "In 1992, Junko Tabei was the first woman to reach the summits of the highest peaks on each continent."

4 How does the time line help you better understand Junko Tabei's involvement in the world of mountain climbing? Include words or sentences from the text that relate to the time line.

_____

_____

_____

_____

_____

_____

_____

_____

LESSON 26
Explaining an Author's Purpose

 **Introduction**

THEME: >>> **Finding the Facts**

An **author's purpose** in writing a text is to express information to a reader. To persuade readers to believe the information, the author includes reasons and evidence that support it. **Reasons** might include ideas about why the main idea is positive or negative, or why it should be put into practice. **Evidence** might include facts or details from studies, experts, or other sources that back up the main idea.

Read the paragraph.

Sometimes, it's the simple habits that keep us healthy and happy. For example, reading a book for just 30 minutes a day can be extremely good for you. Studies have shown that reading regularly helps you concentrate better. It also increases your ability to understand matters, especially complicated topics. Reading regularly may also make you a better friend, because reading improves your listening skills. A book may seem less interesting than a computer or a video game, but don't let its outward appearance fool you. Reading regularly reduces stress levels, which is great for your heart and mind, and it increases your vocabulary, making it easier for you to express yourself!

Complete the table with information about the author's main point and the reasons and evidence that support the idea.

Author's Main Point	Reasons	Evidence
	• increases comprehension • improves listening skills • •	

Read the first part of the speech. Then answer the questions.

excerpt from President Obama's "Back to School" Event

In 2009, President Obama spoke at Wakefield High School in Arlington, Virginia. Here is part of his speech.

1   I know that for many of you, today is the first day of school. And for those of you in kindergarten, or starting middle or high school, it's your first day in a new school, so it's understandable if you're a little nervous. I imagine there are some seniors out there who are feeling pretty good right now, with just one more year to go. And no matter what grade you're in, some of you are probably wishing it were still summer, and you could've stayed in bed just a little longer this morning.

2   I know that feeling. When I was young my mother decided to teach me extra lessons herself, Monday through Friday—at 4:30 in the morning.

3   Now, I wasn't too happy about getting up that early. A lot of times, I'd fall asleep right there at the kitchen table. But whenever I'd complain, my mother would just give me one of those looks and say, "This is no picnic for me either, buster...."

4   Now, I've given a lot of speeches about education. And I've talked a lot about responsibility.

5   I've talked about your teachers' responsibility for inspiring you, and pushing you to learn.

6   I've talked about your parents' responsibility for making sure you stay on track, and get your homework done, and don't spend every waking hour in front of the TV or with that Xbox.

7   I've talked a lot about your government's responsibility for setting high standards, supporting teachers and principals, and turning around schools that aren't working....

8   And that's what I want to focus on today: the responsibility each of you has for your education. I want to start with the responsibility you have to yourself.

Think About It

What point is the president trying to make in this speech? The question asks
you to analyze the speech to determine the author's main point.

To whom is President Obama delivering the speech? _____

_____

On what day is President Obama making the speech? _____

_____

What memory does President Obama share during his speech? _____

_____

_____

_____

After discussing his childhood memory, President Obama explains that he has given
many speeches about education and responsibility. Whose responsibility has he

talked about in the past? _____

_____

_____

Whose responsibility does he want to focus on in this speech? _____

_____

What point is President Obama trying to make in this speech? _____

_____

_____

A CLOSER LOOK

Why does the author believe that students must take responsibility for themselves? Underline the reasons and evidence the author provides to support his point.

Continue reading the speech. Then answer the question.

9 Every single one of you has something you're good at. Every single one of you has something to offer. And you have a responsibility to yourself to discover what that is. That's the opportunity an education can provide.

10 Where you are right now doesn't have to determine where you'll end up. No one's written your destiny for you. Here in America, you write your own destiny. You make your own future....

11 The story of America isn't about people who quit when things got tough. It's about people who kept going, who tried harder, who loved their country too much to do anything less than their best.

12 It's the story of students who sat where you sit 250 years ago, and went on to wage a revolution and found this nation. Students who sat where you sit 75 years ago who overcame a Depression and won a world war; who fought for civil rights and put a man on the moon. Students who sat where you sit 20 years ago who founded Google, Twitter, and Facebook and changed the way we communicate with each other....

13 So I expect you to get serious this year. I expect you to put your best effort into everything you do. I expect great things from each of you. So don't let us down—don't let your family or your country or yourself down. Make us all proud. I know you can do it.

What is the author's motivation for giving this speech?

The author discusses the history of the United States in order to _____.

A convince students to study United States history

B give a reason for why it's important to make your country proud

C explain the principals the United States was founded upon

D provide evidence that hard work pays off

 DISCUSS IT

Think about the reasons the author gives to support the main point. Talk with another student about these reasons. Which reasons do you find most convincing? Why?

A CLOSER LOOK

Several main topics related to caring for a pet turtle are included in the passage. In the margin, note the main topic presented in each paragraph.

Read the passage. Then answer the questions.

Caring for a Pet Turtle

1　Turtles are beloved by many people. But when you decide to make a turtle your pet, you're making a commitment for a very long time. Some turtles live longer than humans do! Therefore, it's important to know the specific care a pet turtle needs.

2　To care for a pet turtle, you need the proper equipment. Small turtles can be kept indoors in tanks or outdoors in closed off areas that have a pond. Large turtles can be kept indoors in large tanks or outdoors. However, turtles kept outdoors often need to hibernate during the winter. They can also be kept inside until the weather gets warmer.

3　A turtle needs a place to swim, a place to dry off, and a place to soak up sunlight. Turtles that live indoors must have access to artificial lighting that gives off UVB radiation, like the sun does naturally. To set up a tank or pond for a turtle, you need gravel, logs, or islands so the turtle can get out of the water, a water filter, and a water heater. A gravel vacuum cleaner makes cleaning a turtle's tank much easier.

4　Turtles need a good deal of exercise. Therefore, you need to provide a pet turtle with a place to move around. Most turtles appear to move awkwardly on land, but they are actually fast runners and good climbers. A turtle's tank or outdoor area needs to have enough room for them to swim and climb. If it doesn't, you should take them to a wading pool a few times every week.

5　Turtles need a variety of options when it comes to food. Young turtles eat meat only. Older turtles eat meat and vegetables. Experts recommend having at least six different kinds of food for a pet turtle. They agree that turtle pellets can be the main food, but it should be supplemented with other types of food. Strawberries, vegetables, fish, and crickets are some good options.

6　Caring for a pet turtle is a serious responsibility. Consider all the advice given here before getting a pet turtle. In addition, develop a relationship with a veterinarian who specializes in caring for these special reptiles.

> How does the title of the passage relate to the author's main point for writing?

1 Part A

Which answer *best* describes the author's main reason for writing the passage?

A   to convince readers to become owners of a pet turtle

B   to inform readers about the dangers of caring for a pet turtle

C   to teach readers that caring for a pet turtle can be fun

D   to explain to readers the proper care a pet turtle requires

> In caring for a pet turtle, what should a pet owner supply?

Part B

Which of the following from the passage *best* supports the answer to Part A?

A   "Most turtles appear to move awkwardly on land, but they are actually fast runners and good climbers."

B   "But when you decide to make a turtle your pet, you're making a commitment for a very long time."

C   "A turtle needs a place to swim, a place to dry off, and a place to soak up sunlight."

D   "Some turtles live longer than humans do!"

> What are the differences between a main point, a reason, and evidence?

2   What evidence does the author provide to support the point about feeding turtles?

A   "Turtles need a variety of options when it comes to food."

B   "Experts recommend having at least six different kinds of food."

C   "Young turtles eat meat only."

D   "Older turtles eat meat and vegetables."

> Often, the topic sentence of a paragraph summarizes the main idea of the paragraph.

3   What is the author's main point in paragraph 4?

_____

_____

_____

_____

Read the passage. Then answer the questions.

Solving the Problems of America's Roads

1   The problems with America's roads were not easy to solve. The country needed strong leadership. Solving these problems took time, money, and hard work.

2   The first step was taken by the police of New York City. They created "rules of the road." Slow vehicles had to keep to the right. Faster vehicles could pass on the left. Drivers must use hand signals when they turned, stopped, or slowed down.

3   Another problem was the many accidents that happened at intersections. The first electric traffic signals were installed in the city of Cleveland, Ohio. A red light meant *stop,* and a green light meant *go.* Other cities added traffic signals that had a third color light. This yellow light signaled *caution* or *slow down.*

4   In the early years of the automobile, there were no drivers' licenses. There were no age limits for drivers. There was no auto insurance. This soon changed. Automobile owners had to register their cars. New York was the first state to give drivers' licenses to certain drivers. Then New Jersey drivers had to have a license to drive. They had to pass an exam to get a license.

5 The US needed a road system. The Bureau of Public Roads was created in Washington, DC, in 1915. It worked with the states to take care of and organize the roads. Old roads were repaired, and new, paved ones were built. Lines were painted on the roads to mark traffic lanes. Speed limits were established. The limits were posted on signs. Roads were given route numbers. Major highways received US highway numbers. Routes that ran north to south were given odd numbers. Routes that ran east to west were given even numbers.

6 President Eisenhower knew there was a need for wide, smooth, well-marked highways. These highways must connect state-to-state and coast-to-coast. He was sure that this type of highway system would improve safety. It could help businesses and small towns grow.

7 The government created the US Interstate Highway System in 1956. Engineers began working on these Interstate highways. They tested road materials. They studied bridge and road plans. They built roads that were the same all across the country.

8 The US Interstate Highway System was to be the largest project in US history. It would take 40 years to build. It would have 54,000 bridges and 100 tunnels. More than 46,500 miles of Interstates would cross America. The roads would pass through every state in the nation.

1 Part A

What is the author's main point in paragraph 5?

A   to describe the road system that was put into place

B   to explain why the US needed a road system

C   to explain how to read a map

D   to describe the leader of the Bureau of Public Roads

Part B

Which of the following from the passage *best* supports the answer to Part A?

A   "The Bureau of Public Roads was created in Washington, DC, in 1915."

B   "Roads were given route numbers."

C   "The US needed a road system."

D   "It worked with the states to take care of and organize the roads."

2 In paragraph 6, which of the following reasons does the author give for why President Eisenhower thought highways were needed?

    A to make driving safer

    B to create a more beautiful driving experience

    C to help people learn how to drive

    D to keep people from getting lost

3 What are two pieces of evidence that support the point that some changes regarding roads began in New York?

_____

_____

_____

_____

4 What is the author's main point in paragraph 1, and what detail in the final paragraph supports that point?

_____

_____

_____

_____

LESSON 27

Integrating Information from Two Texts

Introduction

THEME: ≫ **Finding the Facts**

To learn about a subject, you use more than one source. Then you must **integrate,** or combine, the information you found to tell about the subject. You do this for many class assignments. For example, if you wanted to learn about model airplanes, you could get directions for building one from a book or on the Internet. You could also find books that talk about people's experience building them, operating them, or entering contests with them. Each source includes facts and details that the author thinks are important. Some of the information will be the same in two texts, and sometimes it will be different. You learn more about a subject by using several sources.

Look at two different sources used to write a paper about Roger Williams, the governor of the colony of Rhode Island. Then answer the questions that follow.

A. Biography of Williams
1. born and educated in England
2. became a chaplain
3. became a Puritan (disagreed with the Church of England)
4. went to New World to separate from Church of England (1630)
5. became preacher in Salem and Plymouth colonies (Massachusetts)
6. disagreed with some of the religious ideas of Massachusetts colonies
7. Massachusetts made him leave the colony
8. made friends with Native Americans
9. learned Native American languages
10. wrote book about Native American languages and culture
11. had strong ideas about separation of church and state
12. had 6 children and many grandchildren
13. died in Providence (1683)

B. Book about Roger Williams and colony of Rhode Island
1. Williams was forced to leave Massachusetts because of his beliefs
2. Williams paid Native Americans for land to establish his own colony
3. settlers each got same amount of land, bought from Native Americans
4. colony established trade with Native Americans
5. Williams got charter for Rhode Island from England
6. more people came to live in the colony
7. Williams served as chief officer from 1654–58
8. King Philip's War in Europe spilled into the colonies
9. Williams could not keep the peace, though he tried
10. Native Americans fought with Massachusetts and also in Rhode Island
11. Providence burned in the war, including Williams' house (1676)
12. colony was rebuilt

What information is in both sources? _____

_____

_____

How are the two sources different? _____

_____

_____

Use both sources to write a paragraph about Roger Williams.

_____

_____

_____

_____

Read the first passage. Then answer the questions.

adapted from LOU HENRY HOOVER

1 A woman nicknamed Daisy started the Girl Scouts of the USA, and a tomboy called Lou helped the organization grow.

2 Juliette Gordon was born on October 31, 1860. Her nickname was Daisy. She grew up in Savannah, Georgia. She was artistically talented and high spirited. After marrying William Low, she met Sir Robert Baden-Powell, an Englishman. He was the founder of the Boy Scouts and the English Girl Guides, the name for the girls' scouting program. Baden-Powell asked Daisy to start the Girl Scouts in the US.

3 In 1912, Daisy returned to Savannah from England to bring scouting to American girls. Daisy had never spent one day in an office organizing anything. But she crusaded across the nation. She wouldn't take no for an answer.

4 Lou Henry was born on March 29, 1874. She grew up in Waterloo, Iowa, and enjoyed the outdoor life. She was the first woman to receive a degree in geology from Stanford University. She traveled the world with her husband Herbert Hoover, who later became president of the US.

5 During World War I, Lou met Daisy. Lou believed in the ideas of scouting and became a national leader of the Girl Scouts. It was Lou who led the first national Girl Scout cookie drive in 1935.

6 Daisy and Lou brought together girls from the North and South who were wealthy and poor, black and white, athletic and handicapped. They helped instill confidence that all women can develop their potential to be whatever they wish to be.

Think About It

What information would you use in a report about the Girl Scouts? Ask what facts are most important.

How did Daisy start the Girl Scouts in America? _____

_____

What is special about how Daisy and Lou helped girls succeed? _____

_____

Read the second passage. Then answer the question.

The Cookies

A CLOSER LOOK

Reread the two passages. What information is the same in both passages? Underline important ideas in both.

1 To pay for activities, the Girl Scouts needed to make money. The sale of cookies began in 1917, five years after Juliette Gordon Low started Girl Scouting in the US. The first cookie sale was held by a troop in Oklahoma. The girls baked cookies and sold them in the high school cafeteria.

2 In July 1922, a sugar cookie recipe appeared in the national magazine. The article suggested scouts bake the cookies and sell them at a profit. To make six- to seven-dozen cookies it would cost between 26 and 36 cents. The girls could sell them for 25 to 30 cents per dozen to make a profit of at least $1.50 per dozen.

3 Over the next years, scouts throughout the country continued to bake cookies at home. They put them in wax paper bags, sealed them with a sticker, and sold them door to door for 25 to 35 cents per dozen.

4 In 1934, Girl Scouts in Philadelphia found a company to bake the cookies. This made it possible to make and sell more cookies. By 1936, the national Girl Scouts hired a baker to make the cookies. Now, scouts all over the country would sell the same cookies.

5 By 1935, hundreds of troops were selling the popular cookies. During World War II, there were shortages of sugar, flour, and butter. To raise money during this time, the girls sold calendars.

6 As the popularity of scouting grew, so did sales of cookies. Today, over 3.7 million Girl Scouts sell 200 million boxes of cookies each year. These sales earn the scouts more than $780 million!

Which title brings together ideas from both passages?

What is the *best* title for an essay that integrates the information in passage 1 with passage 2?

A Daisy and Lou

B The History of the Girl Scouts

C Scouting in the US

D Recipe for Success

 DISCUSS IT

Work with another student to integrate the two passages. Make an outline that covers topics in both passages. Discuss how the ideas could be tied together.

3

Read both passages. Then answer the questions.

Sections ☰ BLOG **The White House Blog** 🔍

Posted by Becky Fried at 1:15 PM

adapted from **"Meet Girl Scout Troop 2612 Bridge Designers, STEM Enthusiasts"**

In 2014, the White House held its fourth annual science fair. The focus of the fair was on women and girls in science, technology, engineering, and math (STEM). Five young Girl Scouts were invited to show their science project to President Obama. Here is their story.

1 Girl Scout Troop 2612 of Eastern Oklahoma put their scout motto of "Be Prepared" into action. They remembered the damaging summer floods of 2013 in Colorado. They noticed that because bridges had been washed out, the emergency crew was not able to rescue certain communities. The troop's robotics team set out to design a solution.

2 The team worked on the problem for months as part of a contest challenging students to create a solution to a natural disaster. Thousands of elementary-school-aged students from across the country were invited to take part in the contest. For the challenge, they had to explore how simple machines, motorized parts, engineering, and math can help solve the problems presented by natural disasters like floods or earthquakes.

3 The girls learned about robotics. Then they invented a Flood-Proof Bridge. To build a model of the bridge, they used motors and gears that worked just like the bridge. The girls learned how to write a simple computer program. A motion sensor in the riverbed gives instructions to the program. The program makes the bridge pull up when the water gets too high.

Total Views: 756

Blog Archive
▼ 2015
  ▶ December
  ▶ November
  ▶ October
  ▶ September

ADVERTISEMENT

Print   Share

A CLOSER LOOK

How are the two passages related? Circle at least two details in each text that you would combine to tell about the topic.

4 The girls' invention got them an invitation to the White House Science Fair in May 2014. The five who went to Washington were the only Girl Scouts at the fair. These 8-year-old girls were also the youngest students there. They proudly showed off their Flood-Proof Bridge and were excited to meet the president.

5 We asked a few members of the team some questions about their project and love of all things STEM.

6 *What inspires you? How do you hope to inspire others?*

- **Lucy Claire McGarrah Sharp, age 8.** "I am inspired when I read about biographies of women who have made things. I hope to inspire others by doing science and engineering and inventing so that girls can believe in themselves."

- **Claire Winton, age 8.** "I think about what I need to solve a problem. I would like to talk to other people about inventing."

- **Avery Dodson, age 8.** "I love seeing other people invent cool stuff. I've been reading about inventors like Kellogg, Levi Strauss, and Bette Nesmith Graham in school. They all invented really cool stuff that we use every day. I want to inspire others by letting them play with my inventions. It's cool to like girly stuff and building stuff at the same time."

Please Sign In to Comment

Comment Section 💬 15 Comments

▼ Newest First

Office of the President of the United States
Washington, DC
May 27, 2014

THE WHITE HOUSE

White House Announces Science Fair 2014

The White House Science Fair, being held today, brings together student winners of science, technology, engineering, and math (STEM) competitions from across the country. This year's fair is centered on women and girls in STEM. The fair is part of the president's efforts to get more girls and boys interested in STEM subjects. The president believes that support for STEM programs will help students succeed.

The fair will include over 100 students from more than 30 states. These students originally took part in more than 40 different STEM competitions and groups.

The president will view students' work. He will speak about the important role of STEM education in the country's future.

The president will also announce plans to support education and training in STEM subjects. Funding will help train teachers, and add programs for students.

"When students excel in math and science, they're laying the groundwork for helping America compete for the jobs and industries of the future," said President Obama. "That's why I'm proud to celebrate outstanding students at the White House Science Fair, and to announce new steps we are taking to help more young people succeed in these critical subjects."

The president will also announce a new program that connects STEM students around the world and puts them in touch with leading scientists. Using technology, students in the US, Malaysia, Australia, and the city of Barcelona will be able to interact and discuss ideas. Students will also learn about a day in the life of a scientist.

Some of the projects the president will see include:

- Student's "Sandless" Bag Keeps Salt Water off South Florida Streets
- Football Fanatic Seeks Safer Helmet after "Aha" Moment
- Girl Coders Build App to Help Visually Impaired Classmate
- Girl Scout Troop Designs Flood-Proof Bridge
- Overcoming Odds, North Dakota Kids Imagine City of the Future

Read Claire's quote and the last paragraph of passage 2.

1 Part A

Based on Claire Winton's statement, how might President Obama's program help students like Claire?

A The Girl Scouts will get more funding.

B The girls in Claire's troop will have more competitions they can enter.

C Meeting the president is an experience the girls won't forget.

D A new program will let Claire talk to other students around the world about her ideas for inventions.

Part B

What details from both texts *best* support the answer to Part A?

_____

_____

_____

_____

Look for similarities in each passage.

2 Which detail would *most likely* be in a report that integrates information from both passages?

A The title of the Girl Scouts' project, Flood-Proof Bridge.

B Information about how the girls learned how to write a simple computer program.

C Information about students in the US, Malaysia, Australia, and the city of Barcelona.

D Avery Dodson's quote about famous inventors.

What might the girls do in the future?

3 What does Avery Dodson's statement show about why the 2014 science fair was focused on girls?

_____

_____

_____

_____

Read the passages. Then answer the questions.

America's First Roads

1   Did you know that the first roads in America were rivers? In colonial America, towns grew along the seacoast and large rivers. Water travel was the way to move people and goods from place to place. People did not travel for fun—very few went far from home. Sometimes overland travel could not be avoided. Rivers did not flow in all the directions people needed to go.

2   Most paths followed Native American trails. Farmers used these paths to carry goods to market. Narrow dirt paths made travel very difficult and slow. People usually walked. Many roads were so small that carts, even horses, were too big for them. A traveler had to walk and lead the horse down the path!

3   Dirt roads were rough. They were full of ruts and holes, and many people wanted to fix them. Roads near waterways and swamps were fixed first. Rain made these roads extra muddy. Dry weather made other roads dusty. In winter, most roads could not be used.

4   The first American toll road was paved with wooden planks. It was built in 1786. The wooden planks allowed wheeled carts to roll easily. It kept them from getting stuck in the mud. The traveler paid a fee. Then he went through a turnstile to use the road. Toll roads were built by companies. These companies hoped to get the money they spent building the roads back in tolls.

5   In the 1800s, businessmen needed shorter, cheaper ways to send goods across America.

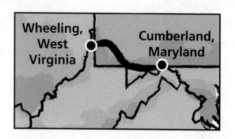

In 1818, the first National Road opened to travelers. It was the first federal road. Its nickname was "The Main Street of America." The National Road linked Cumberland, Maryland, to Wheeling, West Virginia (then part of Virginia). Later, it became Route 40.

6   Cities began to pave their busy roads with gravel and cobblestones. They built bridges. However, most roads were still muddy, bumpy dirt tracks. People, horses, bicycles, stray dogs, and other animals shared narrow streets. Roads were crowded.

7   By 1905, thousands of Americans owned automobiles. Streets were more crowded and more dangerous. New noises frightened horses and pedestrians. Automobiles stalled or broke down. They got stuck in ruts and mud. Roads were too narrow for two cars to move around each other. There were no rules of the road. There were lots of accidents. People and animals were hurt or killed. Drivers were scared. Across the country, people demanded better roads. State governments began to listen. Today, we have roads that connect just about every place you could imagine.

Traffic Safety Comes First

The town of Longview has a problem with traffic safety at their middle school. The school formed a committee to try to find a solution. This is a letter the committee wrote to the town.

March 12, 2015

Longview Traffic Committee
Longview Town Hall
Longview, OH 43215

To the Longview Traffic Committee:

Members of the Longview Middle School community are worried about the safety of our students. The driveway of our Middle School runs directly into the intersection of Route 8 and Maple Street. This is dangerous for anyone crossing the driveway on foot, in a car, or on a bicycle. In the last year, there have been several accidents here. One was serious. Too often, there are many near-accidents.

Right now, the county board and the town council are studying the problem. We are thankful that this intersection is part of a larger study of traffic flow along Route 8. However, we also recognize that this type of study takes time. Meanwhile, we are worried about the immediate safety of our community.

Both parents and community members share our views. Our students at the Middle School are at risk every day. There is no traffic signal at the intersection. There is no easy way to cross the street safely. It is dangerous all the time, especially during school drop-off and pick-up hours. School buses using the driveway add to the problem. The bus drivers have complained about this intersection. They, too, worry about safety.

Our school bus drivers often have to wait for a very long time before they can safely turn into or out of the driveway. Sometimes, this has caused students to be late to class. It also often causes a traffic jam at the end of the school day.

Essentially, we have a four-way intersection with no traffic signals. This is a problem that needs attention now.

We hope that you can look at some short-term solutions while we are waiting for the final report from the county board. Our school committee has come up with several ideas. We hope you will find some of them acceptable.

We look forward to working with the town committee. We all want to find solutions to keep our community and our students safe.

Sincerely,
Longview Middle School
Safety Committee

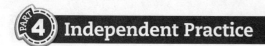

1 What was the biggest problem with the early roads in the US?

  A They were not paved and difficult for any kind of travel.

  B They were only for horses.

  C There was too much traffic on them.

  D They cost too much money.

2 Part A

What detail in the final paragraph of passage 1 would you include in an oral report that combines the topics of both passages?

  A "By 1905, thousands of Americans owned automobiles."

  B "New noises frightened horses and pedestrians."

  C "Automobiles stalled or broke down."

  D "Across the country, people demanded better roads."

Part B

What detail from passage 2 *best* supports the answer to Part A?

_____

_____

_____

_____

3 What idea links the two passages?

  A road safety

  B the cost of building roads

  C the importance of roads

  D problems with roads

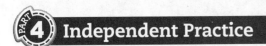

4 Explain what roads in the early days of the country have in common with the intersection at Longview Middle School. Give details that you would include in an essay.

_____

_____

_____

_____

_____

_____

CCLS RI.4.7–9

Integration of Knowledge and Ideas in Informational Text

Read both passages. Then answer the questions.

Tips for Using Your Digital Camera

- Know your camera! Always read the instruction book. Find out what all the different switches, buttons, and controls do. Learn how to use the flash.
- First, set the date and time! Every week or so, check the time setting.
- Practice taking photographs before using the camera.
- Use the camera's highest resolution. This setting gives the sharpest pictures. Check the instruction book for how to do this.
- Keep your camera battery charged. Be sure to have a spare battery handy.
- Make sure the camera's lens is clean! Use lens paper to carefully wipe it off.
- Learn about the camera's scene settings. This helps you quickly switch between a close-up of an object and a picture of a larger scene.
- Experiment with the settings on the camera's zoom lens.
- Usually, the optical zoom is better than digital zoom. Digital zoom can increase or decrease the size of the image. You can do the same thing with software.

- Check the camera's viewfinder (the little window you look through). The camera sees more than you see. Experiment to find out the difference. Every camera is a little different.
- Use the camera's flash to brighten nearby subjects that are in the shade. The flash can help remove shadows.
- Always have a spare memory card handy. You never know when you will need it.
- A tripod is very important in dim light. The camera needs more time to take a photo in dim light. A tripod will hold the camera steady. If you don't have a tripod, rest the camera on something that doesn't move, for example a fence post or a car roof.

- Regularly download your photos to a computer disk drive. Be sure to back up these photos onto a second computer or disk. A CD-ROM can store hundreds of photos.
- It's very easy to use software to touch up and change your photos. But remember for a science project, you must always explain why you made these changes.

Have Fun Doing Science with a Camera

adapted from My NASA Data
contributed by Forrest M. Mims III

1. Make a Cloud Photo Album

   Make photographs of various kinds of clouds. Practice with different settings in different kinds of light. See how many different kinds of clouds you can find. Print out your pictures and organize them. Which ones are high in the sky? Which ones are low in the sky? Are they different colors? Look up the names and label your photos.

2. Make a Tree Photo Album

   There are hundreds of types of trees. Take a picture of each kind you find. Make a note of where the tree is so you can photograph it again later.

   Try to get a shot of the whole tree. Don't forget to take a picture of a leaf from each tree. You might also want to take a close-up of the bark. Print out your photos. Put the shots of the leaf, bark, and whole tree together in one group. Do this for each kind of tree you have. Then label each group with the name of the tree. Use the Internet or books about trees to help you match the names with the trees.

3. Make a Sunset Photo Album

   Find the spot you want to photograph and set up your camera 30 minutes before sunset. You never know when the best and most beautiful light will be. The light changes very quickly as the sun sinks lower and lower. If you have a tripod, use it. Make as many photographs as you can during that time.

   Keep an eye on the weather. Sunsets can have different colors and patterns in the sky. Clear days can have pretty sunsets, but often the sunsets on days when there is dust or smoke in the air make even prettier sunsets. Try to zoom in on these sunsets. Take some photographs that include the cloud patterns.

Arrange your photographs according to the kind of clouds in the sunset. What can you tell about the sunset from the cloud patterns? Compare the sunset photos to your photos of clouds at different times of the day. Use the Internet or other books to get more information about how dust in the air affects sunsets.

1 What is an appropriate title for a report that integrates information from both passages?

   A   How to Protect and Use a Camera

   B   How to Make Cloud and Tree Photo Albums

   C   Using a Camera's Settings for Science Projects

   D   Using a Camera's Features and Settings

2 Which tips from passage 1 would be the *most* useful for making a tree photo album?

   A   tips about using a tripod

   B   tips about using batteries

   C   tips about posting photos

   D   tips about using a zoom lens

3 What kind of photographs will a tripod help take? Use the picture and details from the text to explain your answer.

   _____

   _____

   _____

4 How could you use the tips in passage 1 to do one of the projects in passage 2? Use specific examples from the text.

   _____

   _____

   _____

   _____

Read the passage. Then answer the questions.

Codes & Ciphers

1   Throughout history, world events have changed because of secret messages—secrets that were kept and secrets that were not. In the world of diplomacy, knowing what your enemy is planning helps you to prepare. But it is also important that your enemies do not know what you have planned.

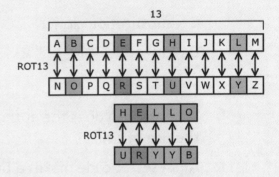

What are codes?

2   Message codes are any symbol or signal used to represent or communicate something else. Any word could be considered a code word. The code word given to a four-legged furry creature that barks is the letters D-O-G. Because you know that those three letters represent a real dog, you understand the code!

3   Sometimes, however, it is important that only a few people understand the message. In the world of cryptology, codes are used to make messages secret by changing the words into something else. But, in order for your friends to understand the coded message, they need the key! If your friends have the key, and others do not, your messages become secret.

4   How well you've created your code and key will determine how long your message stays a secret from others.

What is a cipher?

5   A cipher is a way to make a word or message secret by changing or rearranging the letters in the message. (A code affects the word, not the individual letters.) One type of cipher, called a transposition cipher, is created by simply rearranging the letters in the word itself. For example, the letters CHYPRAGTOPRY can be unscrambled to reveal the word CRYPTOGRAPHY. Another cipher, the substitution cipher, is more difficult. It involves changing the letters of your message into something else by substituting other letters, numbers, or symbols. Using a substitution cipher, the word CRYPTOGRAHY might look like DOHQMRZOFQYH. In this example C=D, R=O, Y=H, and so on.

6   To understand the message, they must know how you created the cipher. In our substitution cipher, your friend would need to know the key, or how the system is set up (A=F, etc.). If only you and your friend have the key, then it is very difficult for others to read your message.

5 What kind of cipher is shown in the figure?

    A transposition cipher

    B code

    C substitution cipher

    D cipher key

6 What reason does the author give for the importance of secrecy in the use of codes?

    A A secret code makes a puzzle fun to solve.

    B A secret code can keep information from an enemy.

    C A strong key can prevent others from breaking the code.

    D A secret code can change events of the world.

7 What evidence supports the point that a substitution cipher is more difficult to decode than a transposition cipher?

    A A transposition cipher rearranges the letters in a word.

    B A substitution cipher requires a key.

    C A substitution cipher keeps messages secret from others.

    D A transposition cipher matches one letter with a different letter.

8 What is the main point of this passage?

_____

_____

_____

_____

This unit will help you with all your writing. You will learn why it is important to edit your work. You will learn more about the different types of writing. All writers write with a purpose, and these lessons will help you understand these different types of writing. You will also learn more about the rules of English. These rules help make your writing clear for the reader.

LESSON 28 The Writing Process takes you through the five steps of the writing process. You will learn about prewriting, drafting, revising, editing, and publishing. You use this process every time you write.

LESSON 29 Argumentative Writing helps you learn more about argumentative writing. It will explain how to write a piece that persuades someone to take action or to respond. It will help you determine your argument and support it with facts and examples.

LESSON 30 Informational Writing is about the type of writing you do most in class. You will learn about the characteristics of this type of writing. You will also learn how to organize your writing so it is clear to the reader.

LESSON 31 Narrative Writing will help you write a story with a clear beginning, middle, and end.

LESSON 32 Rules of English reviews the grammar and writing conventions that help you write clear and well-thought-out sentences.

LESSON 33 Vocabulary focuses on vocabulary development. You will learn about word relationships and context clues. You will also create new words by using affixes.

LESSON 28

The Writing Process

 Introduction

The writing process is the series of steps you follow to shape your words into writing that is clear and interesting. Most writers follow these five steps:

Prewriting → Drafting → Revising → Editing → Publishing

An easy way to remember the writing process is to think of what you do in each step. In the prewriting step, you **plan** what you will write. The drafting step is when you actually **write.** Then you go back and **revise,** or make changes in the revising step. Next, you check, or **edit,** your writing. You check your writing for spelling, grammar, capitalization, and punctuation errors. Finally, you show, or **publish,** your work.

Step 1: Prewriting

In the prewriting stage, you need to think about these things to plan what you will write:

- Why are you writing? This is called your purpose.
- What will you write about? This is called your subject.
- What will you say? This is called your content.
- How will you say it? This is called your voice.
- Who will read it? This is called your audience.

Sometimes, however, you are writing for a test. Then some of these things are already decided for you. Here is a question from a test.

> Think about a time when you were excited about something that you learned, discovered, or saw. Write a story for your class about what you learned and how you felt about it. In your paper, be sure to:
>
> - write about a specific experience you had
> - arrange the details in time order
> - include a conclusion

The question tells you the purpose is to write a story. It also tells you the subject is a time you were excited about something that you learned, discovered, or saw. The audience is your class. The rest is up to you. You need to think about what you will write about and how you will say it. Many writers begin by underlining important words. Look at the words underlined in the question. Writers also make notes about what they will write.

You can use a graphic organizer to plan your writing. A graphic organizer helps you arrange your ideas. A sequence chart is helpful when you write a story. It helps you map out events in the order in which they happen.

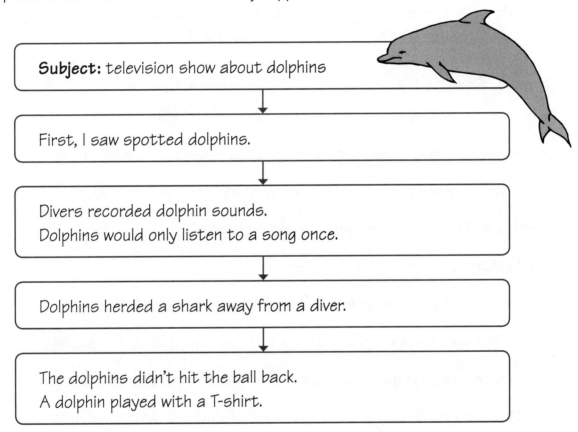

Subject: television show about dolphins

First, I saw spotted dolphins.

Divers recorded dolphin sounds.
Dolphins would only listen to a song once.

Dolphins herded a shark away from a diver.

The dolphins didn't hit the ball back.
A dolphin played with a T-shirt.

There are other types of graphic organizers you can use depending on what you are writing. Here are some examples:

- **Cluster map or web**—This organizer works for many kinds of writing. It can help you to get your ideas on paper.
- **Venn diagram**—A Venn diagram is a way to organize your ideas when you want to compare and contrast two things.
- **Time line**—A time line works well when you are writing a narrative. It helps you map out events in the order they happen.
- **Cause-and-effect chart**—This shows you the connection between what happened and the effect it had on other things.

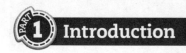

Step 2: Drafting

After you have made a plan, it is time for the next step. Now, it is time to write. This step is called **drafting.** Put your ideas into sentences and paragraphs. Don't worry about spelling and grammar yet. You can change your writing later. In this step, you just write down your ideas. You use the prewriting plan as a guide.

There are two ways to make a draft. One way is to just start writing. You let your ideas flow freely, writing them down as you think of them. However, you will probably need to spend more time revising what you have written.

The other way is to work from the prewriting plan you made. Here is a draft that could be written based on the sequence chart on page 291.

Last week, I watched an exciting television show about dolphins. The first thing I saw was spotted dolphins swiming by the divers' boat. It was on the water. I never knew there were spotted dolphins. Then all of the divers went under water to record the dolphins' sounds. The divers whistled and squeaked! I laughed when the divers said that Dolphins would listen to a song, but only once!

After that, I saw a dolphin protect a diver from a shark. The diver was underwater alone when a shark swam near him. Than a few dolphins came and herded the shark away. It was fun to see the divers try to play with the dolphins. First, they tried to play ball, but the dolphins didnt hit the ball back. They played also music for the dolphins to see how they liked it. Then one of the divers let go of a T-shirt and it floated away in the water Pretty soon, a dolphin took the T-shirt in his teeth and swam back near the diver and let go of it.

Step 3: Revising

After you finish writing your draft, the next step is revising. In this step, you read what you have written and decide on the changes you want to make. You edit your writing to make it clear to your readers.

When you revise, you might need to make changes to the content of your work. The content includes the ideas and details. You might also need to revise its structure, or organization. You can ask yourself the following questions to decide what changes to make to improve your draft.

Content

- Does my writing have a main idea?
- Did I include enough supporting details?
- Do I need to add an important detail or example?
- Did I include unimportant details that should come out?
- Does my writing have an introduction and a conclusion?

Structure

- Is my writing organized in a way that fits the topic?
- Are my ideas organized in a way that is easy to follow?
- Do I need to add words, phrases, or sentences to make them clearer?
- Do my sentences clearly express my ideas?
- Are my sentences well written?

Peer Review

The teacher might sometimes have students work in pairs to edit each other's papers. This is called peer editing or peer review. Students use a checklist, or rubric, to do this. The rubric explains what is needed to receive a certain scores on a writing paper.

The rubric tells what is expected for a range of scores. Sometimes one rubric is used for the whole writing task. Other times two rubrics are used. One is for the content and how it is developed. The other is for grammar, punctuation, and capitalization. Rubrics for writing may differ but they should look something like the one on page 294.

SAMPLE RUBRIC

Score 3

- The writing answers all parts of the question.
- The opening sentences clearly convey the topic.
- The supporting details are in time order and all relate directly to the main idea.
- Details about when and where events took place are included.
- Words are used correctly and well.
- There are almost no mistakes in grammar, capitalization, punctuation, and spelling.

Score 2

- The writing answers almost all parts of the question.
- The opening sentences convey the topic.
- Most supporting details relate directly to the main idea and are in time order.
- Some details about when and where events took place are included.
- Some words are misused.
- There are some mistakes in grammar, capitalization, punctuation, and spelling.

Score 1

- The writing answers only part of the question.
- The opening sentences do not relate to the topic.
- Many supporting details do not relate directly to the main idea and are not in time order.
- The writer doesn't include details about when and where events took place.
- Many words are overused or misused.
- There are several mistakes in grammar, capitalization, punctuation, and spelling.

Step 4: Editing

You have revised your work. Once you are happy with it, you can do the next step. You can edit your work. That means you read what you have written. You check to be sure everything is right. You look for grammar mistakes. You also look for mistakes in spelling, capitalization, and punctuation. You edit to make sure that:

- subjects and verbs agree
- the pronoun forms are right
- all words are spelled correctly
- proper nouns are capitalized

When you edit, you go over each sentence. You look for mistakes to be changed. This is called **proofreading.** When you proofread, you use marks to show changes. The chart below shows you some marks to use.

Proofreading Symbols	
∧ Add letters or words.	The dolphins ∧ beautiful. *(were)*
⊙ Add a period.	I heard them whistle⊙
≡ Capitalize a letter.	Then i̲ was scared.
⊂ Close up space.	They swam under‿water.
⌄ Add a comma.	He wanted to play⌄ but the dolphin didn't.
/ Make a capital letter lowercase.	He wanted to play, but the Ðolphin didn't.
¶ Begin a new paragraph.	¶ The diver was all alone.
⌐ᶴ Delete letters or words.	The diver was all al̶l̶ alone.
∿ Switch the position of letters or words.	They played also music.

Step 5: Publishing

Once you have fixed any mistakes or problems with your work, you are ready to publish it. Publishing means to share your work with other people. This is the last stage of writing. You might turn your paper into your teacher. Or, you may read it to the class. Maybe, you are asked to create a poster or PowerPoint presentation with your work. Publishing can take many forms.

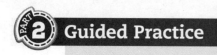

Read the revision. Look for changes. Then answer the questions.

Last week, I watched an exciting television show about

dolphins. The first thing I saw was spotted dolphins swim~~m~~ing by

the divers' boat. ~~It was on the water~~ I never knew there were

spotted dolphins. Then all of the divers went under water to

record the dolphins' sounds. The divers whistled and squeaked!

I laughed when the divers said that Ðolphins would listen to a

song, but only once!

After that, I saw a dolphin protect a diver from a shark. The

diver was underwater alone when a shark swam near him. Th~~a~~n a

few dolphins came and herded the shark away. It was fun to see

the divers try to play with the dolphins. **at the end of the show** First, they tried to play

ball, but the dolphins didn't hit the ball back. They played also

music for the dolphins to see how they liked it. Then one of the

divers let go of a T-shirt and it floated away in the water Pretty

soon, a dolphin took the T-shirt in his teeth and swam back near

the diver and let go of it.

I learned so much about dolphins in this television show. I

wouldn't have missed it for anything! In the fall, there is

going to be another show about the dolphins at Marina Park.

Every sentence should support the main idea with essential information.

1 Why did the writer take out a sentence in paragraph 1?

_____

_____

_____

_____

The idea should relate to the main point or details in a paragraph. The ideas should build on each other.

2 Why was a sentence moved from paragraph 2 to paragraph 1?

_____

_____

_____

_____

Sometimes a writer adds more support for the main idea or to create a stronger argument.

3 Why was a phrase added to paragraph 2?

_____

_____

_____

_____

The writer has introduced his idea and developed it, but something is missing.

4 Why did the writer add the third paragraph?

_____

_____

_____

_____

3 Independent Practice

Read the question carefully. Then answer the questions.

Most people have met someone that they admire greatly. Write an essay for your teacher about a real or an imagined experience you've had with someone you admire. When you write your essay, be sure to do the following:

- follow every step of the writing process
- include a main idea
- put the details of the essay in sequence

1 What are you being asked to write about?

_____

_____

2

┌─────────────────────────┐
│ **Subject:**   │
└─────────────────────────┘
            │
            ▼
┌─────────────────────────┐
│   │
└─────────────────────────┘
            │
            ▼
┌─────────────────────────┐
│   │
└─────────────────────────┘
            │
            ▼
┌─────────────────────────┐
│   │
└─────────────────────────┘
            │
            ▼
┌─────────────────────────┐
│   │
└─────────────────────────┘

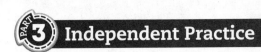

3 Now that you have thought about the topic and organized your ideas, write
a draft of your essay.

_____

_____

_____

_____

_____

_____

_____

_____

_____

_____

_____

_____

_____

_____

Revising, Editing, and Publishing

- Revise your draft to organize your writing. Is your central idea clear? Do
  the facts and details support your central idea? Are your sentences well
  written?

- Proofread to check for correct spelling, grammar, capitalization, and
  punctuation. Have a peer edit your work if appropriate.

- To publish, write or type your final answer on a separate sheet of paper
  and turn it in to your teacher.

LESSON 29

Argumentative Writing

Part 1 Introduction

When you write to **persuade,** you are writing to convince someone to respond or take action. An example of **argumentative writing** is a student's letter to the principal asking her to improve the lunch choices by adding yogurt and sandwich wraps to the menu. An email message, a column in the newspaper, and a letter to the editor of the school newspaper are examples of argumentative writing.

You need a strong argument to persuade the reader to agree with something or take action on an issue. You need to organize your ideas in a logical order. The topic sentence should state your opinion on the subject. Your **opinion** is what you think or feel about a subject. A strong argument is supported with facts, reasons, and examples. **Facts** are statements that can be proven. **Reasons** explain why your argument or opinion makes good sense. If you want the reader to agree with your point of view, you must support it. You should also think about the opposing point of view and offer points of your own that counter these opposing points of view. Your last sentence should be a strong ending that sums up your argument.

Part 2 Guided Practice

Read the question. Then answer the questions.

You have been asked to write a letter to your school newspaper to convince students that wearing a school uniform is a good idea. Be sure to:

- state your opinion clearly in the first sentence
- use facts, reasons, and examples to support your opinion

Here is one student's letter to the school community:

Dear students,

I believe that students should wear uniforms to school. There are many good reasons why it would be better to wear school uniforms. First, we would save time deciding what to wear every morning. We wouldn't go crazy trying on outfits! Second, even with uniforms, students can still show their individuality. They can choose their sneakers, backpacks, and jackets. Third, wearing uniforms helps make students feel like they are part of a community. It's like being on the same team. Another point is that students wouldn't compete over who has the coolest clothes. Students like to fit in. We should have school uniforms so no one will feel left out if they don't have the latest fads. When students aren't judged by their clothes, everyone is happier.

If students wear uniforms, their families will save money. Many families don't have lots of money to spend on clothes. Buying lots of different outfits can add up. Uniforms are not expensive. School uniforms are something that everyone can agree on!

Sincerely,

Zach Ryan

What is the student's opinion?

1 What is the topic sentence?

_____

_____

How does the student introduce his reasons?

2 List the words that lead from one supporting reason to another.

_____

What supporting statements back up the student's opinion?

3 What reason or fact does the student focus on in his last paragraph or conclusion?

_____

_____

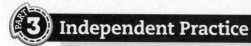

Read the question. Follow the writing process in Lesson 28 to craft your writing. Write your response on a separate piece of paper.

Write a letter to the principal of your school asking him to let the students organize an after-school club. Be sure to:

- describe the club

- state your argument clearly

- support it with facts, reasons, and examples

Informational Writing

 Introduction

Textbooks, newspaper articles, and cookbooks are examples of **informational writing.** When you are asked to write a report on a subject, you are writing an informational piece. You also use this type of writing when you answer a question on a test.

Informational writing is based on facts, examples, and details. It should be clear and easy to read. There are several ways to organize an informational piece. You might use main idea and supporting details or cause and effect. You could also choose to compare and contrast the information or organize it by a sequence of steps.

 Guided Practice

Read the question. Then answer the questions.

Your class has been reading about wildlife and biologists who study it. Using the information you learned, explain how and why biologists identify animals they study. Be sure to:

- include a main idea
- use facts and details to support it
- organize the details in a logical order

Here is what one student wrote:

    Wildlife biologists need to identify individual animals to learn how animals behave. They can tell who the animals are by their markings. For example, each zebra has a unique pattern of stripes. Biologists can identify an individual zebra by the markings on the "saddle area" on its back. They can tell a cheetah by the pattern of dots on its face, chest, and legs. The shape of a rhinoceros's horns helps identify a particular rhino.

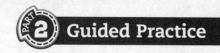

When animals in a group all look alike, scientists give them identification tags. They attach plastic tags to the fins of fish, metal tags to the ears of small animals like foxes, and numbered rings to the legs of birds.

Scientists keep the information about each animal on file cards. They take the cards with them when they go out to track wildlife. Then they know if they have seen the same animal before in a different place. When they meet the same animal a few times, they can learn more about how it behaves. They can find out how far an animal travels and if it stays with the same group or joins a new group. Sometimes biologists identify a new baby and can learn how it behaves as it grows up.

What does paragraph 1 mainly discuss?

1 What is the main idea expressed in paragraph 1? List a detail that supports it.

Paragraph 1: _____

Detail: _____

_____

What examples does paragraph 2 give?

2 What is the main idea expressed in paragraph 2? List a detail that supports it.

Paragraph 2: _____

Detail: _____

_____

How does this paragraph discuss information in other two paragraphs?

3 What is the main idea expressed in paragraph 3? List a detail that supports it.

Paragraph 3: _____

Detail: _____

_____

Read the chart and question. Follow the writing process in Lesson 28 to craft your writing. Write your response on a separate piece of paper.

Your teacher has asked you to give younger students some advice about healthy eating. Write two or three paragraphs explaining how to choose a healthy diet. Base your information on the healthy eating chart. Be sure to:

- have your topic sentence state the main idea of your paragraphs

- arrange the details in a logical order that younger readers will be able to follow

The latest government report advises people to eat more grains, vegetables, and fruit, and less meat. The chart below shows the five main food groups. It also shows how much of each food group people should eat every day.

Grains Make half your grains whole	Vegetables Vary your veggies	Fruits Focus on fruits	Milk Get your calcium	Meat & Beans Go lean with protein
Eat 6 oz. Eat at least 3 oz of whole-wheat grain, cereals, breads, crackers, rice, or pasta. 1 oz is about 1 slice of bread, or $\frac{1}{2}$ cup of cooked rice.	Eat $2\frac{1}{2}$ cups. Eat more dark green veggies like broccoli and other dark leafy greens. Eat more orange vegetables like carrots. Eat more dry beans and peas.	Eat 2 cups. Eat a variety of fruit. Choose fresh, frozen, canned, or dried fruit. Go easy on fruit juices.	Get 3 cups. For kids aged 2–8, it's 2. Go low-fat or fat-free when you choose milk, yogurt, or milk products, choose lactose-free products or other calcium sources, such as fortified foods and vegetables.	Eat $5\frac{1}{2}$ oz. Choose low-fat or lean meats and poultry. Bake it, broil it, or grill it. Vary your protein: choose more fish, beans, peas, nuts, and seeds.

LESSON 31

Narrative Writing

 Introduction

Narrative writing tells a story. Narratives can be a fictional, or make-believe, story or a story based on real events. This is called a **creative narrative.** You can also write about events that have happened to you in story form. This is called a **personal narrative.** A personal narrative is written in first person, using the pronouns *I* and *me.* For instance, you might write a personal narrative about the events of a sleepover you had with a friend or a trip to an amusement park.

When you write a narrative, be sure that it has a clear beginning, middle, and end. Many narratives tell the events in time order. They may also include details about the **setting,** the place and time that the event took place. It may also include **dialogue,** the words the characters speak.

 Guided Practice

Read the question. Then answer the questions.

Write a story about a time when you went on an interesting trip or rode on a bus, a train, a subway, or a plane. Be sure to:

- organize your details in time order
- include details about the time and place and your feelings

Here is what one student wrote:

I took my first train trip by myself last week. I had a few problems. I'd taken the train many times with my dad, but this time I went to visit Aunt Carla alone. Dad walked me to the train car. He embarrassed me by pointing me out to a conductor and telling him I was 10 years old. Then I got on the train and went down the aisle until I found a seat by the window. Dad waved at me until the train left the station at 9:02 a.m.

When we got going, I dove into my backpack for my mp3 player. I pushed "On" and then I realized I left the new batteries on the kitchen table. Then I pulled out a book and looked for my glasses. I thought I felt them but all I came up with was my toothbrush. I forgot my glasses, too. I felt a little upset. If Dad had been with me, we would have talked or played a game.

Finally, I leaned my head on the window and watched the scenery whiz by. The train made that "whump, whump, whump" sound over the tracks. I counted how many snowmen I saw in the backyards we passed. After that I guess I fell asleep. The next thing I knew the conductor was asking me, "Weren't you getting off in Indianapolis?" My eyes popped open and I saw my aunt standing on the train platform. Lucky for me, the train had just pulled in to the station.

What does the student write about?	**1** What specific event is the focus of the student's story? _____ _____
What helps you know when events occurred?	**2** What words or phrases show the order of the events in the story? _____ _____

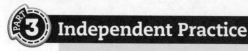
Read the question. Follow the writing process described in Lesson 28 to craft your writing. Write your response on a separate sheet of paper.

Think about a time when you earned something. Write a narrative about a time when you earned something you wanted and how you felt as you worked toward your goal. In your writing, be sure to:

- tell events in time order

- give a sense of the setting

- use details

- include a beginning, middle, and ending

LESSON 32 Rules of English

1 Introduction

Every language has rules to help you become a better writer if you follow them.

Capitalization

Always capitalize the first word of a sentence.

Incorrect	sometimes a map is useful.
Correct	Sometimes a map is useful.

Capitalize the names of people, places, and particular things, such as days of the week, holidays, and months of the year.

People	**Places**	**Things, Ideas, Groups**
Spanish	Ohio	October
Peyton Manning	New Zealand	Sunday
Sacajawea	Missouri River	Thanksgiving

Punctuation

A sentence begins with a capital letter and ends with a punctuation mark.

A sentence that makes a statement or gives a command ends with a period.

Statement	I like strawberries and cereal for breakfast**.**
Command	Don't forget to take an umbrella**.**

A sentence that asks a question ends with a question mark.

Question	Are you going to try out for the school play**?**

A sentence that expresses a strong feeling ends with an exclamation mark.

Exclamation	I can't believe I lost my backpack**!**

Commas

A **comma** is used to separate the speaker and what is said.

Jeremy said**,** "Caroline is at the store."

A comma is used to separate the city and state in an address. It is also used to separate the street and the city.

143 Sunset Strip**,** Los Angeles**,** California
58 Plymouth Road**,** Bristol**,** Connecticut

You use commas in compound sentences. A compound sentence is two complete sentences joined by a comma and a conjunction such as *and, or, but,* or *so.*

> **Compound Sentence**   I built a birdhouse**, and** a sparrow came to live in it.

Quotation Marks

Quotation marks are used to separate what is said from the speaker.

> Robbie asked, **"**Are you coming to the baseball game?**"**

Quotation marks are used to set off something that is quoted.

> The author wrote that **"**the sun was streaked with red and orange.**"**

Subject and Predicate

Every sentence has two parts: a complete subject and a complete predicate.

The **subject** tells the person, place, thing, or idea the sentence is about. It is a noun or a pronoun.

> **People** work to keep the ocean clean.

The **predicate** tells what the subject of the sentence is, has, or does. It is a verb.

> The oceans **cover** about three quarters of Earth.

A **complete subject** is one or more words that tell who or what is doing the action in the sentence. The key word in the complete subject is the simple subject. The simple subject is often a **noun,** but it can be a pronoun.

In the following sentences, the complete subject is underlined and the simple subject is in bold type.

> <u>**Jill**</u> went to band rehearsal.
> <u>**She**</u> went to band rehearsal.
>
> <u>The tallest **boy**</u> played the tuba.
> <u>**He**</u> played the tuba.

A **complete predicate** can be one word or several words that tell what the subject of the sentence does or is. The key word in the complete predicate is the simple predicate, or **verb.** Sometimes the verb may be one word, or it may have a helping verb. Some examples are *has* carried, *were* seen, *was* going, and *can* jump.

In the following sentences, the complete predicate is underlined and the simple predicate is in bold type.

Ana **pitched** the ball fast.
Ana **has pitched** the game today.

Verbs such as *pitched* are called **action verbs.** Action verbs tell about doing something. Often, a noun follows an action verb. This noun is called the object of the verb. It tells *what* or *whom* receives the action of the verb. In these sentences, the action verb is underlined and the object of the verb is in bold type.

What *did I buy?*
I bought six **tickets.**

Whom *did the crowd applaud?*
The crowd applauded the **band.**

Verbs such as *is, were,* and *seem* are called **linking verbs.** These verbs link the subject to a noun or adjective that comes after it. In these sentences, each linking verb is underlined. The word that the verb connects to the subject is in bold type.

The conductor is a funny **man.** (*is* links *man* and *conductor*)
The instruments are **old.** (*are* links *instruments* and *old*)

Relative Pronouns

Relative clauses begin with a question word and they modify a noun or pronoun.

Relative pronouns are *who, whose, whom, which,* and *that.* These pronouns relate back to persons or things that were referred to earlier.

We saw **that** the car that won the race.
The woman **whose** dinner was late became angry.

The pronouns *who, whose,* and *whom* are used to refer to a person.

The pronoun *that* is used to refer to an animal or thing.

The pronoun *which* is used to refer to animals, things, and ideas.

Relative Adverbs

Relative adverbs are *where, when,* and *why.* They modify a noun by telling where something happened, when it happened, or why it happened.

Adverbs tell about a verb. They answer the question how, when, or why.

There is a castle in the town **where** I lived.
I will be happy **when** school is out.
I understand **why** you are mad.

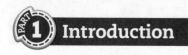

Adjectives

Adjectives are words that describe or tell about a noun or a pronoun. They can give an opinion. They can tell the size, age, or shape of something. Adjectives can tell what it is made of and its purpose. Choosing specific, colorful adjectives makes your writing come alive for readers. The more exact your adjectives are, the better your writing will be. In the examples below, the adjective is in bold type, and the noun it describes is underlined.

Adjective   The **red** <u>sun</u> dropped into the sea.

When two adjectives describe a noun, use a comma to separate them.

Adjectives   The **fiery, red** <u>sun</u> sank below the horizon.

You can tell when to use a comma. If you would place *and* or *but* between two adjectives, then use a comma.

Sometimes you use more than one adjective to describe something. Then it is important to put the adjectives in order. There is a general order for placing adjectives.

Adjectives that offer an **opinion** about something come first. These are followed by adjectives that give a **physical description.** These are adjectives that tell the size, shape, age, and color of something. Adjectives that tell where something came from are next in the order. These are followed by adjectives that tell what material it is made of and its purpose.

Opinion	Size	Age	Shape	Color	Origin	Material	Purpose	Noun
a beautiful,		old,			Irish,	knit		sweater
Opinion		**Age**			**Origin**	**Material**		

May, Must, and Can

The words *may, must,* and *can* tell the condition of something.

Can means "to be able to." It means that you are able to do something.

Can Jessie drive?

May means "to be allowed to." It means to have permission to do something.

May Jessie borrow the car?

May also shows that there something is likely or possible.

It **may** rain on Saturday.

Must means "have to." It is something that has to be done.

I **must** wash my clothes.

Prepositional Phrases

A prepositional phrase is a group of words that begins with a preposition and ends with the noun or pronoun that is the object of the preposition. Adjectives that describe the object are also part of the prepositional phrase.

Compare the following prepositional phrases. In each phrase, the preposition is in bold type and its object is underlined. In the second example for each phrase, notice the words that describe the object.

in the <u>house</u>   **in** Walter's old <u>house</u>
with a <u>jacket</u>   **with** a big, warm <u>jacket</u>

Common prepositions include:

about	behind	down	near	to
above	beneath	for	of	through
across	beside	from	on	under
around	between	in	out	up
at	by	inside	over	with

Sometimes you can combine two sentences by turning one into a prepositional phrase. Then you add the phrase to the sentence that comes before or after it.

Two Sentences   Dad has a tool shed. It is in the backyard.
One Sentence   Dad has a tool shed in the backyard.

Frequently Confused Words

Homophones are words that sound alike. However, they are spelled differently. They also have different meanings.

To means "toward" or is used with a verb like *to walk.*
Too means "also" or "more than enough."
Two means "the sum of 1 + 1."

Here means "in this place."
Hear means "to listen."

There means "in that place."
Their means "belonging to them."
They're means "they are."

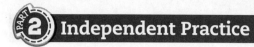

Place the adjectives in the proper order to complete the sentence.

1   The _____ crowd encouraged the
                        (large, noisy)

_____ runners.
        (young, exhausted)

2   We took a _____ ferry boat to the
                        (tourist, small, slow)

_____ beach.
        (white, famous, tiny)

Circle the word that is the best replacement for the bold words.

3   Abdul **knows how to** swim.   (may, can, must)

4   Rafael **has to** do his homework.   (may, can, must)

Write the homophone to complete the sentences.

5   _____ here.
        (There, Their, They're)

6   I _____ them laughing.
        (here, hear)

Circle each complete subject and underline each complete predicate.

7   Trisha took a picture with an underwater camera.

8   The group wore snorkels and masks.

Underline the words in each sentence that need a capital letter.

9 The maps clark drew of the american west are not at Yale university.

10 few europeans had traveled west of the mississippi river.

Edit the following paragraph to correct all the mistakes in capitalization and punctuation. Cross out each mistake and write your correction above it.

11

> What is a Yellow Bike. If you lived in austin, texas, you might know. yellow Bikes are public bikes that anyone can use. The bikes are free to ride but you can't keep a bike. After using one for a few hours, you leave it on the street for the next person. What a great idea. a group called the Yellow Bike Project put the first free bikes on the street in january, 1997. They want to help austin cut down on pollution? People donate bicycles to the project! then the project fixes them up and paints them bright yellow.

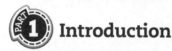

LESSON 33 Vocabulary

① Introduction

Many words are made up of different parts. A word may have a **prefix**, a **word base**, and a **suffix**. If you know what some or all of the parts mean, you can usually figure out the meaning of the word.

un-   friend   -ly

friend is the word base

un- is a prefix that means "not"   -ly is a suffix that means "like"

So, the word *unfriendly* means "not like a friend."

Prefixes

A **prefix** is a word part added to the beginning of a word. A prefix changes the meaning of the word base to make a new word. The prefix *un-* means "not." If you add the prefix *un-* to the word *happy,* you make a new word that means "not happy."

Most prefixes come from Latin or Greek words. For example, the prefix *tri-* is from the Latin word that means "three."

Prefix Chart

Prefix	Meaning	Example
bi-	two	bicycle
dis-	opposite of, not	disappear
ex-	out	exclude
il-, im-, ir-	not	illegal, impossible
in-	in, not	independent
over-	too much, too long	overdone
pre-	before	prepackage
re-	back, again	replay
tri-	three	tricycle
un-	not	unpleasant

Match a prefix with each of these word bases to make a word that fits the new meaning.

Prefix	Word Base	New Meaning	New Word
	record	before making a recording	
	use	use too much	
	regular	not regular	
	able	not able to do	
	visit	visit again	

Suffixes

A **suffix** is a word part added to the end of the word. Like a prefix, a suffix changes the meaning of the word.

> Your *friendship* means a lot to me.

You know what *friend* means. The suffix *-ship* means "the quality or state of something." *Friendship* is the state of being friends.

Some suffixes change words to different parts of speech. When you add the suffix *-ly* to the word *friend,* a noun, you make the word *friendly,* an adjective.

Suffix Chart

Suffix	Meaning	Example
-able, -ible	able to	break<u>able</u>
-al	being like, having to do with	natur<u>al</u>
-ance	act or fact of	import<u>ance</u>, reluct<u>ance</u>
-ar, -er, -or	one who	li<u>ar</u>, paint<u>er</u>, inspect<u>or</u>
-en	make	tight<u>en</u>
-er	more	bright<u>er</u>
-ful	full of, likely to	rest<u>ful</u>
-ic, -ish	being like, having the quality of	hero<u>ic</u>, child<u>ish</u>
-less	without	home<u>less</u>
-ly	like, in that way	perfect<u>ly</u>
-ness	quality or state of	kind<u>ness</u>

Match a suffix with each of these words to make a word that fits the new meaning.

Root	Suffix	New Meaning	New Word
care		without care	
thank		full of thanks	
train		one who trains	
dark		make dark	
dark		more dark	
correct		in a correct way	

Roots

Prefixes and suffixes must be added to **roots** in order to make new words. If you know what the root means and you know what different prefixes and suffixes mean, you can often figure out the meaning of new words. Remember this word?

un-   friend   -ly

friend is the root

un- is a prefix that means "not"   *-ly* is a suffix that means "like"

Roots can be combined with prefixes and suffixes to create new words.

Root	Meaning	New Word	New Word Meaning
fact	make	factory	a place where things are made
geo	earth	geometry	measuring of the earth
port	carry	transportation	act of carrying
struct	build	structure	building

Here is a web of words with the base **do.**

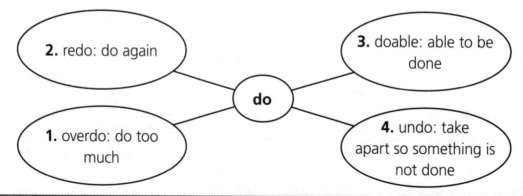

Choose the correct word from the web for each sentence below.

1 Don't _____ the gardening or you will be tired.

2 Rhan thinks the project is _____ in ten days.

3 I will have to _____ the homework I lost.

4 Can you _____ the knot you tied?

Synonyms and Antonyms

Synonyms are words that mean the same, or almost the same.

Look for a pair of synonyms in this sentence:

> Emily will display her scrapbook at the school fair, and Jawan will show his car collection.

If you did not know the word *display,* you could figure it out from the synonym *show* in the second part of the sentence. You could exchange the synonyms, and the sentence would mean the same thing.

Antonyms are words that mean the opposite of one another. Look for a pair of antonyms in this sentence.

> Mom forbids us from playing soccer in the street, but she allows us to play in the alley.

The words *forbids* and *allows* are antonyms. The word <u>but</u> tells you that forbidding something is the **opposite** of allowing it.

Read the passage. Then answer the questions.

1   People aren't the only creatures who use ladders. Some salmon do, too. These fish live most of their lives in the sea, but in the spring they swim up large streams and rivers. The salmon travel to small, quiet streams where they lay their eggs. Just any quiet stream won't do. Salmon like to lay their eggs in the same stream where they were born.

2   Streams and rivers often form waterfalls as they tumble out of mountains. Salmon defeat this hilly *geography* by leaping as high as ten feet at a time on their way upstream. Yet recently, dams have been constructed to block many waterways. Some of them stand 50 feet or higher. That's too high even for these champion *jumpers*.

3   The builders had to *rethink* the design of the dams. They decided to build a kind of ladder into them. A fish ladder looks like a stairway filled with water. Each concrete step has a pool that is about a foot higher than the one below it. The ladder is *specially* built so that the water flows slowly down the steps. The salmon jump from step to step. If they get overtired, they can swim around for a while in large resting pools.

1   The word *specially* means _____.

  A   in a special way

  B   in a special place

  C   with special tools

  D   for a special person

2   What does the word *jumpers* mean in this selection?

  A   able to jump

  B   without jumping

  C   fish that can jump

  D   things to jump over

3 To *rethink* means to _____.

   A not think

   B think again

   C think about

   D stop thinking

4 The word *geography* has to do with _____.

   A fish

   B water

   C the earth

   D protecting animals

Read the passage. Then answer the questions.

1 The continent of Antarctica *encircles* the South Pole. This *site* is colder and lonelier than any other place on Earth. The land of this forlorn continent lies under a mile of ice and snow. *Glaciers* are everywhere. Some of these rivers of ice are thousands of feet thick. It is no wonder that there are no native Antarcticans. But there are people living in Antarctica. Scientists from many countries live and work there even in the deepest winter.

2 Explorers were the first people to reach Antarctica, followed much later by scientists. They built stations to study plants, animals, and *weather.* Life in Antarctica isn't easy. It is rarely warm enough to go outside. The stations have heat and electricity. But food may be *stale* or come from cans. And mail from family and friends is slow to arrive. The stations play old radio and TV programs for fun. Yet no one thinks of Antarctica as home. Scientists stay because there is so much to learn.

3 One feature of life in Antarctica is most unusual. Many countries have stations there—the United States, Russia, Japan, Britain, Australia, Argentina, France, and others. But no nation claims the continent as its own. All of the countries follow the same rules and share what they discover. In that way, Antarctica is a model society. A hundred years ago, explorers of different nations *vied* for the honor of "discovering" the South Pole. Newspapers described their efforts as a race. Today, scientists of many nations share the research station at the South Pole. Antarctica shows us how to live together in peace.

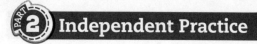

5 The word *encircles* means _____.

   A includes

   B is named

   C surrounds

   D belongs to

6 Which of these words means the same thing as *site?*

   A place

   B river

   C home

   D continent

7 *Glaciers* are _____.

   A rivers of ice

   B research stations

   C snow-covered mountains

   D people who live in cold places

8 In the second paragraph, the word *weather* means _____.

   A where

   B a word expressing choice

   C to expose to the sun and rain

   D conditions of air and temperature

9 What does the word *vied* mean in the last paragraph?

   A ran

   B died

   C shared

   D competed

UNIT 7 REVIEW
Writing on Demand

Write answers to the following questions on separate sheets of paper. For each question, take a few minutes to plan what you are going to write. Use notes, outlines, and other prewriting ideas from the writing process. Write the best first draft you can. Then allow yourself one revision. Each final draft should be about two pages long.

QUESTION 1

Imagine that you are going to spend a year on a remote island. You may bring two of your favorite games with you. They cannot be electronic or video games because there is no electricity on the island. There will be plenty of people to play with, but you will have to teach them the games. Write a letter to the people on the island describing the two games. Be sure to explain:

- why you chose the two games

- similarities and differences between the two games

- what makes the games fun to play

QUESTION 2

Your teacher would like to create a time capsule of items from the 21st century to be buried for future generations to uncover years from now. She has asked your class to create a list of items that should be included. Write a persuasive letter to your teacher and classmates about an item that you feel should be included. Write your opinion of the item and provide reasons why you think it should be included. In your argumentative writing, be sure to:

- include a topic sentence that clearly states your opinion

- support your opinion with a least three good reasons

GLOSSARY

A

Acts: the divisions of a play

Allusion: author uses a word or phrase from another story or myth

Antonyms: words with an opposite meaning

B

Biography: a story that tells about a person's life

C

Cast: the characters in a play

Cause: the reason something happens or what made it happen

Characters: who a story is about

Chronological order: the order in which things happen

Comparison: how two things, actions, or ideas are alike

Conclusions: details figured out by putting together information from a story

Conflict: a problem or struggle in a story

Connotation: a suggested idea or feeling toward a word

Contrast: how two things, actions, or ideas are different

Convince: to make someone feel sure

D

Definitions: words that tell what another word means

Descriptions: words that tell you more about another word

Details: important information in a story or article

Dialogue: the words characters speak in a play

E

Effect: the result or thing that happens

Evidence: proof

Example: word description that helps show what a word means

F **Fable:** a story, usually involving animals, that teaches a lesson

Fact: a statement or information that can be proven true or false

Fairy tale: a story with imaginary qualities and qualities of magic

Fiction: a made-up story

Figurative language: language that is not meant literally

Firsthand account: written by someone who experienced an event

Folktale: a story that teaches a lesson or explains how something came about

I **Illustrations:** pictures

Imagery: visually descriptive language

Inferences: information figured out with details from the story and what you know

J **Judgments:** personal opinions

L **Legend:** a story from the past about people, places, and events

Literal: word means exactly what it says

M **Main idea:** the most important idea of a paragraph or story

Metaphor: the comparison of two like things without using the words *like* or *as*

Meter: the number and types of sound in a line of poetry

Mood: the feeling of a story, poem, or play

Moral: concerned with principles of right and wrong

Myth: a story that explains something about nature or a people's customs or beliefs

N **Narrator:** the person who tells the story or describes the events to the audience in a play

Nonfiction: a true story with facts

O   **Opinion:** something that someone believes or thinks

P   **Personification:** giving human characteristics to a concept or object

Play: a story performed by actors on a stage

Plot: the events or actions of a story

Poetry: a story full of musical language with rhyming or rhythm

Point of view: who is telling the story

> **First-person:** the main character is telling the story; uses first-person pronouns *I* and *we*
>
> **Third-person:** narrator is limited to knowledge of the thoughts and feelings of only one of the characters; uses third-person pronouns *he, she,* and *they*

Prefix: part of a word added to the beginning of another word that changes the meaning of the word

Prior knowledge: what you already know about a topic before reading

Props: objects used by characters in a play

R   **Realistic fiction:** a made-up story that could have happened

Rhyme: repeated sounds at the ends of words

Rhythm: pattern of stressed and unstressed beats in a line of poetry

S   **Scene:** a division of an act in a play

Scenery: backgrounds and larger objects that create the setting of the play

Script: the written text of a play

Secondhand account: written about an event by someone who did not experience it

Sequence: the order in which things happen

Setting: where and when a story happens

Simile: a type of figurative language that compares two unlike things using the words *like* and *as*

Stage directions: how actors should move and speak on stage

Stanza: a group of lines within a poem, similar to a chapter in a book

Suffix: part of a word added to the end of another word that changes the meaning of the word

Summary: a few sentences that tell the main idea and most important details of a story

Synonyms: words that have a similar meaning

Text structure: how an article is organized

Theme: the lesson or main idea of a story

Tone: the mood or feeling of a story

Topic: what the story is about

V

Verses: lines of poetry